Conversion to Islam

CONVERSION TO ISLAM

A Study of Native British Converts

Ali Köse

Routledge
Taylor & Francis Group

LONDON AND NEW YORK

First published in 1996 by
Kegan Paul International

This edition first published in 2010 by
Routledge
2 Park Square, Milton Park, Abingdon, Oxfordshire OX14 4RN

Simultaneously published in the USA and Canada
by Routledge
711 Third Avenue, New York, NY 10017

First issued in paperback 2014

Routledge is an imprint of the Taylor & Francis Group, an informa business

British Library Cataloguing in Publication Data
A catalogue record for this book is available from the British Library

ISBN 13: 978-0-7103-0546-6 (hbk)
ISBN 13: 978-1-138-01074-1 (pbk)

Publisher's Note
The publisher has gone to great lengths to ensure the quality of this reprint
but points out that some imperfections in the original copies may be
apparent. The publisher has made every effort to contact original copyright
holders and would welcome correspondence from those they have been
unable to trace.

To Bosnian women
who have suffered horribly

CONTENTS

Acknowledgements   xi

Introduction   1

1 Muslims in Britain   5

2 On the Way to Conversion   31

3 Conversion Process   67

4 Postconversion   125

5 Conversion through Sufism   142

Conclusion   189

Glossary   195
Notes   197
Bibliography   201
Index   213

TABLES

Table 2.1   Perception of relations with parents in childhood   33
Table 2.2   Fathering in childhood and adolescence   35
Table 2.3   Conversion age groups   47
Table 3.1   Religion of origin   67
Table 3.2a Religious affiliation before conversion   68
Table 3.2b Belief in God prior to conversion   68
Table 3.3   Religion or religious group involved other
            than religion of origin   69
Table 3.4a Levels of completed education   80
Table 3.4b Social class   80
Table 3.5   Reported traumatic events in life before
            conversion   83
Table 3.6   Conversion motifs (patterns)   98
Table 3.7   Most motivating factor in conversion process   109
Table 3.8   First contact with Islam   112

ACKNOWLEDGEMENTS

This book is not the product of months or years of isolation in a library. It has had to rely on the help of tens of people who have come to my assistance by talking to me. I am grateful to the people I have interviewed. They allowed me to enter their lives. None of my work would have been possible without the help of these people who gave me their time and hospitality.

It is impossible for me to thank all the people who have contributed to the research, but there are certain categories of people to whom I must express my gratitude and debt. In the first place, with all sincerity and however inadequate the words, I should like to express my deep gratitude to Dr. C. M. Loewenthal who was a steadfast source of suggestions and criticism throughout the research. Secondly, I am grateful for the financial support that I received from Türkiye Diyanet Vakfı. Thirdly, I wish to record my thanks to Louise Baker and Talip Kücükcan who read the manuscript in its final stages and made helpful suggestions, and Daoud Owen, the president of the Association for British Muslims, who provided a substantial amount of information on native British converts to Islam. Finally, my biggest debt is to my wife without whose encouragement and bullying this book could not have been prepared.

INTRODUCTION

Religious conversion is an immensely complex phenomenon. The term religious conversion comprises three experiences. It may be an experience of increased devotion within the same religious structure, a shift from no religious commitment to a devout religious life, or a change from one religion to another. Conversion experiences may come about in different circumstances, in different ways, and with different outcomes. They may occur in the soul-searching, sincere man/woman, who may find greater values in beliefs other than those s/he was exposed to in his/her childhood or in an individual who wishes to marry an adherent of a religion other than his/hers.

Since the turn of the century social scientists and religionists have adopted different perspectives when explaining the nature of the conversion experience. Social scientists have proposed a range of social and psychological forces at work, while believers have emphasised the nature of divine-human encounter. Social scientists have also differed among themselves as to the causes of conversion. Their differences may be categorised under three themes (see Heirich, 1977: 654–6); the *first* sees conversion as a fantasy solution to stress, in which the threatening situation is overcome either by making an alliance with supernatural forces or by changing one's frame of reference so that previously distressing material no longer seems important. Much of the psychological literature on religion favour this perspective. The *second* focuses on previous conditioning rather than the circumstances which produce the immediate result (e.g. stress). Thus it looks for socialisation circumstances that should leave one ripe for plucking. It looks at parental orientations, sex-role education, and the impact of schooling. The *third* emphasises interactions

1

that make a different understanding of one's experience possible. It focuses upon conditions that lead one to take a particular frame of reference seriously. It involves analysis of patterns of interpersonal influence, whereby inputs from others become so mutually consistent and reinforcing that one begins to see things through the others' eyes. Many social scientists have focused their attention on a single 'causal explanation', but some have seen conversion as involving all three processes in interaction, as in Lofland-Stark's (1965: 874) seven-step conversion process model.

The present book is the outcome of an interview study based on the accounts of 70 converts to Islam, 50 males and 20 females, during 1990–91 in various parts of England. The sample consists of 66 English, 3 Irish, and 1 Welsh. 51 were Church of England, 12 were Catholics, 3 were Methodists, and 4 were Jews. Their ages range from 17 to 66 years, and had been converted between 1 week and 48 years prior to participating in the study. 23 (33%) are currently involved in *Sufism*. The group of *Shaykh Nazim* and *Abd al-Qadir as-Sufi (al-Murabit)* were observed and 23 native British converts from these groups were interviewed.

The major objective of this research is to record the conversion experiences of 70 native British converts to Islam and to provide, to a certain extent, the reasons underlying them. It endeavours to understand the psychological and sociological roots of their conversion experience. What has provoked these people? What are the backgrounds of the converts? What are the patterns of conversion to Islam? What is the nature of this transformation? What are the processes involved? Are there long-term predispositions? And how far are existing conversion theories applicable to native British converts to Islam?

A questionnaire which covered the whole lifespan of the converts, i.e. childhood, adolescence experiences, and conversion process, etc. was prepared. Though the source of information was primarily the interviews, available published and unpublished records and books, newspapers, magazines, and journals were also used. To aid in the construction of the interview questionnaire the literature on religious experience and conversion in the domain of psychology and sociology was reviewed (e.g. Starbuck, 1911; Pratt, 1948; Salzman, 1953; Heirich, 1977; Downton, 1980, Ullman, 1989; Poston, 1992; Gillespie, 1991). The growing literature about the new religious movements was also examined

2

(e.g. Bellah, 1976; Lofland, 1977a; Greil, 1977; Barker, 1984 and 1989; Wallis, 1984; Robbins, 1988). In choosing the questions the results of previous studies were taken into account. For example, Ullman (1989: 11–16) found that converts characterised their childhood as unhappy reporting specific, disturbing, traumatic events. So, to test the validity of this finding for the present sample questions on childhood experiences like 'Can you describe your relationship with your parents when a child?', or 'Did anything unusual like separation from either parents happen to you?' were included.

The methods which were used to select the subjects were snowball and convenience sampling. At the outset finding converts to Islam seemed to present some difficulty since converts are scattered across Britain and they do not clump together in ghetto-like enclaves. Yet being already familiar with the Muslim community in Britain, and also being acquainted with several converts was an advantage. In the end, around 100 converts were met, but only 70 participated in this research which provided the basis for this book. Of those who were met but not interviewed, contact with 20 was lost although they had agreed to participate, and 10 for various reasons did not want to be interviewed.

Converts were contacted through three channels. *First*, help from various Islamic organisations was sought to provide the names and addresses of converts (n=12). *Second*, a substantial amount of time was spent in mosques and other Muslim meeting places to identify native British converts who would be obvious through their physical features (n=45). *Third*, converts already known or interviewed were asked to introduce the researcher to any other convert that they knew (n=13). To meet and interview converts various parts of England were travelled to. London, Norwich, Oxford, Plymouth, Bournemouth, and Nottingham are among other places where the converts were met.

Chapter 1 is about Muslims in Britain. It looks at both life-long Muslims and converts as well as presenting their history. It also deals with the differences within the Muslim community regarding da'wah strategy. Chapter 2 focuses on childhood and adolescence experiences reviewing the psychological and socio-logical theories of conversion and attempts to find out how far these theories are applicable to the converts to Islam. Chapter 3 examines the backgrounds of the converts regarding religion and

3

then analyses the immediate antecedents of the conversion as well as conversion process focusing on conversion motifs. A conversion process model is also developed in this chapter. Chapter 4 looks at the postconversion period to find out the changes the converts went through regarding beliefs, practices, etc. It also examines converts' present relationships with their parents and wider society. Chapter 5 reveals the findings on conversion through Sufism as far as the above mentioned Sufi groups are concerned. It elucidates the characteristics of conversion through Sufism.

This research is necessarily limited to a particular sample of converts which may not be representative of all conversions to Islam. Therefore caution should be exercised when generalising from the present findings. When Lofland and Stark, studying conversion to Divine Precepts, developed their model of conversion in 1965, they had few models and theoretical and substantive material to guide them. In fact, Lofland (1977b: 817) in a later paper admitted that it was a setback for their study. This research is in a similar position except that conversion in general has been more widely studied since their time. Yet, as far as conversion to Islam is concerned there is limited theoretical and substantive material available. However, I hope that readers will gain an insight into the experience of those converts to Islam who were interviewed.

ONE

MUSLIMS IN BRITAIN

A Immigrant Muslims of Britain

1 Their history

Muslim migration and settlement in Britain dates from the middle years of the 19th century when Muslim seamen from Yemen, Somalia and South Asia came to settle in such ports as Cardiff, Liverpool, and London (Collins, 1957: 11). In more recent times, due to the industrial growth in Britain in the 1950s and 1960s large industrial cities such as London, Birmingham and Manchester have been attracting a rapidly increasing Muslim population. This period has brought a large number of Muslim migrants to this country from the Indian subcontinent. After the Second World War, Muslims, particularly from the Commonwealth countries, found their way to Britain in connection with trade, commerce, education and service. By the end of the war the number of Indian Muslims in Britain had exceeded 30,000. In 1949 it was estimated that there were more than 43,000 Pakistanis in Britain (Hunter, 1962: 17–18).

Muslim migration and settlement in the 1950s, after the Second World War, has many different characteristics in comparison to that which took place during the late 19th and early 20th century. It is different not only in terms of the nature and size of the migratory movement, but also the geographical and religious backgrounds of the migrants. Unlike the Muslim settlements in the dockland areas of seaports a century ago, it is characterised by a substantial Muslim settlement in the industrialised inner cities (Ally,1982: 90). After the war due to rapid economic growth and post-war reconstruction there was an intense shortage of

5

labour in Britain as well as Europe and the colonies became the best recruiting market. To this end Britain made attempts to attract workers from abroad, and exploited its historical links with India and Pakistan (Rose, et al, 1969: 78–81; Shaw, 1988: 12). Further, in the post-war period, due to the creation of the new independent states of Pakistan and Bangladesh, these countries were facing serious economical, social and political problems which was a catalyst for emigration (Allen, 1971: 36–7). Regarding religious background, in contrast to the West African origin Sufi oriented Arab groups, the Muslims of India and Pakistan were much more influenced by the 20th century religious groups, like the Jamaat-i Islami and the Tablighi Jamaat.

Turkish Cypriots were the second largest Muslim community migrating to Britain. As the Greeks began to seek political union with Greece the tension between the Greek and the Turkish community was exacerbated in the 1950s and many Turks migrated to Britain. Many East and West Africans also came to Britain in the 1960s (Ally, 1982: 97, 103).

In analysing the history of Muslims in Britain one can identify that the primary motivating factor for the migratory movements in 1950s and 1960s was economic (Anwar, 1979: 25). Most of those who migrated at the beginning were unskilled workers. They were hardly educated in their own language and basic culture. They came alone with the ultimate intention of returning home after a few years. The most overriding character of Muslim migration as a whole is that it followed the pattern of the husband arriving first and being joined later by his wife and family. So there was a preponderance of male Muslims in the 1950s and 1960s in Britain (Rex and Moore, 1967: 116). However, when Britain introduced the Commonwealth Immigration Act of 1962 to put an end to its 'open door' policy, many non-working dependants and more workers arrived due to the threat of immigration control by the British government. The 1962 Act then imposed a system of regulation through the issue of employment vouchers according to their skills and qualifications. Finally, the 1971 Immigration Act made it impossible for all but the wealthiest entrepreneurs to enter the UK from the 'New Commonwealth', thus ending the migration of single men. This Act still permitted the entry of dependants, although the mode of its operation and subsequent further restrictions delayed the arrival of many and prevented others from coming altogether (Rose, et al, 1969:

82–5). So the migration of a substantial number of dependants of workers already in Britain meant more permanent settlement for Muslims and the concern for community increased. Religion in terms of establishing organisations; thus education became the primary concern.

2 The contemporary Muslim community

Britain's Muslims could be classified broadly as: (a) immigrant workers; (b) students (there are about 30,000 Muslim students in British Universities) (Kettani, 1986: 41); (c) professionals and businessmen; (d) diplomatic business personnel; and (e) native British Muslims. It is the first group that is by far the most numerous and these are mainly persons intending to stay in Britain permanently (Johnstone, 1981: 169).

There is no accurate figure for the total number of Muslims in Britain since Britain does not keep religious statistics. The estimates range from 750,000 to 1 million. The majority of the Muslim community, between 300,000 and 400,000 is from Pakistan. Other groups of Muslims include Bengalis (60,000), Indians (80,000), Turkish Cypriots (50,000), Turks (5,000–20,000), Arabs (120,000), Malaysians (30,000), East Africans (30,000–90,000), Iranians (25,000–50,000), Nigerians (20,000) and others (30,000) (see Neilsen, 1992: 41). The vast majority of Muslims in Britain are *Sunni* but Britain also has around 25,000 *Shi'ite* Muslims from Iran and around 15,000 *Ahmadis* from India (McHugh, 1990: 36), who are considered to be outside the pale of Islam.

Geographically, the Muslim population is not uniformly spread throughout Britain. The majority is resident in the largest industrial cities such as London, Birmingham, Liverpool, Manchester, Sheffield, and Bradford. The regional pattern varies considerably from one Muslim nationality to another, for instance, while Bengalis are settled in East London, Oldham, and Bradford, Turkish Cypriots live in North and South East London (Ally, 1982: 120–2; Nielsen, 1992: 42–3).

During the first years of their migration, Muslims did not intend to settle permanently and they knew they were coming to a strange society and their expectations were limited. This attitude led to a lack of desire to learn English or to set up social organisations. However, with the arrival of the families in the 1960s and 1970s this orientation changed in favour of settlement.

7

Consequently the second generation now does not feel they are immigrants at all, and consider Britain their home. So this growing tendency towards settlement brought the establishment of ethnic, socio-economic and religious institutions to cater for the community's need (Dahya, 1973: 245; Ally, 1982: 127). The Muslims began to take steps to emphasise their religious and cultural traditions and they built mosques and made religious instruction available to their children by running weekend schools, and occasionally full-time private primary/secondary schools.

Although religious identification is generally strong among Muslims in Britain, the degree of religious observance and attending worship seem to be in decline when compared to that of home. For some it may be stronger than it would be back home because some who regard themselves as exiles in a strange land may identify more strongly with their religion. On the other hand, some who practised their religion in their homeland may sometimes throw it to the wind when they come to Britain (Hunter, 1985: xi). The Muslim community seems to consist of both extremes. Some Muslims apparently take great pride in being anglicised, proving their 'modernity' through adopting an English life-style in their homes. They gradually develop a self-centred, individualistic and secularist approach. One example for this is the Turkish Cypriot community that is more secularised than any other ethnic Muslim community. What is very obvious is that there is a trend towards a weakening in religious observance within the community as far as the second generation is concerned. Anwar (1986: 17), in a survey, covering nearly 8,000 Muslims, found that a higher percentage (35%) of young Muslims as compared with parents (20%) never go to a mosque. In their survey of Pakistanis Rex and Moore (1967: 170) concluded:

> Although the Pakistani community remains apart socially and culturally from the host society, there are none the less some signs at the margins of lapsing both from Islam and from Pakistani culture. Religious duties are overlooked. An increasing number of Pakistanis drink alcohol.

Due to their ethnic and religious background, the Muslim community in Britain today faces problems relating to determining its identity and establishing itself as a community. Among them religious, racial, and educational problems as well as unemployment,[1] and lack of leadership can be highlighted. Problems concerning religious education of Muslim children and lack of proper leadership have always been the areas that Muslims talk about most.

In the last five decades Muslims have established their own places of worship and organisations of which the vast majority have their roots in the country of origin. Most of them have a local character and their activities are very limited, but some have a nationwide effect within the community. There were about 80 mosques in 1970 (Hiro, 1971: 146), and around 250–300 in the 1980s (Anwar, 1980: 111; Neilsen, 1992: 45). Now their number is estimated at over 1,000; most being small and located in terraced houses (Mohammad, 1991: 49). Religious activities taking place in the mosques are organised by Muslim organisations. The mosque has often been used as an instrument of sectarianism and a forum ground for power politics back in the country of origin. In every city where there is a Muslim community there are tens of Muslim organisations. The majority of these organisations are small existing mainly on paper, but there are larger national organisations concerned with welfare, education, and *da'wah* (mission). Some of these organisations are popular because they are a reflection of the movements or political parties that exist in the homeland. Some of the most well-known organisations are: UK Islamic Mission, Islamic Foundation, Islamic Propagation Centre, Islamic Cultural Centre, the Tablighi Jamaat, Ahli Hadith, and the Muslim Parliament.

Apart from sectarian and mission organisations there are a number of service and publishing or media organisations. The former includes a few charities such as Muslim Aid, London, and Islamic Relief, Birmingham, and such organisations as the Muslim Women's Association and Muslim Educational Trust. The latter type of organisations are specialised in publishing books and papers about Islam and Muslims in Britain. The Islamic Foundation, for example, is one of them which concerns itself with the publication of Islamic literature in English.

The Muslim organisations lack a strong central organisational set-up. There is almost no institutional relationship between different organisations. This leads to a lack of recognition by the British authorities. In the course of this research it is observed that organisations are making little progress in their mission towards both Muslims and non-Muslims. So far as non-Muslims are concerned the findings of this research prove that their mission is far from being successful. Of the 70 converts, who were interviewed for this research, only 23 (32.8%) got in touch with or were introduced to Muslim organisations or groups in Britain during the process of conversion and their introduction was not the result of a direct missionary activity. Most of the organisations have also failed to gain the support of the Muslim community. There are several reasons for their failure: (a) The same divisions in the motherland still exist in Britain; (b) the immigrant founders of organisations who belong to a generation of a different background have failed to develop a structure for the new generation; and (c) these organisations have failed to grasp the dynamics of western society.

It may be concluded then that though the Muslims of Britain are a religious and cultural entity, they are not yet an organised community. It has been suggested that there are three options for Muslims in Britain: *assimilation, isolation* and *integration* (Mohammad, 1991: 107). Muslims do live in isolation to some extent in terms of living according to their tradition and religion, but politically and economically they seem to have integrated into British structure. It appears that there is a willingness among Muslims in Britain to adapt to the social structure of this country without losing their identity as Muslims. As a community they have become a part of the social structure of the new society (Anwar, 1986: 6, 20). In this respect, Muslims can be classified as an integrating community in general.

In the late 19th century, and in the early 20th century, while Britain was witnessing the migration of the Muslim population the number of converts to Islam was relatively increasing. Now I turn to the history of native British Muslims who converted to Islam.

B Native British Muslims

1 Their history

When Islam emerged in the seventh century in the Arab Peninsula, Arabs were not aware of the existence of England; and the Prophet Muhammad was a young man when the English converted to Christianity (Daniel, 1975: 10). There was a story of St Willibald (Bishop of Eichstadt) who went on a pilgrimage towards the middle of the eighth century. Landing at Tortosa in Syria from Cyprus, St Willibald and seven other Englishmen were soon arrested by 'pagan Saracens', who 'did not know what people they were, and thought they must be spies.' They were rescued by the intervention of a Spanish chamberlain of the 'Saracen king' and they were brought in front of the caliph; he asked them where they came from, and was told that 'these men come from the Western shore, where the sunset takes place, and we do not know of any land beyond, and nothing but waters.' The ruler answered, 'Why should we punish them? They have not committed any offence against us. Put them on the road . . .' (Daniel, 1975: 49).

Then in the following centuries Islam was seen as an offshoot or heresy of Christianity (Hourani, 1991: 10; Daniel, 1975: 231). However, at the beginning of the 13th century England came very near conversion to Islam. According to Matthew Paris,[2] King John (1199–1216) of England in 1213 sent a secret embassy, three envoys; one cleric called Master Robert of London and two laymen to the ruler of Morocco, Muhammad an-Nasser, to seek his military support for John against his rebellious barons. King John's relationship with papacy may have also motivated him in his decision to seek help from the ruler of Morocco since the time of King John was the climax and watershed in the history of the political relations of England with the papacy (Knowles, 1958: 418). Matthew Paris writes that the envoys were instructed to tell the King of Morocco that he would voluntarily give up to him himself and his Kingdom and he would abandon the Christian faith, which he considered false, and would faithfully adhere to Islam. Yet the request was turned down by the ruler of Morocco.[3] By the time of King John, the British also became familiar with Muslim powers in Spain. Many Englishmen had returned home from studying in Spain (Daniel, 1975: 108, 273). In the same century the Koran was available to the English in Latin translation (Hourani, 1991: 8).

Throughout the Middle Ages, during or after the Crusades, the image of Islam and Muslims in the European or British mind was being built on misinformation about Islam that was described as a form of polytheistic idol worship. The West perceived the East as a dangerous region where Islam flourished and monstrous races multiplied and thrived (Kabbani, 1986: 14). It was also supposed to be an ordinance of the religion of the Saracens 'to rob, to make prisoner and to kill the adversaries of God and their prophet, and to persecute and destroy them in

11

every way' (Watt, 1972: 75). The image of violent Arabs was mixed with the image of Islam and this image remained throughout the Middle Ages.

The reports on the first large-scale conversion to Islam do not trace back before the late 19th century. In the late 19th and early 20th centuries there were a relatively large number of English converts to Islam in Britain and the first two Islamic organisations led by converts were growing. At that time in Britain, there were a substantial amount of Muslim students and professionals. Since the students and professionals came from a high class in their own society and they had a good command of English, they easily moved among British middle and upper class society. They were able to attract the interest of the British more than the seamen settled in dockland areas (Ally, 1982: 48). The first conversion of an Englishman in this period was that of a peer called Lord Stanley of Alderley, an uncle of Bertrand Russell (Clark, 1986: 41). This was followed by the conversion of William H. Quilliam of Liverpool, a well-known lawyer and an eloquent speaker. Quilliam's journey to Morocco in 1887 gave him the opportunity to study Islam and he soon became Muslim.[4] He went on to become the founder of the Liverpool Mosque and Muslim Institute.

(a) The Liverpool Mosque and Muslim Institute   After his conversion Quilliam began to spread the message of Islam and steadily made converts. His first converts were his own family, including his mother and his three sons. He published a number of booklets and from 1893 to 1908 he issued a weekly, *The Crescent* (Clark, 1986: 39). The first booklet ran into three editions in English and was translated into 13 languages. After publishing these booklets he became a well-known name in the Muslim world. His efforts resulted in prominent scientists, teachers and people in the professions as well as a few spinsters and widows accepting Islam (Ally, 1982: 49). Quilliam undertook social work in the interest of spreading Islam and he founded a house called *Medina House* which was a home for 20 or 30 foundlings who were brought up as Muslims (Ally, 1982: 56). Mothers of the babies were required to sign a special clause that stated that they would be brought up as Muslims.[5] Quilliam travelled around Britain and lectured on Islam, using non-Islamic networks like *Manx clubs*

and *Temperance Societies* and he claimed up to 150 British adherents (Clark, 1986: 39).

Quilliam had international Islamic contacts as well. The Shah of Persia nominated him as Persian consul for Liverpool and he received a personal gift from the *Ameer* of Afghanistan. He purchased the West Derby premises which was used as an Islamic Institute and a residence for himself and his family. In 1890, he was invited by the Ottoman Sultan to visit Istanbul and the Sultan soon appointed him *Shaykh al-Islam* of the British Isles. In 1891 Quilliam became Shaykh Abdullah Quilliam after he established the 'Liverpool Mosque and Institute'. The institute was able to establish a 'Muslim College' and offer full-time courses to both Muslim and non-Muslim students. There were courses in the pure sciences, history, and languages (Arabic and European).[6] Through running these educational programmes one of the aims of the institute was to attract the attention of non-Muslims. For this purpose the institute also ran a weekly literary and debating society (Ally, 1982: 50–6).

Quilliam followed an appropriate strategy in his missionary activity. He always bore in mind the background of the people he was addressing and tried to make potential converts feel at home while they were given *da'wah*. For this end he organised morning and evening services on Sundays. He acknowledged that:

> Most of the people in this country are Christians and are accustomed in their churches and chapels to a certain form of service, consisting generally of the singing of a chant, some hymns, the reading of a chapter from the Bible and a sermon from the clergyman. These people had to be brought gradually into the faith: consequently to make them feel more at home at the missionary meetings, we held a service something like the one they had been accustomed to.[7]

On Sunday mornings prayer and meditation were held and this was followed by a congregational meeting in the evening. Both services were held in the lecture hall of the institute.[8] The congregational meeting consisted of singing of hymns in English and was specifically designed for potential converts. Quilliam himself compiled some hymns and entitled it 'Hymns suitable for English-speaking Muslim congregation'. Many of them were taken from Evangelical poets and divines. Some of them were adapted to conform to Islamic beliefs (Ally, 1982: 58).

In the early part of the 20th century, Quilliam's activities began to attract antagonism and pressure from both the local community and from some of the churches. According to *The Islamic World* this antagonism was largely because of Quilliam's ability to attract a significant number of converts.[9] This hostility towards Quilliam was also caused by his public condemnation of the church. He wrote letters to the church criticising their missionary activities in Muslim countries (Ally, 1982: 62). He also issued a proclamation to Egyptian soldiers in 1896, criticising the British policy over Sudan and urging Muslim soldiers in the British army to refrain from taking up arms against the Muslims of Sudan.[10] In the end Quilliam had to leave Britain and he was reported to have gone to the East in 1908. After Quilliam had left Liverpool, the mosque and the institution declined and eventually closed (Siddiq, 1934, 14). Quilliam's son, Bilal, sold off the West Derby premises which was registered in Quilliam's name. It is not known what happened to Quilliam after that, but it was assumed that he and his sons went to Turkey with other converts. There was also a rumour that Quilliam came back to Britain under a pseudo name in the 1920s. While the movement was in decline in Liverpool there was another mission growing up in Woking. This mission consisted of many converts too, and it was led by them in its later years.

(b) The Woking Mission The Woking Mission began with the building of a mosque in Woking in 1889, which was to be the first mosque in the London area and Muslims were the first non-Judea-Christian community in Britain to establish a place of worship of their own (Hiro, 1971, 146). The mosque was established by Dr. Leitner, a Hungarian orientalist who settled in Britain after retirement from the post of registrar at the University of Punjab. Leitner also arranged for the building of an Indian student hostel and an institute for oriental studies (Haqq, 1930: 242). The mosque in Woking would become a centre for an Islamic mission and witness many conversions to Islam (Siddiq, 1934: 16). After the death of Leitner in 1899 the mosque and adjacent building were left in a neglected state for many years until a Lahore barrister, Khwaja Kamal-ud-Din of India came to

England in 1912 as a Muslim missionary with the objective of removing misconceptions about Islam in Britain and working for conversions. Kamal-ud-Din based himself at Richmond, Surrey, and held meetings at Hyde Park (Ally, 1982: 64; Clark, 1986: 40). He started a monthly called *Muslim India and Islamic Review*. In 1913 he moved to Woking and took possession of the mosque from the heirs of Leitner. He had the building repaired and within months the Woking mission was established. Kamal-ud-Din kept on publishing the monthly, which in the following years changed its name to *Islamic Review and Modern India* first, then to the *Islamic Review* in 1921 (Siddiq, 1934: 19; Clark, 1986: 41).

The Woking Mission's first success came when an English lord, Lord Headley who later took the name of al-Haj al-Farooq, converted to Islam in 1913.[11] His conversion drew the attention of the British public to Islam as a faith that might be personally relevant to British individuals (Ally, 1982: 70; Clark, 1986: 41). Lord Headley was an engineer until he succeeded his cousin in 1913 to become the fifth Baron and the 11th holder of the baronetcy of Nostell, Yorkshire, and the fifth holder of the baronetcy of Little Warsely, Essex. He was brought up as a Protestant; but also studied Roman Catholicism at Trinity College, Cambridge, and was struck by what he called Catholics' 'believe this or be damned!' attitude. His contact with Islam came about when he went to India in 1896 as a contract engineer. After his return to England he met Khwaja Kamal-ud-Din and decided to announce publicly his conversion to Islam, as he wrote in an article after the death of Kamal-Din (Headley, 1933: 109–114).

Lord Headley's conversion was followed by a group of British converts to Islam, amongst whom were John (Yehya) Parkinson, S. Musgrave, Khalid Sheldrake, Dr N. J. Whyment, Noor-ed-Din Stephen, and Prof. H. Marcel (Mustafa) Leon (Sheldrake, 1915: 4–7). Prof. Leon was a former lecturer at the Liverpool Mosque and a long time associate of A. Quilliam. After meeting Lord Headley he became a close colleague of Headley, and together they developed the Woking mission through an autonomous body called *the British Muslim Society* under the presidency of Headley in 1914 to propagate Islam in Britain (Sheldrake, 1915: 4). The society which had many members from the middle class and the aristocracy of British society with experience of India or other Muslim countries as servicemen or as their families met

15

regularly for Friday prayers and for Sunday services at Woking Mosque. Sunday services were held in the form of a ceremony for those who wished to announce their acceptance of Islam. It organised public meetings and lectures on a weekly basis. On some occasions like the birthday of the Prophet Muhammad, the society organised celebratory meetings at London's leading hotels and many new or potential converts attended these meetings (Siddiq, 1934: 20–1; Ally, 1982: 73).

The strategy they used to carry out missionary work was very important. The society and its president Lord Headley, presented Islam in a very delicate way. The objective of the society was to show that Islam was not 'antagonistic or hostile' to Christianity (Ally, 1982: 75). Islam would be shown as easy to the potential convert, or to the new convert. They thought, for example, it might be too much to expect 'the busy city man' to pray five times a day at the appointed times. It would be all right for him to send up his silent prayer. Lord Headley's remark on these points was that, 'There are many things in this world desirable but not essential.'[12] He was of the opinion that if insistence were made on the strict observance of 'minor' points then they would be laying themselves open to the charges they themselves make against Christians who insist that certain ceremonies and beliefs are essential (Headley, 1927: 238). He was also very careful about politics. He would not involve himself in politics as Quilliam of Liverpool did. In his presidential address in 1915 he made it clear that the society should not involve itself in politics since Britain was at war with the Ottomans at the time.[13]

The Mission's monthly journal, the *Islamic Review,* was its mouthpiece. It contained writings on religions and articles on various aspects of Islam; mostly in comparison with Christianity. Announcements were also made to attract discussions from non-Muslims, in which it was said: 'The Muslim church welcomes Non-Muslims as well. Collections are dispensed with and healthy criticism is encouraged.'[14] Most of the writings in the journal were done by converts. One other feature of the journal was that it announced the name and the number of new converts, sometimes accompanied with their pictures. Nearly each issue consisted of one or two converts' biography (or autobiography) as well as their reasons for converting to Islam:

The English brotherhood is growing steadily. Several people

joined Islam formally this month. A young Londoner, who has been given Abdulaziz as his Islamic name, bids fair to develop into an earnest worker. Madam Bloch, of Brighton, also deserves particular mention for the devotion that she displayed for her co-religionist and newly-adopted faith on her visit to the mosque. The Muslim name given to her is Noor-Jahan (i.e., the light of the world). It is hoped that she will put forth efforts to spread the light and show the truth to those among whom she is living.[15]

People intending to convert were invited either to call at the mosque (it may be the prayer hall) or they were given the option of writing to the mission. Some converts sent their declaration of faith and transcriptions of these letters were published in the journal. A letter from a convert named Sarah is as follows:

Dear Mr. Deen, I enclose my announcement. I hope you will allow me to join the Muslim faith. I do hereby testify that there is no other God or object of worship and to be served but One-Allah; I do testify that Muhammad is the prophet of God. I do not believe in the divinity of Jesus, but I accept him as a prophet of God with other prophets, like Abraham, Moses, Solomon, and David and others. I believe in the Divine Message of all prophets of the world. I do not make any distinction between them. I do accept the Koran as the last book of God to perfect religion. I do promise to act according to the injunction of the Koran, and lead a Muslim life. God help me so. Amen.[16]

The *Islamic Review* kept its readers informed of activities, religious or social. It also functioned as a community newsletter in which news about the members were announced. As understood from the *Islamic Review* in 1924 the number of Muslims in Britain was estimated at 10,000 and the estimated figure of British converts from Christianity was approximately 1,000 who were scattered around the country.[17] But there is no other written testimony available confirming those figures.

The activities of the mission also included preparing literature for the British public expounding the teaching of Islam. A long list of publications was issued on such subjects as 'Muhammad and Jesus'. The mission also collaborated with other Muslim organisations. One of them was the *Muslim Literary Society* that developed under the presidency of Abdullah Yusuf Ali famed as a translator of the Koran into English. The famous Koran translator M. Pickthall, a convert to Islam, was also among members of this society. (Ally, 1982: 78; Clark, 1986: 40).

After the death of the two key figures, Khwaja Kamal-ud-Din in 1932 and Lord Headley in 1933, the mission was taken over by a new committee. Although it continued after the Second World War till the 1960s it has lost its popularity for two reasons (Ally, 1982: 82). *Firstly,* because of the allegations about the mission being an Ahmadiyyah movement due to Kamal-ud-Din's *Ahmadi* background, though the allegations were previously denied.[18] *Secondly,* with the development of the *Central Mosque* and *East London Mosque* in London its influence weakened.

The Woking mission seems to have been successful in attracting many conversions among middle and upper class society in Britain. The answer to the question of 'Why was the mission successful?' lies within the fact that its president and first members were prominent Englishmen and they, making use of being Englishmen, used a methodology which was not alien to British people, such as holding morning and evening assemblies or giving parties at London's big hotels on special occasions or sometimes calling the Woking Mosque, a 'Muslim Church'. The message was from Englishmen to Englishmen. In addition, Islam was presented to the potential convert as compatible with being a Westerner. Being a convert had always been presented as being a 'better Christian' rather than denouncing Christianity. To take an example, having given his reasons for embracing Islam Lord Headley declared that: 'I consider myself by that very act a far better Christian than I was before . . .' (Bawany, 1961: 19).

While the Woking mission was in action, another prominent Englishman, Marmaduke Pickthall, announced his conversion to Islam in London in 1917 at the age of 42 and took the name Muhammad. A few years later his wife followed him into Islam. Pickthall (1875–1936) is famous among Muslims as a translator of the Koran. He was also a novelist. He published 15 novels and short stories mainly about the Near East. His last two novels after his conversion are considered the first English Islamic novels. Pickthall was an English Tory and opposed British schemes and the war against the Ottoman Empire, which estranged him from his fellow countrymen. He was interested in the Middle East and lived in Muslim countries for many years.

Pickthall came from a devout Church of England family. His father was a clergyman. Soon after his conversion he was able to lead prayers at the mosque in Notting Hill Gate, West London. He devoted his time to Islam by writing, lecturing, and publishing pamphlets. In London he formed an Islamic information bureau and published a journal entitled *Muslim Outlook* (Clark, 1986: 23–39).

The most overriding character of the first converts to Islam is that many of them had worked in Muslim lands, especially in India, and had been impressed by the faith and conduct of Muslim colleagues. Also there was a large number of transient visitors to Britain, often students from the Muslim world (Clark, 1986: 41).

In the period between the two World Wars Islam was identified with these groups of people in Liverpool, Woking, and London. There may have been isolated cases of conversions that are not known. It is also not known what happened to the families and descendants of those people. It is still to be known what happened to them or whether their descendants were brought up as Muslims.

2 The contemporary native British Muslims

The current number of English converts to Islam is estimated at around 3,000–5,000[19] and their number seems to be relatively increasing (McHugh, 1990: 36; Britain 1990: An Official Handbook, H.M.S.O., 231). Any accurate number would be difficult to obtain due to two facts. *First*, being Muslim does not require that one should register officially with a mosque or an organisation although some organisations, like the Islamic Cultural Centre in London, issue *conversion certificates* on application. *Second*, converts are scattered around the country and they do not live as a community.

Converts range from local women who have adopted Islam to a greater or lesser extent of commitment upon marrying a Muslim to British intellectuals who are highly articulate in expressing their views on a variety of matters (Johnstone, 1981: 181). Most converts came to know Islam through personal contact and it plays a great role in their conversion. Many women get involved with Muslims and they turn to Islam through marrying Arabs and Pakistanis particularly (McHugh, 1990: 36; Ball, 1987:

21). They do not necessarily have to convert for marriage since Islamic law permits Muslim men to marry *Ahl al-Kitab* (People of the Book). The proportion of men to women seems to be almost equal. A significant number of them are middle-aged people who lived through the hippie generation of the sixties and seventies. Disgusted with Western materialism, they came to Islam in search of spiritual enlightenment and after their conversion some assumed influential positions within the Muslim community. Sardar (1991: 19) explains why some converts gain these positions:

> . . . it has been aided by two factors. *First*, most Muslims in Britain originate from the Indian subcontinent and suffer from a 'Raj mentality'. They treat a white convert to Islam as an extended family treats a new bride: she is put on a pedestal and admired from a distance. Many white converts have been offered positions of authority. *Second*, the convert leaders are propped up by rich Arabs. Despite the rhetoric of Islamic equality, many Gulf Arabs indulge in a form of racism. They look down on Muslims from the subcontinent and look up to white converts.

British converts believe that Islam is a universal religion and it must be beyond national and ethnic boundaries. In Muslim countries, they think, Islam is mixed with local culture and tradition and they want to practise an Islam that is more Koranic and accords with authentic traditions of the Prophet. To achieve their understanding of Islam some converts attempted to start their own groups/movements. One such convert was Abd al-Qadir as-Sufi (Ian Dallas) who became Muslim in 1967. Abd al-Qadir started a Sufic movement in the seventies which then used to be called the *Darqawiyya*, but now it is called the *Murabitun: European Muslim Movement*. He attracted many converts to Islam and made an unsuccessful attempt to start a self-sufficient Muslim village in Britain. Sufism seems to attract many converts to Islam. It is believed to be the major force behind conversion to Islam in Britain (Murghani, 1987: 46). Such a Sufi movement, apart from the *Murabitun*, in which converts are involved, is that of Shaykh Nazim, a Turkish Cypriot based in North Cyprus (see chapter 5).

Some converts like Yusuf Islam (formerly pop singer Cat Stevens) are actively engaged in helping the Muslim community and converts. Yusuf Islam arranges a meeting called the *Islamic Circle* every Saturday afternoon in the Islamic Cultural Centre in London. He also opened the Islamia Primary School, which allots 20 percent of its time to religious education and has a fully integrated Islamic curriculum, and lately a secondary school for girls in the London Borough of Brent. Many converts including well-known names such as Martin Lings, Gai Eaton, Ahmad Thomson, Abdul Hakim Winter, Meryl wyn Davis, Sarah Malik, Ruqayah Khalil and Harfiyah Ball have contributed by writing books, and many others by giving talks on Islam (Mohammad, 1991: 98–9). It is observed that indigenous Muslims are more liberal and dynamic in their interpretation of the role of Islam in Britain than their immigrant fellow Muslims who are more traditionally oriented due to their historical and cultural background.

Indigenous Muslims have also formed other organisations under different names such as the *Islamic Party of Britain* and *Association for British Muslims* which will now be dealt with respectively. While the groups of Abd al-Qadir as-Sufi and Shaykh Nazim have the objective of attracting non-Muslims into Islam, these organisations aim to organise Muslims/convert Muslims, or meeting their ends in Britain.

(a) The Islamic Party of Britain In Britain some Muslims think that to wield some control they have to have political power and they feel there is no political party in Britain that represents their interests (Evans, 1989: 11). Political consciousness in this way was raised after the Salman Rushdie affair and some Muslims reacted by starting a party called the Islamic Party of Britain in September 1989 which was to be the first Islamic party formed in a non-Muslim country. They thought demonstrations and political pressure have been quite ineffective for Muslims in Britain. The main personality for the initiation of the Islamic party was Sahib Mustaqim Bleher, a German convert to Islam, the general secretary of the party, who thought that the time was appropriate for greater political action by Muslims in Britain.

The party claims its membership has reached 8,000 and is aiming for 250,000 in five years. The party's reasons for establishing and some of its objectives to achieve are as follows: (a) To lobby for political support among the existing members of councils and parliament on issues which concern Muslims as a whole and on behalf of other members of society regardless of race, colour or creed who are too weak to defend themselves; (b) to establish unity and leadership within the Muslim community; (c) to actively confront the media and correct historical inaccuracy and prejudice; (d) to campaign vigorously to provide interest-free banking facilities, enterprise-support and legal indemnification; (e) to present a viable political and social alternative to the British people based on the abiding Islamic principles of justice, benevolence and tolerance; (f) to establish regular regional and national rallies/seminars to call people to Islam and participation in action through support or membership.[20]

According to the party's spokesman on economy, A. Hankin, who is an English convert to Islam, one of the aims of the party was to make other parties feel that there is this alternative Islamic party if they do not take the view of Muslims:

> We didn't expect to be swept to power in the next general election. We didn't even expect to have an MP or any kind of representative. The main impact or the main benefit we had from it is the fact of the formation of the party has forced the other political parties to take the views of the Muslims much more seriously because there is now always that alternative in the background. If the Muslims view that their rights are being walked over or they are not being listened to, then there is always this alternative of Islamic party. Both the Labour party and the Conservatives know this. And perhaps the second major reason for the establishment of the party was in terms of da'wah. Being a political party we will automatically get a certain degree of press coverage. When reporting Islamic party policies I always report Islamic teachings. And this allows many people who otherwise would never have a chance to have any idea what Islam is saying to learn a few things about Islam. And this already has had quite a significant effect on many people.[21]

Before the general election of 9 April 1992 the party took part in several local elections where many Muslims are resident such as Bradford where it came fourth after the three big parties, but failed to attract a substantial number of Muslim votes.[22] The general election of 9 April 1992 also brought failure for the party.

For example, in Bradford West where the president of the party, Daoud Pidcock, was a candidate it was able to get only one percent of the votes.[23]

The executive body of the party mainly consists of converts to Islam. The president Daoud Pidcock, the general secretary Sahib Mustaqim Bleher, transport and education spokesman Abdur-rahim Green, spokesman on economics Abd as-Salam Hankin are all converts to Islam. Since the party is mainly run by converts it is criticised by some Muslims and leaders of the Muslim community are deeply divided about the launch of the party. Zaki Badawi, chair of the *Council of Imams and Mosques* commented: 'It is the converts who are taking the lead in all this. Few have no roots in the community.'[24]

In an article on a national paper over the leadership problem of British Muslims Sardar (1991: 19) has severely criticised the position of converts in the party:

In following the *Sunnah* example of Muhammad, the converts came to see themselves as personifying the Prophet; only they could interpret Islam for other Muslims. So they sought to impose their often authoritarian version of Islam and the *Sunnah*. In this respect, no one would be surprised that while converts have a disproportionate influence within the Islamic Party of Britain.

It is also proposed that the convert leadership would not understand the real problems of Asians like racism. However, the spokesman A. Hankin explains why the party had to be set up by converts:

The reality of the Muslim organisations in this country is that they are really disjointed. There is a lot of competition, there is a lot of petty personal rivalries between different organisations. And to try and bring them together was really a hopeless task from the beginning. So it might be a benefit that in the party there are converts because they do not have any allegiance to any ethnic or racial group. Converts are fairly neutral in this.

The headquarters of the party was in Birmingham but it has now been moved to Milton Keynes. The party is trying to set up branches in areas where there is a significant number of Muslim population. The executive body of the party believes that it would probably be a number of years before the party can have a solid significant impact on British politics by having votes from the Muslim community.

(b) The Association for British Muslims   Since none of the existing organisations air the problems of converts and none has a programme especially for them some converts decided to establish an organisation called the *Association for British Muslims* which was set up in London in 1974. It is a continuation of William Quilliam's organisation in Liverpool and the one that functioned in Notting Hill Gate, West London, during the 1920s and 1930s. The objectives of the association are to represent the interests of all Muslim converts and to project a better understanding of Islam in Britain. Although the association mainly aims to help converts to adjust to being Muslim Britons, it also aims at the descendants of immigrants to adjust equally to being British Muslims. According to the president of the association they do not see any contradiction between British traditions and Islam. He states that the association represents the majority of converts, and a typical profile is middle class, professional, often public school educated, monarchist, conservative, and involved with genuine mystic paths and masters (Owen, 1991: 14).

The association has had a lot of criticism, not least from other converts on the basis that there is no racial grouping in Islam and so they can not split off. The president, Daoud Owen, answers the criticisms by accusing other Muslim organisations of not being able to understand converts and the British mentality:

> The problem has been that a lot of the organisations in Britain don't address the specific needs of converts who have particular problems. And also they don't understand the British culture. Some of the organisations were set up to bring Islam to British people, but none of them has actually understood the British culture, the British mind. It was all very well belonging to these organisations, but nobody was helping somebody who had converted come to terms with the social consequences of it. And very simple practical things of how to help somebody, say, stop drinking, stop eating pork, and why these things are necessary. As a result there are a lot of converts who are not getting the aftercare that they need.[25]

24

The president also accuses Muslims who discourage converts to join the association:

> People are talking to converts saying, 'You can't join them because we are Muslim and all Muslims are brothers, and there is no nation in Islam.' This is foolish. Why is it right to have, say, a Sri Lankan or a Pakistani Muslim association, but not to have a British Muslim association?

To conclude then, although some converts seem to be taking the lead on many occasions and in organisational matters, they, however, are not as publicly active as pre-War period converts who had exclusively taken the matters of the Muslim community in their hands (see Murghani, 1987: 46). The reasons for this change are two-fold. *First*, before the War, the number of Muslims were very small. With the influx of immigration in the 1950s and 1960s the philosophical and political ideas of Muslim thinkers from the home countries of immigrants were brought in. *Second*, Muslims brought in their religious leaders with them as well as community leaders. This situation led to immigrants having less consultation with converts over the matters of the Muslim community. Now we turn to the da'wah activities of Muslims in Britain and their strategy in the West in general.

C Da'wah strategy in Britain

In terms of missionary activities, Muslims in Britain have been unenthusiastic even though da'wah (mission, spreading the message of Islam) is stated as one of the priorities in the objectives of many organisations. However, the majority of Muslims living in Britain believe that the emergence of a distinctive Muslim identity is essential for effective da'wah and this can be achieved through the example of moral excellence set by Muslims. According to them the stability of Muslim family life, the absence of drinks, drugs, etc., and the overall discipline of Muslims living in the West will itself send powerful signals to non-Muslims. In his address to British Muslims during the annual conference of the UK Islamic Mission in 1985, Faruqi (1986: 7, 19) spelt out that the family is the 'best tool' for Islamic da'wah in the West to present the value of Islam and urged Muslims to make it a rule to invite a non-Muslim to visit their family once a week.

The Muslim who wishes to perform da'wah activity in Britain faces a complex situation. He is on the one hand, commanded by the Koran (16: 125) to *'Invite (all) to the way of thy Lord with wisdom and beautiful preaching.'* On the other hand, he lives in a non-Muslim surrounding where his religion is not recognised by the state. So the activist Muslim in such a position has two options. He may choose to abandon his mission, or he may choose the way of calling individuals to Islam if he wants to fulfil his religious responsibility. For those activists who chooses the latter way there seems to be two main strategies. There are those who favour an indirect da'wah approach and those who prefer direct missionary work.

1 Indirect da'wah approach

Most Muslims believe that living a Muslim life-style is sufficient to attract others to the religion. To use a Christian concept this approach may be called 'life-style evangelism' (Poston, 1992: 117). According to those who advocate this type of missionary activity, God has not given power to man to convert anybody. Hence, a Muslim should not worry himself whether other people will accept or reject his message (Islahi, 1978: 151ff). Instead they ought to behave as Muslims. They believe that 'action speaks louder than words' and criticise direct da'wah activists for utilising the agency of the word of mouth as the only means of propagation of the faith and avoiding the importance of demonstrating practically. Mawdudi (1967: 31), who is the founder of Jamaat-i Islami and has a significant following in Britain, advocates indirect da'wah strategy, though he does not exclude direct da'wah, to Muslims living in Britain and invites them to be ambassadors of Islam. By doing so, he says, they will manage to invoke an interest on the part of non-Muslims.

One characteristic of indirect da'wah proponents is that if they, by chance, engage in conversation with non-Muslims, they prefer to point out common grounds that Islam shares with other religions rather than claiming that Islam is superior to others. Life-style proponents are more likely to be introversionist in the sense that they are concerned primarily with the maintenance of their religion than conveying the message of Islam to non-Muslims. The first generation of immigrants are mainly to be classified into this group because they were more concerned with obtaining a comfortable standard of living in Britain. Having migrated to a non-Muslim country and having faced ensuing uncertainty they have tended to be defensive and passivist. This passivist attitude may have led Muslims to be isolationists and have less interaction with non-Muslims.

2 Direct da'wah approach

Some Muslims find life-style da'wah strategy insufficient although they regard it as supportive of one's mission. They see it as being too·passive. They think that in a pluralistic society the Muslim life-style will not even be noticed by non-Muslims (Yakan, 1984: 111). Instead they advocate that to bring non-Muslims into the fold of Islam a Muslim should inform a non-Muslim of the specific precepts of Islam.

Direct da'wah proponents are more extrovertly oriented and more activist as opposed to introvert, passivist indirect da'wah proponents. The new generation of Muslims, who consider Britain their home in contrast to their parents, are more likely to fall into this category. They believe that if Islam is presented to British society, many people will not find difficulty in accepting it because Islam offers alternatives to British society (western societies in general) which has a high crime rate, drug problems, etc.

The most important qualification for Muslim activists according to some strategists is that they must be equipped with a full-knowledge of Islamic teachings and a full mastery of the techniques of modern propaganda as well as competence in at least some of the main academic disciplines of today (al-Fasi, 1967: 3–4). Mawdudi (1967: 31) urges Muslims living in Britain to have a body of bright and studious young Muslims who should prepare themselves for highly scientific pursuits and they should be able to suggest reasonable solutions, according to Islamic concepts and theories, of all problems that crop up in present day life. Otherwise, Mawdudi suggests, nothing will be accepted by English people since they have reached a high standard of development in philosophy, physical and social sciences. Some strategists also favour utilising proper communication techniques in order to facilitate da'wah activity. They are aware of the fact that much could be learnt from Christian missionary methodology such as distribution of literature in various lan-

27

guages and establishing of Islamic broadcasting stations (Sicard, 1976: 354).

Along this line of precepts of direct da'wah methodology in Britain, facilities such as seminars, lectures and the like are arranged in mosques, schools and Islamic organisations to draw different kinds of people. On these occasions Muslims have the chance of engaging in conversation with non-Muslims during refreshments which are often made available following such gatherings. Islamic societies in universities make use of this type of gathering more successfully than any other kind of organisation.

Since there is no institution in Britain and throughout the Muslim world similar to Christian missionary institutions, the Muslim mission relies on printed work more than anything else. Apart from the organisations' own publishing there are several publishing houses that print books adapted to da'wah objectives. Some of the literature consists of booklets, some full-length books, and magazines which are more applicable to those who are interested in Islam. Many books and magazines discuss Christian-Muslim relations and target Christian audiences attempting to bridge the gap between the two faiths. Emphasis has always been made about Jesus being a prophet of Islam as well as Islam being an Abrahamic religion. Free copies of the Koran with English translation are also made available to non-Muslims by several organisations.

Some converts involved in this study expressed their opinions as to whether Muslims should take a more proselytising approach to da'wah. Most of them believe that if Islam is made known to British people objectively, there will be more converts. One convert remarked rather eagerly: 'I can't imagine any one reason why anybody should reject Islam if they really understand what Islam is all about. It is something perfectly reasonable and rational.' Another convert had a slightly different view:

'I think there is always this fear in most people that you are trying to con them and things like that as Jehovah's Witnesses and Mormons coming to the door. They think you are just another one of them. And so this is why I'm taking a softly, softly approach. But I think nevertheless you do have to make an effort to let them learn something about Islam at any possible time.'

28

Psychologically the indirect da'wah view is certainly a more comfortable means of propagating since there is little chance of confrontation with a targeted individual. On the other hand, indirect missionary activity may create a situation in which a Muslim is religiously devout and socially emphatic in his surrounding and may be appreciated as simply 'a good neighbour' without inquiry as to the causes of the observed devotion and empathy (Poston, 1992: 117ff). So direct da'wah activists are of the opinion that some intellectual interaction must inevitably occur since non-Muslims also need to be aware of the doctrines of Islam to commit to it, whereas indirect da'wah activists are of the opinion 'get hold of the heart and the head yields easily.'

In general the Muslims of Britain are often criticised for not finding a proper da'wah methodology and for their failure to contextualise Islam for the Western audience. Khurram Murad for the first time specified da'wah strategy for Muslims living in Britain/the West. Murad is involved in the Jamaat-i Islami movement in Pakistan and he was a disciple of Mawdudi. He came to Britain to succeed Khurshid Ahmad, the founder of the Islamic Foundation in Leicester, in 1978. He remained in this position until 1986 when he had to go back to Pakistan due to health reasons. During his stay in Britain he has served as an inspirational force for Islamic workers in the West. His booklets and speeches are considered as textbooks for Islamic workers in Britain and elsewhere (Abdullah, 1986: 63). His experience in Britain enabled him to understand the special problems connected with the establishment of an Islamic movement and da'wah in a non-Muslim context and he collected his views in two main works entitled *Da'wah Among Non-Muslims in the West* and *Islamic Movement in the West*. For Murad da'wah among non-Muslims cannot, and should not, be treated as an isolated phenomenon. Muslims should recognise its proper place at the centre of Islamic life that they must live. In his view, da'wah in Islam is not a profession. It is a state of mind, a world view, an attitude to life, thus it is integral to Islam. There are elements of both the direct and indirect da'wah approach in Murad's thinking. He sees both types of approaches as complementing one another. Having stated the central place of da'wah in Islam, Khurram Murad tries to determine the concepts and methodologies and points to three basic concepts which, in his view, provide the essential framework for the important attitudes and approaches that Muslims should follow concerning da'wah. *Firstly,* Islam is not a new religion; it is the eternal message of God. The basic message of Islam, that was given to the first Prophet, was the same as that given to the last Prophet. So coming to Islam is like going back to one's own roots – in nature and in history. *Secondly,* the *Muslim Ummah* has not been constituted to become just another nation among nations, Islam has been raised for all mankind. *Thirdly,* the objective of da'wah is not to win an argument, it is to win and activate a heart (Murad, 1986: 16–17).

Not much has been put forward on Muslim missionary activity in Britain apart from Murad's effort to form a strategy for da'wah. And not many organisations give priority to missionary work. Those which give priority to missionary work are inadequate in developing a programme. In the light of the above stated facts it may be concluded that Muslim missionary work in Britain has not been successful. There are many reasons for this failure which one can easily detect upon observing the Muslim community and listening to British converts to Islam. Some of the significant reasons, as Mohammad (1991: 99, 103) outlines can be counted as follows: (a) The Muslims in Britain have had a low self image for they had neither an Islamic state to look up to around the world nor any significant achievements in Britain; (b) most Muslims cannot step out of their cultural boundaries to accept Muslims from other cultures; (c) they are ignorant of the basic values of English people and the fundamentals of Christian theology; (d) they are engrossed in petty disputes and do not project a clear-cut world view and perspective of Islam; (e) they have failed to evolve a language for da'wah or an appropriate strategy of communication which could appeal to the people in Britain; (f) Muslim youth who interact with non-Muslims do not know how to present their religion to non-Muslims since they learn religion from their elders who try to convince only the convinced.

Taken altogether the above mentioned facts with the fact that Muslims in Britain are viewed as 'ex-colonials' who have received the additional favour of being allowed to settle in mainland Britain, the future of conversion to Islam in Britain does not seem to be promising. Yet the present number of native British converts around 3,000–5,000 may be treated as significant though it is not as significant as in some European countries.[26]

TWO

ON THE WAY TO CONVERSION

'At school one day our English master asked us all in turn what we wanted to be when we grew up. The hasty answers he received covered the usual small boy choice: "engine driver", "policeman", "sailor", and all the rest. When it came to my turn, however, I simply blurted out, "I should like to be a clergyman". The entire class rocked with laughter and the master joined in.'

Abraham Carmel

A Childhood experiences

Most of the literature on conversion suggest that to understand conversion experience one should look at the developing person throughout his/her lifespan, also taking into consideration psycho-social factors. In this way the claim that the conversion as part of a lifelong search for ultimate meaning can be examined.[1] Thus the structure of the interview was organised to examine the whole lifespan of the converts, beginning with childhood and adolescence experiences. In this chapter the reported childhood and adolescence experiences of the converts to Islam will be described. The characteristics of the group interviewed will be compared with those of other groups whose conversion biographies have been similarly studied.

1 Happiness versus unhappiness

It has long been established that the family is principal among the social relationships that contribute to religious growth (Meadow and Kahoe, 1984: 37). Christensen (1963: 210) found evidence that distorted interfamilial relationships unconsciously affect the development of religious experience. Studies on converts to new religious movements generally indicate that they have a special appeal to disorganised, disturbed youth alienated from their family of origin. Deutsch (1975: 166), for example, studied 14 members of the New York-based Meher Baba cult and described virtually all gave histories of 'chronic unhappiness and unsatisfactory parental relations'. He found that all but a few of the parental marriages were described as unhappy. Ullman (1989: 11–16; 1982: 189), studying 40 converts from various groups; born-again Christians, the repentant Jews, the Hare Krishna devotees, and the Bahai converts, with a control group of 30 nonconverts, found that converts characterised their childhood as unhappy more often than nonconverts. About one-half of converts (47.5%) in Ullman's sample were judged as describing an extremely unhappy childhood while only 6 (15%) were judged as describing a normal or happy childhood. They reported specific, disturbing, traumatic events experiencing early parental divorce or death, or witnessing a parent attempt suicide, violent fights, or recurrent mental breakdowns of parents.

To examine these issues the interview questions intended to discover converts' emotional well-being during childhood, and adolescence. They referred to the person's perception of both parents, and to specific traumatic events during childhood and adolescence.

In general the converts to Islam drew a normal or happy (but rarely very happy) picture of their childhood although there were extreme cases which were described as 'horrible'. 31 (44%) reported a 'happy' childhood, 18 (26%) described it as 'moderate'. Only 21 (30%) reported an unhappy childhood. As for traumatic events in childhood or early adolescence, 11 (16%) stated that their parents were divorced (one woman was adopted never knowing who her true parents were), 3 (4%) said their parents were on the verge of breakup, 9 (13%) had at least one parent who died before they were 16 years of age. Parental divorce seems to have been the major trauma (16%) of childhood. In most cases it was the father whom they blamed for disturbances in the family. Kathleen, for example, like Jimmy recalled how she hated her father:

32

'My father was alcoholic and he used to beat my mother. I was always witnessing this alone since I had no brothers and sisters. And I prayed many times that he should die . . . When I was a young girl I used to pray God saying that "the only thing that I want from you is a man who does not drink since I saw what alcohol does to family." '

When describing how they perceived their relationships with their fathers in childhood (table 2.1), 21 reported bad relations while 4 had no relation whatsoever with their father. It was an average relationship for 25, while it was good or very good for 20. As for relations with the mother 11 reported bad relations. It was average for 28, and was good or very good for 31. 19 reported separations of over 1 year from either parent in childhood (separation covered father being away, death, divorce, etc.).

The father problem appeared with similar frequency in men and women. 40 percent of women as against 34 percent of men reported bad relations with their fathers. As for the mother problem it also appeared with similar frequency in men and women. 20 percent of women reported bad relations as against 41 percent of men.

Table 2.1 Perception of relations with parents in childhood

	relation with father (n=70)	relation with mother (n=70)
no relation	4 (5.7%)	0 (0%)
bad	21 (30%)	11 (15.7%)
average	25 (35.7%)	28 (40%)
good/very good	20 (28.6%)	31 (44.3%)

2 Father figure in childhood: absent or withdrawn father

Some studies on religious conversion from the psychoanalytic perspective hypothesised that the religious conversion experience may serve to supply a benevolent, protective, strong and firm paternal figure to replace a father who was seen as deficient in these respects. Allison (1969: 23, 31) studying male college students who experienced conversion found that four out of seven subjects had fathers who were 'either adulterers, alcoholics or committed suicide'. Allison concluded that 'the conversion experience serves to alter a perception of the actual father as weak, ineffective, or absent by supplying instead an internal representation of a strong and principled substitute paternal figure with clear values and firm judgements.' Salzman (1953: 186), suggesting a distinction between 'progressive' and 'regressive' conversions, traced the regressive conversion back to a hated father figure or father symbols. The majority of Deutsch's (1975: 168) sample described their fathers as hostile and critical. Deutsch also found that at least four of the 14 converts' fathers were absent. Similarly, in Ullman's study the importance of father figure stood out in interviews with 40 converts. Almost 80 percent of Ullman's sample were judged as experiencing an extremely stressful relationship with their fathers and from the converts' childhood memories their fathers emerged as either absent, extremely passive, or actively rejecting. About one-third of them had had very little or no contact with their biological fathers since the ages of four/five. 45 percent had fathers whom they perceived as weak, withdrawn, or hostile. Only 18 percent were judged as describing a positive relationship with their fathers (Ullman, 1989: 30). In the light of these findings Ullman concluded that 'The absence, withdrawal, or hostility of the father places specific obstacles in the individual's development. It may affect children's perspective on moral prohibitions and may hamper their perception of the environment as safe and masterable. Thus the father figure is indeed implicated not only in the converts' memories of childhood but in the very process of conversion and important changes preceding conversion may intensify the need for a protective father figure for a religious conversion, whereby an inhibitory structure is imposed and the protection of an omnipotent authority figure is supplied, offering ways of by-passing these obstacles while simultaneously reflecting them.' (Ullman, 1989: 59).

The present study provides limited support of a problem regarding relationship with the father as the above studies speculated. As presented earlier only less than one third of the converts reported bad or stressful relations with their father. Their childhood or adolescent experiences in terms of absent, withdrawn, or normal fathering were also examined. 18 reported father absence while 25 described their father as withdrawn. 27 reported normal fathering[2] (table 2.2).

Table 2.2 Fathering in childhood
and adolescence (n=70)

Father absent	18 (26%)
Father withdrawn	25 (36%)
Normal fathering	27 (38%)

Father absence (26%) in most cases were caused by divorce. However, death and being away from home for occupational reasons were also among the reasons. 4 converts had little or no contact with their fathers. This seems merely to have accentuated the estrangement between them since childhood. Raymond has no knowledge of his father's personality, background or occupation: 'I don't know anything about my father. I think he is somewhere in London. It doesn't really bother me. He is not really my father anyway, is he? He has only slept with my mother. Father is someone who brings you up.'

Passive and withdrawn fathers are more frequent (36%) than father absence (26%) in the childhood memories of the converts to Islam. They are remembered by their children as distant and ineffectual, too withdrawn for guidance and support. Debbie, a 20 years old college student, portrayed her father as punishing: 'My relations with my father was very poor. The only contact I had with him was that of a father punishing his daughter. Never ever have we had a private conversation. With my mother it has never been deep either.'

Taken together 62 per cent reported either absent or withdrawn fathers as against 38 percent who reported normal fathering. This finding with the majority having a history of nonexistent or turbulent relationships raises the question of 'How is the want of fathering implicated in the actual conversion process? What is the chain of events through which ineffectual fathering may participate in bringing about a conversion experience?'[3] The lack of paternal protection may exacerbate the child's perception of reality outside the home as unreliable. Evidently many of those who did not receive adequate fathering regarded society as unreliable and some had, rebellious feelings when they reached adolescence. The cases of Raymond, Steve, and Tony that will be presented in the following pages give examples of the importance of fathering. In their eyes the world out there is populated with hypocrites, manipulators, etc. They believe that conversion gave them the chance to leave this sinister world. As Ullman

35

(1989: 54–5) puts it the father may serve as a mediator between the family and the outside world and aids in securing the child's perception of reality outside the home as safe and malleable. A father who is absent, withdrawn, harsh or rejecting may cause the child to wish to change these consequential aspects of social-isation, and therefore induce a search for protection and a mean-ingful structure. Religious conversion may be an expression of an attempted solution for these consequences of inadequate fathering. Religion, however, provides guidelines for behaviour, inhibits impulses and produces structure and stability.

However, these findings do not necessarily suggest that all who have absent or withdrawn fathers will be religious converts. It may only suggest that difficulties in relating to father may only be one of the antecedents of religious conversion among many. Besides, some converts like Pam also tended to express anger towards their mothers: 'I have always had a very good relationship with my father, but I had a difficult and rocky relationship with my mother.'

3 Mother: father's substitute and independence from her

When the father is absent or withdrawn the chances of an over-dependence on the mother may increase. Allison's (1969: 31) research suggested that the father's actual absence or unavail-ability or perception of him as weak or immoral is associated with a special closeness between the subjects and their mothers. Allison found that even in the case of the subjects whose fathers were less obviously absent or inadequate, there is a suggestion that the subjects felt particularly close to their mothers and rela-tively remote from their fathers during much of their lives. Ullman (1989: 56) also wrote that converts whose father were absent or withdrawn tended to report positive and close relation-ships with their mothers. This pattern of relations with the mother naturally occurs with some (7%) of the converts to Islam, since many experienced early parental divorce and almost all continued to stay with their mothers, which eventually led to estrangement from the father. In these cases the mother often emerges as supportive, understanding, and warmer than the father. It seems likely that the lack of paternal guidance or sup-port had enforced, in these cases, a reliance on the mother as the only source of security and had intensified the intimate bond with her. However some still described their mother as good-natured and warm-hearted but also found them ignorant and inadequate. Raymond, a 22 years old college student, does not even know his father's whereabouts. He has lived with his mother all his life. Though he has always been dependent on his mother he saw her as inadequate. His mother was a drug-user and she did not even send Raymond to school until 13 years of age. He hated his mother as well as his father. When he started to talk about his mother he said he did not like to say she was his mother and blamed her for not giving him a normal upbringing and for being an 'agnostic' and trying to indoctrinate him with that. Raymond converted when 18 which is well below the average conversion age (29.7) for the present sample. Merging with his mother due to lack of paternal guidance seems to have precipitated his conversion process but he also wanted to separate himself from his mother although he intellectually had his own reasons for conversion.

Some of the existing literature on conversion in adolescence suggest that the adolescent moves via conversion towards independence from his mother. If the father is absent or withdrawn and the mother is the only source of security, the process of separation and the individuation becomes more urgent and more difficult. Overdependence on the mother may blur the boundaries of the relationship with her. Allison (1969: 24, 36) claimed that the conversion experience provides a substitute father, and it may also provide 'a protector against the regressive nostalgia for the undifferentiated union with the mother and serves thereby in aiding the process of individuation and differentiation.' Levin and Zegans (1974: 75) also showed that with a weak-father figure as an object for identification the adolescent may not develop a firm sexual identity and therefore he can not establish for himself a 'self' truly separate from his mother. Ullman (1989: 57) suggested that the convert, through the conversion, finds not only an inhibitor and protector to replace a father who is deficient in these respects but also a shield from the seductive unity with the mother. Thus the conversion experience helps consolidate the converts' previously shaky sense of identity.

4 (6%) converts who had their father absent in childhood recounted that they wanted to be independent of their mothers. As quoted above Raymond had a strong need to separate from

his mother. John also had a difficult relationship with his mother when he was an adolescent:

'I went through quite a traumatic stage from the age of about 11 to 15. In that my mother separated from my father. I was given the choice of whether to live with my mother or stay with my father. As I felt closer to my mother I went to live with her. But my relationship with her, apart from the first few years, was very difficult. She developed an alcohol problem. And my relationship with her distanced. It became increasingly hard to communicate with her.'

This pattern of differentiation from the mother is sometimes present in the sample studied. Yet they are rare cases. The hypothesis that through conversion those who have a weak father figure may gain individuation from the mother does not seem to be a crucial factor in the conversion experiences of the converts to Islam. Freddie and John converted in their mid-twenties, and Raymond converted when 18. However, the interviews suggest that the need to break maternal bonds may have been something of a precipitating factor for conversion.

4 Parents' affiliation and upbringing regarding religion

The likelihood of adopting parental religion has been found to be higher if religion is important for the parents; if both parents share the same religious beliefs; and if the child identifies with the parents. The child then experiences strong social pressure to conform to their wishes with regard to religion (Batson and Ventis, 1982: 46–7).

The converts to Islam seem to have come from families where there was no strong identification with any religion. They mostly (85%) come from families that did not belong to a church, or were not active participants in a church. Most of the interviewees gave the following or a similar account about their parents: 'My parents are not church-goers, but basically just believers.' Most described their parents' connection with the church in terms of ceremonial attendance like weddings and funerals.

When classified according to religion of upbringing the present sample consists of 51 Church of England, 12 Catholics, 3 Methodists, and 4 Jews (table 3.1). Significantly, 17 (24%) had parents religiously heterogeneous such as the mother being Church of

England and the father Agnostic, or the mother being Catholic and the father Church of England. Three converts had one parent who converted to their partner's religion or denomination. And five described one parent as being atheist or agnostic.

36 (51%) described that they had 'no' or 'weak' religious upbringing. Twenty (29%) answered 'normal' while only 14 (20%) described it as 'strong'. Even some of those who had religious upbringing reported not being happy with it at the time. They were confused with what they were taught. Anne recollects her confusion:

> 'I had a very religious upbringing in the family, I used to go to Church every Sunday and to Catholic school where they taught us, when I was five, that three gods is one God and one God is three. And when I was a teenager I used to go to a Convent school . . . I ignored what I didn't understand in Christianity. I picked up the bits which I liked from the Bible like 'love your neighbour as yourself' and 'you can tell a good tree by its fruit' and all the things in the Bible which made sense. But I never thought about the Trinity and I never thought about when it said 'this is my body, eat it in memory of Me,' and 'this is my blood, drink it in memory of Me,' and things like that.'

Although relative religiosity of the parents was not specifically examined, interviews revealed that converts described their mothers as more religious than their fathers, and they learnt their religion through their mothers rather than their fathers. This, in fact, is in congruent with the finding that Christian women are more religious than Christian men (Argyle and Beit-Hallahmi, 1975: 71). Of the four different backgrounds; Church of England, Catholics, Methodists, and Jews of which the present sample consists, converts of Jewish origin seem to have the least religious upbringing in the family. Parents who were Church of England seem to have not been strongly religious although they did not particularly oppose religion in general, and they sent their children to Sunday school. Of the 3 Methodists, only one reported religious upbringing. Catholics seemed to have had the most strict religious upbringing compared to others.

5 Freud and religious conversion

Freud's interpretation of religious experience places the father in the centre. He maintains that humans endow God with features that they have attributed to their own fathers in childhood. He claimed that a human's relationship to God is always modelled after his relationship with his biological father, fluctuating and changing with it. The psychoanalytic view which Freud developed suggests that one source of the need for religious beliefs lies in children's disappointments in their parents. Children get disappointed with parents whom they have perceived as omnipotent and unconditionally protective. According to the psychoanalytic view children transfer these perceptions and expectations to a new superior figure and the child's wish for utter protection by an invincible power lives on in the religious beliefs of the adult. Freud claims that a second source of the need for religious beliefs lies in the Oedipal situation. Religious beliefs and the rituals may be viewed as an expression of the body's efforts to atone for his guilt over his desire to displace his actual father.[4] Freud's interpretation of a religious conversion that will be dealt with below is a logical extension of his ideas by which he depicted religious belief as a fantasy wish fulfilment, as an illusion which distorts the reality of the human condition. He argued that the belief in an omnipotent God provides people with an illusory father, sparing them the recognition of their own helplessness (Freud, 1978).

Freud's only article (1961) dealing directly with the experience of religious conversion is his response to a letter he received from a young American physician who protested psychoanalysis' disparaging views of religion, criticised Freud, and described his own conversion experience that he had in the year he graduated at the University. Before his experience, the physician admits, the doctrines of Christianity had been the subject of doubts in his mind. One afternoon while passing through the dissecting room the physician had seen the corpses of a 'sweet-faced dear old woman' being carried onto the dissecting table and was bothered by the thought that: 'There is no God: if there were a God, he would not have allowed this dear old woman to be brought into the dissecting room.' When he got home he had decided to stop going to church. While meditating on this matter, he heard a voice warning him that he should consider the step he was about to take. In the course of the next few days unsettling religious doubts followed and culminated in a religious experience in which the physician accepted Christianity again.

In dealing with this conversion experience Freud, first of all, deals with the matter of 'how come an omnipotent God allows such a terrible thing as the physician thinks?' He purports that the physician's experience is based on bad logic and his interpretation is based on emotional motives. God, as we know, Freud says, allows horrors to take place of a kind very different from the removal of a dead body of a pleasant-looking old woman to a dissecting room. Then Freud asks the question 'why was it, then, that the physician's indignation against God broke out precisely when he received this particular impression in the dissecting room?' Freud believes that the dead woman's face had reminded the physician of his own mother and gives the evidence of the physician's affectionately phrased description of the 'sweet-faced dear old woman'. The significance of the episode at the morgue, in Freud's view, lies in its symbolic tie to the Oedipal situation in which the male child perceives his father as a threatening rival for the mother's love. The physician's undue indignation, according to Freud, is the remnant of this archaic competition with the father. The sight of a 'sweet old woman' aroused in the young physician a longing for his own mother. Freud suggested that this longing was derived from the Oedipus complex, and that this was immediately completed by a feeling of indignation and anger against his father. It stirred the complementing emotion of anger towards his father for 'taking her away' and a wish to dispose of him as a rival. The physician's idea of 'God' and 'father' were not widely separated unconsciously, so his desire to destroy his father manifested itself unconsciously as doubt in the existence of God and sought 'to justify itself in the eyes of reason as indignation about the ill-treatment of a mother-object.' (Freud, 1961: 171). Freud believes that since these religious sentiments are conscious manifestations of a rearoused Oedipal wish to save the mother from the father, they are anxiety-laden and cannot continue. The intense anxiety is caused by the young man's childish fears that his father will retaliate. This anxiety is manifested in the inner voices which warn against resistance to God. The male child resolves the original Oedipal struggle by a complete submission to the will of the father. The new impulse, which is displaced into the sphere of religion by religious doubts, is only a repetition of the Oedipus situation and consequently met with a similar fate. The doubts are quelled by inner voices warning against resistance to God, and the young man feels that he has to submit to the will of God and return to the religious teachings of his childhood. So Freud describes the conversion experience as a defensive process used to reduce anxiety and as an attempt to control anxiety over childhood conflicts between rearoused Oedipal rage towards the father and the fear of his retaliation which is stirred again before conversion. He sees the doubts and ensuing change of heart as by-products of archaic needs. In short, Freud theorised that since the man's understanding of God and father is basically interrelated, he expresses his anger and rebellious feelings in atheistic form. But for fear of the omnipotence of God he is forced to a sudden return to faith.

Freud's hypothesis has found considerable acceptance, especially from psychoanalytically oriented investigators of religious conversion. In a case study of conversion Salzman (1953: 187) interpreted conversion experience as a method of solving the conflict arising from hatred towards the father. Yet he also concluded that a conversion experience may be used as a solution for conflict with any authority figure, whether the father, the mother, or other significant persons. Rizzuto (1979: 51) wrote that the Freudian interpretation was consistent with the findings associating the father figure with the experience of conversion.

To sum up, much of psychoanalysis sees conversion as an attempt to handle repressed material seeking consciousness which are within the framework of religious beliefs; and thus Freud's theories reflect an attempt in conversion to resolve the Oedipal conflict (Gillespie, 1991: 124). The material from the sample studied here has not found evidence to confirm Freud's interpretation of conversion. Though there are converts who expressed anger towards their father the number of those who expressed anger towards their mother was also not insignificant. They are both male and female converts and their indignation towards their father/mother did not seem to have come about as a result of repressed material, but simply caused by their parents not giving them a happy childhood. So Freud's interpretation of religious conversion based on one sudden conversion experience involving one person's return to his religion of upbringing after a few days of hesitation between belief and disbelief does not necessarily reflect the whole nature of religious conversion. It cannot be an explanation for the conversion experiences of those studied here either, since they involve gradual inter-faith conversion. In fact, as Freud (1961: 172) himself admitted '. . . every case of conversion cannot be understood as easily as this one.' Ullman also concluded that Freudian interpretation does not fully explain the conversion experience of her 40 convert subjects. Ullman, after dealing with Freud's interpretation of the physician's conversion experience wrote that Freudian explanation of conversion 'is concerned with the internal dynamics immediately preceding the experience and with the universal psychological themes thereby revealed. Emanating from universal Oedipal longings, the experience of the physician could have been the experience of any male, irrespective of his particular, unique relationship with his father.' (Ullman, 1989: 49). Kildahl's (1977: 245) study of conversion intended to examine the hypothesis which resulted from the Freudian and Psychoanalytic literature. Since the physician's case was a sudden conversion experience Kildahl looked at the Oedipal situation in both sudden and gradual converts. He found nothing in his data to indicate that sudden converts perceive father figures or authority figures any differently than persons of a gradual religious development. His data did not support the idea that the Oedipal situation is handled in any distinctive way by the sudden converts.

B Conversion and adolescence

It is possible that religious conversional change may particularly occur at certain times in the life cycle and during certain stages of development. Gillespie describes adolescence as 'a time for adjusting conformities and trying to sort out what is to be instituted into one's ideological framework and what is to be rejected totally. Various motivations for change exist within the adolescent. They include: physically, emotionally, intellectually . . . motivated actions' (Gillespie, 1991: 104). Psychologists who were interested in conversion phenomenon (James, 1962: 194ff; Coe, 1917: 163; Christensen, 1963: 209; Gillespie, 1991: 94) have suggested that adolescence, a prime time for conflict, identity crisis, searching, reevaluation, and value selection, is the most favourable time for conversion. Developmental psychologists have observed how adolescents are not only capable of abstract thought, but also have a desire for a rational explanation of everything. They believe that religion helps to provide this age group with a solution to individual problems of identity and purpose in life (Argyle and Beit-Hallahmi, 1975: 181).

American psychologists (Starbuck, 1911: 38; Coe, 1917: 163; Hall, 1920: 288–292) studying conversion at the turn of the century described the experience as a typical adolescent phenomenon connected with the normative changes of this age and with tendency to succumb to the power of groups. All of these studies focused on Christian conversion. In most cases, they concluded, conversions were a part of the inevitably intense social and psychological changes of adolescence which is essentially a normal form of adolescent development. For example, Starbuck found that conversion shortens the period of stress and crisis and it prepares the adolescent for entry into adulthood.

The conversion experiences of the typical contemporary converts significantly differ from those of converts studied at the turn of the century. So do experiences of the converts to Islam. The early studies included converts returning to the original teachings from childhood later rejected in adolescence, or moving from one Christian denomination to another which in the end did not bring major changes in terms of core beliefs, life-style, etc. The phenomenon was then seen as a part of the process of becoming an adult and moving from a 'divided self' into a 'unified self', and of securing 'a better life'. Fear, sense of sin, despair, feeling of guilt, and anger were some of the characteristics of the preconversion state (James, 1962: 202ff; Starbuck, 1911: 63). Literature on religious conversion then mainly concentrated on the elated mystical experience and the struggle involved in the process, but it made no attempt to distinguish between different kinds of conversion in terms of their motivations or dynamics of the struggle before conversion (see Salzman, 1953: 181). Furthermore, the early Christian experience of conversions at the turn of the century mostly came about in some large group settings, such as revival meetings and church retreats, attended by the convert's community where young participants were expected to have a conversion experience by which the convert would be rewarded in his social environment. As Coe (1917: 164) pointed out, this expectation of a religious conversion provides a 'psychological set' essential to the experience. The psychological set was also a significant factor in the conversions that occurred in Billy Graham's revivalist meetings during 1950s. However, psychological set for conversion even to one's parents' or environment's religious beliefs does not seem to exist any more, let alone to an alien religion. Society has gradually become secularised and having a conversion experience, or taking one's religion too seriously is considered something weird. Jason's recollection of his childhood and adolescent years may be evidence for this proposal:

> 'The school I went to in London was a totally secular oriented private school. So, like most people in modern Britain I never had a chance either to accept or reject Christianity, simply because it has never been presented to me. And this is generally the case with the younger generation in England. They have not rejected Christianity, they simply don't know what it is. It's never been made clear to them either through schools or from parents or from the society at large. I think the reasons for this is partly the secular society and partly specifically the Anglo-Saxon weakness which regards it is a little bit rude to discuss this area. (It is exactly the opposite in the Muslim world, it is something people love to talk about.) In particularly cultured or educated English circles it is not talked and hence children never talk about it.'

Accounts of converts to other religions confirm our subjects' testimonies of how religion in Britain became a laughing matter in people's mind. Abraham Carmel (1964: 17–8), an Anglican clergyman converted to Catholicism first, then to Judaism, recollects how his school friends laughed at him when he told them he wanted to be a priest when he grew up:

> 'At school one day our English master asked us all in turn what we wanted to be when we grew up. The hasty answers he received covered the usual small boy choice: 'engine driver', 'policeman', 'sailor', and all the rest. When it came to my turn, however, I simply blurted out, 'I should like to be a clergyman.' The entire class rocked with a laughter and the master joined in.'

In contrast to converts at the turn of the century, contemporary converts within Christianity, especially those involved in new movements like the Unification Church adopt beliefs, cognitive changes, and a life-style different from their mainstream culture. They shy away from their parents' religious orientation and adopt new views, often severing their ties with their former social milieu.[5]

In sum, the material from the sample studied suggests that for the vast majority of the subjects interviewed adolescence was not the prime time for conversion. However, it was the period when they partly rejected the religion of childhood. Now the issue of conversion age will be investigated in detail.

1 Conversion age

Although it is evident that religious conversions may occur at any age, the majority of the research on conversion agrees that it is most likely to occur during adolescence. Records of 15,471 conversion cases between 1899 and 1950s show that the average age is 15 years.[6] Early studies, at the turn of the century, among Christian converts by Starbuck (1911: 38), Coe (1917: 163), and Hall (1920: 288–92), found that religious conversion is indeed an adolescent phenomenon. Starbuck, for example, found that it occurred most frequently at the age of 16 for boys and age 13 for girls. Pratt (1948: 122) saw adolescence as a normal period for the experience although he minimised the violent and sudden adolescent religious conversion experience in suggesting that the entire 'moral and religious process of the adolescent period may well be called conversion.' By and large this trend seems to continue today (Argyle and Beit-Hallahmi, 1975: 61; Francis, 1984:69; Paloutzian, 1983: 99). Levin and Zegans (1974: 80) have documented how religious conversion can be a positive factor in the crisis of adolescent turmoil. Christensen (1963: 209) clinically studied 22 men with a history of religious conversion who were under psychotherapy because of incapacitating mental disorders. All of Christensen's subjects were adolescents at the time of conversion. Christensen found an unconscious conflict which related to distorted identifications, a depreciated self-concept, and psychosexual pathology. His study also revealed that a fundamentalistic religious belief was an important part of their early environment and psychic life. Contrary to Christensen's finding, our interviewees' accounts of their childhood experiences and

46

their parents' attitudes towards religion showed that fundamentalistic religious belief was not an important part of their early environment and they rejected the religious beliefs of their childhood in adolescence.

Conversion age for the present sample presents a great deviation from the previously mentioned studies of religious conversion in the West. The average conversion age is 29.7; ranging from 15 to 61 with the vast majority falling into 23–45 years age group (table 2.3). Only 1 (1.4%) experienced conversion before 17. Eighteen (26%) converted between 17 and 22. Forty three (61%) fell into 23–45 age group. And eight (11%) experienced conversion between 46 and 65. Poston's (1992: 166) questionnaire study of European and American converts to Islam found the average conversion age to be 31.4 years.

Table 2.3   Conversion age groups

Age groups	Total n=70 (100%)	Male n=50 (71%)	Female n=20 (29%)
11–16	1 (1.4%)	1 (1.4%)	0 (0%)
17–22	18 (25.7%)	14 (20%)	4 (5.7%)
23–45	43 (61.5%)	30 (42.9%)	13 (18.6%)
46–65	8 (11.4%)	5 (7.1%)	3 (4.3%)

However, as opposed to early and contemporary studies on conversion within Christianity some studies on conversion to contemporary religious cults indicate that conversions take place at a later age, during late teens or early 20s. The average age for Ullman's (1989: 110) sample was 21. Johnson's (1977: 40) study, which covered four groups; Meher Baba, Zen Buddhism, Divine Light Mission and Hare Krishna, found that the average conversion age was in the early 20s ranging anywhere from 18 to 35. Deutsch's (1975: 168) subjects converted between 19–35 with a median age of 25. Galanter's (1980: 1577) study of converts to the Unification Church revealed that they convert in their early 20s. There are other studies which support the proposal that conversion may occur at older ages. Bouquet (1932: 120) writes that seeing conversion as only an adolescent phenomenon 'is too severe a restriction of the field, since conversion, though certainly natural, is a complex and gradual psychic process which is prepared by individual conditions over a long period. It is much more than the moral and religious crisis of adolescence. It may happen that the completion of the process is reached long after adolescence, and even in late middle life.' Jung (1973: 109–31) emphasised that middle age and after were the prime years for religious concern. He emphasised mid-to-late thirties as a period of moving from an extroverted, external-reality-mastery orientation to an introverted inner-reality-understanding orientation. A large number of great Christian figures like St Paul, St Augustine, and Tolstoy converted late in life.

2 Emotional and cognitive issues in adolescence

According to most theorists, identity formation and the time of youth go hand in hand. Youth are involved in many emotional, cognitive, behavioural issues. They struggle with life or have ideological conflicts regarding altruism or emotional intensity. Many youths reflect this tension and quest for identity, and look for the 'right choice' in these years. Their cognitive development impacts their religious concerns. This context may be a time of faith development for youth, and it may be perfect for religious conversion to come to the fore, which may provide an answer to identity confusion (Gillespie, 1991: 180). However, scholars like Baumeister (1986: 170) have suggested that the religious conversion in the form of solving adolescent identity crisis is something of the past. The decline of religious faith and religious experience among youth has deprived them of means of solving identity crises. Now, whether it was emotional or cognitive matters that the converts to Islam were concerned with during adolescence will be examined.

As discussed earlier recent studies report that a history of problem relationships with parents and an unhappy childhood and adolescence are characteristics of religious converts regardless of their religion of origin or the group that they got involved. It is purported that although the different religious groups have many theological and sociological differences among them, they seem to respond to similar psychological needs. Ullman's (1989: 122–3) study of conversion concluded that 'it is not the "typical" but emotionally troubled adolescent who is likely to become a religious convert'. 65 percent of Ullman's sample characterised their adolescence as extremely unhappy. So a turbulent adolescence is associated with conversion. However, 64 percent of those who characterised their adolescence as extremely unhappy also characterised their childhood as extremely unhappy. For the majority of them the psychological upheaval of childhood continued during their adolescence.

The accounts given by the converts to Islam do not strongly support Ullman's finding associating adolescence with turmoil. 36 (51%) of the 70 reported no emotional stress during adolescence. 17 (24%) described their adolescence as moderate or mixed, and 17 (24%) said they had an unhappy adolescence. Yet the data confirms Ullman's finding with regard to the connection between an unhappy childhood and adolescent turmoil. Significantly, 16 of those 17 who reported stressful adolescence also reported an unhappy childhood. The association between an unhappy childhood and emotional stress during adolescence is highly significant (chi-square with continuity correction = 20.259, df=1, p<.001). And more significantly, all of them also reported father absence or father being withdrawn. (There is also a highly significant association between reported emotional stress during adolescence and reported father absence/withdrawn: chi-square with continuity correction = 12.03, df=1, p<.001). These findings clearly illustrate that their turmoil during adolescence was a continuation of their childhood experiences, such as parental divorce. On the other hand, those who reported happy adolescence had a stable childhood. Offer and Offer's[7] study of adolescent boys lends support to the present finding. Offer and Offer found that those who were viewed as in a state of turmoil had a common background of family crisis such as divorce and overt marital conflicts. However, some of the converts to Islam have experienced a tormented adolescence period as a result of their relationship with the outside world, which has eventually precipitated their conversion. Steve, Raymond, Tony, and Henry are among those who have gone through such experiences. Consider the case of Henry:

Henry described his relationship with his parents as good when he was a child. Then he went to boarding school from the age of 11 to 16 and that soured the relationship with his parents and made them distant and 'also', Henry said: '. . . because coming towards adolescence was a difficult time. So I was a bit rebellious and that led me to leave home at the age of 16.' Henry came to London first from a small village where he was brought up. He was not prepared for what he encountered in London,

49

and got himself into a lot of trouble merely by lack of familiarity with London and indeed he became ill. At that time very large numbers of young people were smoking hashish and he took part as well. He described himself then as unstable, and having no roots. He could not concentrate on doing anything and did not have any source of income apart from Social Security. He got pretty ill for six months and was involved in an organisation called *Release* which helped drug users to get off drugs. Fortunately, he ended up in a hospital where a social worker helped him get a scholarship to provide him with funds to do A-levels. As soon as he got his A-levels he left school: 'So that put me in a kind of more balanced situation, but it still wasn't easy. There was a lot going on and changing in the society. I felt incomplete and I had a very strong dissatisfaction with the whole structure of the society at that time.' Henry was struggling to form an identity. He did not have a suitable atmosphere or group around to provide him with this identity achievement. He was yearning to associate himself with something, a group or an ideology. Some of Henry's friends had become members of Divine Light Mission. Henry had a lot of contact with them and went to their meetings to see Guru Maha Raj Ji, but 'it did not feel right', he said. He was living in a hostel then. And there was a couple on the very top floor and another friend of theirs was on the same floor as Henry. He knew them by sight coming up and down the stairs and he heard from his other friends in the same hostel that this couple had become Muslim. Henry was interested just to know what it meant to become a Muslim. He did not even know the word 'Islam'. As he got to know them it occurred to him to ask them if they had books on their religion. The man said that they did not, but he could talk to him about it. Henry went along and they talked about Islam. They were Sufi Muslims involved in the group of Abd al-Qadir as-Sufi. In his second meeting with the man something impressed Henry deeply: 'While we were talking he said, "Sorry, it's time for the prayer now; I have to pray."' There was just one room, so he went into the corner and prayed: 'I think that kind of made an impression, because I saw that somebody was doing something practical and it caught my attention.' Henry was also impressed by the hospitality of the couple. He said: 'It was different. I mean there are many hospitable British people, but it is not that you notice in London.' As their relationship proceeded they invited Henry to come to one of their meetings. Henry found their group very warm and morally much more interesting than most of the people he had been dealing with. He attended their meeting for 4–5 months at the end of which he made up his mind to embrace Islam.

Humans need to have an organised framework within which their life takes on meaning and purpose. Adolescence is precisely that period in which persons begin to orient themselves within some meaningful system. Thus religious systems exist precisely as one type of meaning system in which individuals can orient themselves, understand, interpret, and direct their lives (Spilka, 1985: 200). As well as the emotional side of adolescence the present research also tried to explore converts' interest in religious, political, or other questions, such as concern over social injustice, unresolved specific religious doubts. Twenty three (33%) of the 70 people studied reported cognitive, existential, or religious concerns in adolescence as opposed to those 17 (24%) who reported emotional matters.

In individuals' lives there are some periods that are more crucial than others for change in structural form. Adolescence is one of these periods. It is a period of transition in approach to cognitive tasks and moral issues (Marcia, 1980: 160). Erikson (1968: 128–135) argued that since adolescents attempt to make sense out of the adult world the religious and ideological consistency of a society is very important for them. Part of the motivation for conversion to alien religions, then, involves youthful dissatisfaction with the ideological and religious inconsistencies of society. Adolescence was the time that many of the converts to Islam began questioning the application of their religion in society at large or looking for answers to life's basic questions. It was in adolescence that they attempted to fashion a consistent personal code of moral behaviour in a changing culture of uncertain values. Deutsch's (1975: 168) subjects also reported disinterest or disillusionment with the religion of origin in later adolescence, although a few reported an upsurge of religious interest in early adolescence.

In Britain no more than 15 percent of the population attends church every week. Over half of those who attend at the age of 13 will have ceased to do so by the time they are 20. Some 50 percent of the teenagers attending Roman Catholic services will have given up doing so even before they are 20 and about 75 percent of the Anglicans. Furthermore, by the time of the school leaving age, very few young people would still be claiming allegiance to the Christian churches (Francis, 1984: 10). This is, in fact, what most of the converts to Islam experienced in late adolescence. Some had been religious in their preadolescent years. But this religiosity had disappeared, partially because they had been taught by their teachers at secondary school, or by the society to think in a rational way about religious matters. They lost their capacity for religious experiences, and Christianity lost its plausibility for them. They became restless with the religious tradition of their family or society critically questioning its intellectual, moral and religious adequacy. Tony, 17, who converted 2 weeks before the interview, bitterly criticised society:

'This society doesn't make you know about religion. I don't know why? May be it is wrapped up in the wrong way of life; just working, sleeping, drinking. Religion is not mentioned to people ... I went to a Christian school. They taught us we came from apes. That's the evolution they believed in, not God. So it was a Church of England school believing in Christianity with their own church made us believe in evolution, whereas evolution is about not believing in God. My age-group now is being taught nothing about religion at all. So this society just wants to bring you up not to live in God or not to worry, just to think about the world.'

In his book, *The Crisis of the Modern World*, the French philosopher Guénon (1942: 139) agrees with Tony in his description of the modern Western society as being anti-Christian since its outlook has become anti-religious:

The modern West is said to be Christian, but this is untrue: the modern outlook is anti-Christian, because it is essentially anti-religious; it is anti-religious because, still more generally, it is anti-traditional; this is its distinguishing characteristic and it is what makes it what it is.'

For many of the converts some concepts of Christianity such as Trinity, atonement, Jesus being the Son of God caused confusion in them when adolescents. Henry was one of them:

'From my mother I did have religious upbringing up to the

age of 13. I had to take an active part in the church, but when I was 13 I stopped going to church because I thought it was dead boring. Going to church and singing hymns just didn't appeal to me; I'd rather be out with my mates. I believed there was a God, but I didn't believe the other stuff. This thing with Jesus, God being Jesus and God, and the Holy Spirit, I couldn't accept it. They wouldn't answer my questions. Whenever I went to ask my mother a question she said, "Ask the vicar." If I asked the vicar, he wouldn't answer the question. We used to go round and round, and this circle never actually has come up with a solution. There were other things as well. I said to my mum once: "If the New and the Old Testament are from the same God, how come in the Old Testament He is brutal and in the New He is kind?" It was a total change in personality. Eventually, I rejected everything when I was 15 and I didn't want anything to do with Christianity at all.'

To conclude then, adolescence was the time for most of the converts to Islam to shy away from their childhood religion. And many lost belief in their religion of upbringing and began seeking contentment in other religions. 29 percent of the converts got involved in new religious movements after they broke with the religion of their childhood. When the preconversion period was examined it was found that only 8 (11%) described themselves as practising the religion of upbringing prior to conversion. Others were either nominal or atheist (13%). However, it must be stated that their drift from their religion was part of a general social movement. The 'psychological set' to accept one's parents' or environment's religious beliefs as used to happen in the past did not seem to be the case for them. A firm religious context which can enable the adolescent to interpret his personal experience in terms of religious symbols and the religious framework which may provide a clear model of how to resolve the adolescent phase, by presenting a model of proper Christian life does not seem to be available to the modern adolescent. The Western world lacks a secure ideological context in which experience can be guided and shaped (see Baumeister, 1986: 114).

Although the material from the sample studied confirms that various motivations for physical, emotional, and intellectual change exist within the adolescent, and that adolescence is a time for adjusting conformities and trying to sort out what is to be accepted and what is to be rejected totally, it does not suggest that adolescence is the prime time for conversion. Adolescence, it suggests, prepares the ground for conversional change, not because adolescence is especially traumatic, but because it is the period in which they partly/completely reject the religion of childhood. Even in the cases where the converts had had an emotionally troubled adolescence, it was merely a continuation of the psychological upheaval of childhood.

3 Rebellion conversion

Rebelliousness is another characteristic of adolescent conversion. Allison (1969: 30) found that converts' recollections of their adolescence reveal a history of marked rebelliousness towards religious values and observances during adolescence, following a long period of steady belief during childhood. Heirich, (1977: 655) found among converts to Catholic Pentecostalism that they, though varied widely, rebelled against the church before encountering Pentecostalism. Erikson (1962: 134) described the adolescent as feeling exposed to anarchic manifestations of his drives; needing oversystematised thoughts and overvalued words to give a semblance of order to his inner world.

Some converts involved in this study described their adolescence as a period of rebellion. The interviews with them showed that in some cases, though rare, hatred, resentment, and hostile attitudes towards their parents or society have been involved in adolescence and the preconversion period. In some cases, as a consequence of this rebellion a number of the interviewees had converted to Islam. This type of conversion was found in three cases. These individuals had converted in late adolescence, relatively younger than most of the subjects in the present sample. The emotions cited above have been noted by many observers, yet they have rarely been seen as the focus of a preconversion struggle; nor has conversion itself been interpreted as an attempt to deal with them (see Salzman 1953: 183–4). However, a few have drawn attention to the rebellion type conversion. For example, Heirich (1977: 654) wrote that 'some descriptions of religious conversion involves a dramatic turnabout, either accepting a belief system and behaviours strongly at odds with one's previous cognitive structure and actions or returning to a set of beliefs and commitments against which one has been strongly in rebellion.' Argyle and Beit-Hallahmi (1975: 59) recognised that many adolescent conversions may be understood in the context of rebellion against their parents' superficial religiosity.

Failure in socialisation is considered to be one of the factors in conversion (Dollah, 1979: 58). People who do not undergo a normal process of socialisation during their early personality development may form their own world view, and finally exhibit a behaviour deviant to their society. They may behave against the norms and sanctions of the social world around them.

The case of Steve gives an example of the rebellion type of conversion: Steve left school when 15 and got mixed up for two years with some motorbike gangs who were being influenced by Black Magic and Witchcraft. At the time he drank a lot and smoked hashish. Then he became engaged to a Hindu girl for about three years and read all the Hindu scriptures and literature. But his engagement came to an end, partly because Steve did not like the religion and partly because of his fiancee's parents. From 15 to 19 Steve described himself as not caring about life. He enjoyed being different from other people. He said:

> 'I enjoyed the fact that I would walk into a pub where there were all very ordinary people and I would be dressed in a leather jacket and filthy jeans and looked nasty. But everything was just a game and everything was to try and project an image and to cause some sort of stir amongst other people.'

In 1979 Steve went to New York to stay for a few months. While he was there the Iranian revolution took place and some Americans were held hostage in Iran. Steve always used to find Americans very 'cocky' and 'arrogant'. And with respect to the hostage situation he told them: 'Are you getting some justice back now? This little country over there giving you a kick in the teeth.' While the hostage affair was going on Steve came back to England and the first thing he did was to find out 'what sort of religion can make America come down on its knees?' And he bought a copy of the Koran and read it from front to back. Steve felt that things said in the Koran were almost directed at him. He said: 'It was saying "Don't do this, don't do that!" And I was thinking "Well, whoever has written this has been watching me for the last few years. It was written all down what I have been doing wrong. It was really a shock. Things that I thought I had been doing quite private were all there and were open. It was also this thing about Jesus that struck me because suddenly there was this alternative view.' First Steve rejected what the Koran was saying, but then the more he thought about it, the more it made sense. And also the fact that it has mentioned all other Prophets was appealing as well because he thought he was not losing anything. After a few weeks Steve decided to go to a mosque to find out more and spoke to an *imam* who gave him some books. He read them and thought some were 'silly', some were quite 'sensible'. From the mosque he met a number of people and one took him to his house and he stayed with him for about two weeks. The way this Muslim man treated Steve had an enormous effect on him. The following week Steve prayed in the mosque by just copying everyone, and after the prayer the man who had hosted Steve came in and said: 'If you want to become a Muslim, now you can do the *shahadah*.' Steve did not turn him down and became Muslim when he was 21.

So far Steve's conversion seems to have arisen out of intellect and affection, and was quicker than the normal conversion process for the majority of the converts to Islam. However, Steve recounted that there was a background to his conversion latent in his personality. His rebellious feelings stimulated his conversion as much as his intellect and affection:

'I think throughout everything with me there is an element of rebellion. I've always rebelled against something. If it wasn't my father, it would have to be something else when he died. So I rebelled against the society. So I've joined this motorbike gang; we called ourselves "The Outlaws." It was rebellion. And then once that ended it had been another rebellion. So the next rebellion perhaps was initially the thought of joining a religion (Islam) which was obviously so hated by the people in the West. I thought that's that; that will get up their nose if I join a religion they despise. But that was, may be, just the prod, that wouldn't have been enough to keep me in the religion; that might have been enough to push me towards it. But the fact that I stayed here was really because what the religion had to offer. If someone has come and said to me, "Right, you have only become Muslim because you were rebelling against the society." I would have said, "Fine, that might have been true for the six months, then not much longer than that because I would have found a new method of rebelling against this society. Some friends just thought I was mad and went into another thing. I don't have to remain in a cult of people with a leader in order to stay as a Muslim. What these people (my ex-friends) have to do they have to remain attached to their cult because the minute they are removed from the cult the effect goes. To me, that means they haven't got a true belief. They are only doing it because of the pressure put upon them by the cult. Now whereas with me if you stuck me on the middle of the mountain on my own, I would still be a Muslim. I don't need to have this cult around me and all these people forcing me to believe anything.'

Another example of this type of rebellion is provided by Salzman (1953: 183). One of Salzman's patients under psychotherapy, who had been raised as a moderate Protestant was planning to convert to Catholicism at the time of the therapy. The patient was full of both subtle and direct hostility directed at his parents, primarily his father. His family had always been quite antagonistic towards the Catholic Church and his conversion to Catholicism, he assumed, would come as a double blow to his parents, since he would both join a church they disliked, and he would remove himself from contact with them.

Commitment by the adolescent to views and beliefs other than those of his parents is an indicator of autonomy. Josselson (1980: 190–7) distinguishes four subphases of adolescent individuation of which the first two are often indicative of adolescent conversions: (1) differentiation; (2) practice and experimentation; (3) rapprochement; and (4) consolidation. During the *first* phase the adolescent's psychological needs begin and he attempts to detach himself from parental authority and search for other sources. He starts questioning parental values and concludes that they have their own attributes and flaws and realises that their advice may not be relevant to him. In the *second* phase the adolescent exercises rebelliousness. By practising his separateness he likes opposing, contradicting, and provoking his parents. In the *third* phase the adolescent feels ready to reaccept his parents guidance and endeavours to reestablish the bond with his parents. New cooperative views and selective acceptance replace the outright rebellion. The *final* phase leads to identity formation which involves the consolidation of a sense of personal identity that incorporates independent choices with a selective acceptance of past identification.

Erik had similar feelings towards his parents as those of Salzman's patient. Erick's conversion seemed largely to reflect Josselson's four subphases of adolescent individualisation. Erick rebelled against his parents' heavy disciplinarian attitude and therefore the community they associated with. Erick's parents were Jews who practised the traditional side of Judaism rather than the actual belief. Erick went to Jewish day school till he was about nine and then was sent to boarding school till 17. He described boarding school as 'a whole world within a world, like a prison.' He was not happy with the way he was brought up. He even started smoking at a young age thinking that it was a form of rebellion: 'I was in the position of having it forced on me, rammed down my throat. I disliked the idea of being forced to keep things, I don't like being told to do something.' When Erick was 15 his father died and his mother who was more strict than his father was in total charge of him. His father's death brought him into the real world with a 'bang' and Erick tried to be religious for 3–4 months: 'That's when I really started to think and use my brain. I started to question things. And I was feeling incomplete. Essentially I was wondering what are we here for? To earn money, to try and enjoy ourselves as much as possible? What is the reason for this, what is the point of life, what am I doing all these for? And I wanted to turn to the Jewish religion more.' Yet it did not take long before Erick totally abandoned Judaism deciding that it is not compatible with the 20th century life. When he was still at boarding school his uncle, a solicitor, who wanted Erick to make more friends, sent him to stay with one of his clients who was a Muslim during the summer vacation. Erick stayed with them for a few days and spoke to their children of his age on Islam: 'They seemed to have a very stable life and they were very happy. I saw them praying and I was asking inevitable questions. They were content. They lived life for a reason and they had a stable good household. And I saw these people once or twice because my grandma stopped me seeing them, she didn't want her grandson mixing with Muslims.' From this meeting with Muslims Erick had gained a chance to upset his mother and the rest of the family, and he soon got in touch with an Islamic organisation which provided him with some information and literature. He decided to convert nine months after he met this Muslim family. Erick, as his story suggests, did not deny Judaism. It was the autocracy of the clergy or the strictness of his parents that he rebelled against. 'Judaism in its original, if you look at what the Torah says,' he said, 'is good and clear, but if you look at what has been done to it in the name of tradition, and the law of rabbis, that's where it has gone wrong. I don't want any priests, rabbis or anything to intermediate with. I pray to God, for God sees everything I do.'

As the above accounts illustrate, by adopting a religion or a world view opposed to that of their parents these young people wished to separate from their parents. Conversion, therefore, dissociated them from influences such as parental authority that dominated their lives. According to Erikson's concept of identity formation through conversion they may be classified as 'identity achieved' for they formed a new commitment after having questioned parental values.

4 Eriksonian concept of identity: moratorium and conversion at a later age

Conversion may provide the adolescent with exploration of the self in new commitments in the context of a group, tradition, or religion. It may also give some central perspective, direction, personal fulfilment and goal orientation in moments of identity crisis or ideological confusion. In this sense Erikson's notion of identity seems relevant to the understanding of the conversion phenomenon of adolescence. Erikson places identity within the context of ego-psychoanalytic theory, viewing it as the epigenetically based psychosocial task distinctive, but not exclusive, to adolescence (Marcia, 1980: 159). Erikson's notion of identity consists of subjective experiences of unity, continuity, and autonomy that arise in the search for one's 'true' nature, with objective behavioural manifestations at the personal as well as the societal level (Ullman, 1989: 112). Identity here refers to an existential position, to an inner organisation of needs, abilities, and self-perceptions as well as to a sociopolitical stance.

'Identity achievement' and 'identity diffusion' are polar alternatives of status in Erikson's theory, which hypothesises psycho-logical crisis occurring in late adolescence. A major result of advanced civilisation has been the extension of the term 'social adolescence' which delays the time at which many young people assume adult roles and responsibilities. As society increases in complexity, educational demands on the young also increase. Erikson (1968: 143, 156) refers to this intermediary period as a kind of 'psychological moratorium' in human development. Erikson sees this phase of the life cycle as a time of growing occupational and ideological commitment. The individual who faces imminent adult tasks like getting a job is required to syn-thesise childhood identifications in such a way that he can estab-lish a reciprocal relationship with his society as well as maintaining a feeling of continuity within himself. Marcia (1966, 552), studying 86 college boys attempted to examine Erikson's notion of identity concerning 'objective' manifestations of ident-ity, primarily focusing on the process of crisis and commitment in the domain of ideology, and occupation defining identity by presence or absence of period of questioning and the formation of a commitment in these areas. Marcia described four identity status: (1) 'Identity-achieved' individuals have arrived at their own clear-cut decisions after experiencing a period of question-ing and exploration in the domains of occupation and ideology. With respect to ideology they have reevaluated past beliefs and achieved a resolution; (2) 'identity-diffused' individuals seem to have made little progress towards commitments in these areas, some experiencing no crisis, some being unable to resolve it. They are either uninterested in ideological matters or takes a smorgasbord approach in which one outlook seems as good to them as another and they are not averse to sampling from all; (3) Individuals grouped as 'moratorium' seem to be in the middle of exploring alternative directions concerning these domains and have not yet arrived at definite commitments. They are in the crisis period with commitments rather vague; they are distin-guished from the identity-diffused subjects by the appearance of an active struggle to make commitments; (4) 'foreclosure' individuals are distinguished by not having experienced a crisis, yet expressing commitment. For them it is difficult to tell where their parents' goals for them leave off and where their own goals begin. They become what others have prepared or intended them to become as a child. Marcia also found that most adolescents change in their identity status between the ages of 18 and 22, shifting from foreclosure or identity diffusion to identity achievement.

The Eriksonian concept of identity may help us understand conversion beyond adolescence although Erikson does not detail conversion experience specifically. Among the products of conversion are new beliefs and values. Identity often results in values which include religious ideas. Religion provides for youth and adults a theology (or ideology) (Erikson, 1962: 52; Wright, 1982; 148–150; Gillespie, 1991: 162). Erikson believed that the identity crisis interacts with ideology. It may, therefore, be concluded from Erikson's theories that both the identity crisis in adolescence and the integrity crisis in the middle years are prime times for conversion (Erikson, 1964: 86, 102, 115, 180; Scroggs and Douglas, 1977: 260).

Moratorium may be defined as a time when the near young adult avoids premature overcommitment either by taking time out, or by committing himself to an arduous apprenticeship in some field of endeavour (Fowler, 1981: 43). The moratorium period may end in young adulthood or adulthood with conversion and therefore with identity achievement. Here Fowler's stages of faith may be helpful to understand how and when the moratorium period ends. Fowler's (1981: 161) analysis of faith development suggests that somewhere between Stage 3 (Conventional-Synthetic Faith, which covers adolescence) and Stage 4 (Individuative-Reflective Faith, which covers young adulthood) the individual begins to make a cognitive shift to a more critical, personal view of their own authority in religious decisions.

As presented earlier, in a Christian context the individual typically experiences conversion at the age 15 or 16 and this becomes a period of maximal commitment to the religion. Yet this commitment is usually followed by a period of lesser commitment during which time the convert concentrates upon other aspects of life such as education, choice of career, and marriage. A renewed commitment to religious values could take place when some measures of occupational, marital and financial security have been obtained (Starbuck, 1911: 357). When many were converting to the religion of their parents in adolescence, the converts to Islam seem to have rejected a religious belief. In contrast they converted to another religion, namely Islam, in the late twenties.

This is when an individual is supposed to renew his commitments to his original religious values. During the time between rejection of childhood religion and conversion, most adopted secular identities by which they accomplished integration without resort to conversion, and some tried to explore other alternatives. Yet this was only a temporary and perhaps incomplete integration, for they eventually searched for a religious alternative. They, as Frederick accounted, 'let the religious thing lie asleep' at the back of their mind for a few years.

During the time between rejection of childhood religion and conversion the subjects involved in this study were, in general, neglectful of religion or was experimenting with other alternatives. This period may well be explained by Erikson's observations regarding 'moratorium' period. Erikson observed that many adolescents struggling with the integration process opt to 'retreat' for a period of time in order to work out a plan of self-reorganisation or integration without disturbance from mundane realities. Erikson posited that moratorium individuals go through a period 'before they come to their crossroads, which they often do in their late twenties'. Erikson believes that in this period the individual comes to a decision as what they are and what they are going to be. In his psychoanalytic analysis of the life of Martin Luther, Erikson describes Luther's experience in monastery, St Augustine's experience with Manichaeism, or Bernard Shaw's personality crisis experience before conversion as a moratorium (Erikson, 1962: 43–4).

Having an unstable childhood because of parental problems or father's absence, etc., or a thorny relationship with parents or the environment may have pushed individuals into a moratorium period before 'identity achievement'. Jacobson,[8] investigating differences between identity achievement and moratorium on college seniors reported that 'identity achievement' men had a higher frequency of supportive paternal relationships and more harmonious authority relationships, in general, than did 'moratorium' men. The data analysis lends support to Jacobson's finding of a relationship between moratorium and parental support. Those who reported conversion after they experienced a long period of moratorium (i.e. those converted after 22) were more likely to have had less parental support, especially from their father. 'Moratorium' was significantly associated with 'relation with father' (chi-square with continuity correction = 6.993, df=1, p<.01).

In the following excerpt from the interview with Todd, formerly a Catholic who became Muslim when 22, the fruits of the conversion experience are described in terms reminiscent of the Eriksonian criteria for 'moratorium'. The conversion seems to help Todd consolidate realistic long-term commitments:

> 'My family were so strict that I couldn't ask questions on religion. I don't think it was because they said, "Don't ask questions!", but it was because I wasn't allowed to speak personal. I wasn't allowed to develop a sort of personality. So I just thought I was best to keep quiet and ask no questions anyway . . . I didn't know what to think. I used to swing from being very right-wing to being very left-wing. When I got to university at the age of 18 I was very left-wing for about 3–4 years before becoming Muslim. I think that helped me become a Muslim because I was very conscious of social values and even moral values. I thought socialism was the most appropriate answer. I thought they were the only honest people trying to solve all these problems by helping the poor and the needy and trying to put the brake on capitalism. I felt that I was trying to find the best answers to society's problems. I still, at the age of 21, didn't have the answer. I felt that I needed to have the answer very much. I tried Christianity again which I'd given up at the age of 15. I studied church history, I studied a fair amount about Christianity, but I still couldn't understand what the church was asking me when I was supposed to take the Communion . . . I'm walking out of this church in five minutes, how is it going to help me? I'm taking this host and eating it and I sit down and do a few prayers and walk out and it is big bad world again. It just didn't have any effect on me. It was too weak for me, I think.'

Through his encounter with Islam Todd came to believe that he found answers to the questions he had been asking himself for so many years. He used to criticise the permissiveness of society with respect to things like homosexuality and Aids, and he was attracted by the moral stand of Islam and the Muslims he met. He said:

'They didn't drink, they didn't have any relationship outside marriage and they were very happy not doing it and
they were very confident in arguing these points . . . I read
the Koran one month before I became Muslim and the
verses about morality and relationships, and there were so
many verses about what is right, what is wrong. This is
the most fundamental part that gives you a framework.
Christianity says, "You must choose right as opposed to
wrong", but it gives you no framework. Islam gives you
the basis. It gives you personal hygiene, five times prayer
a day, etc. There is no way you can avoid Islam during
your day. You have to think about God, you have to think
about your work-mates, your family, etc.'

Having analysed Erikson's concept of personal identity formation and the characteristics of religious conversion, Gillespie
(1991: 183–91) found primary relationships between contexts of
both experiences as they appear in the developmental, emotional,
psychological, and societal milieu of life. Gillespie classified these
relationships as: (1) Both the experience of religious conversion
and identity are centrally associated with change in the lives of
individuals; (2) both experiences are concerned with the changing of behaviour and with the result of a changed frame of
reference. Ethical implications follow changed mental constructs;
(3) these two experiences affect the very centre of awareness in
a person. Religious conversion accomplishes this through a basic
change of viewpoint and a forthcoming commitment to a 'way'
or ideology. Personal identity experiences succeed through the
successful resolution of crisis and the virtues and values formed
in the process; (4) both experiences may have roots within the
conflicts of adolescence; (5) in identity experience and in religious
conversion there is an intensity of feelings towards commitment;
(6) religious conversion and personal identity experience deal
with existential questions.

Other literature on conversion also observed that converts go
through a moratorium-like period before conversion. Lofland
and Stark (1965: 868) mentioned that potential converts 'persist
in stressful situations with little or no relief', or 'take specifically
problem-directed action to change troublesome portions of their
lives, without adopting a different world view to interpret them,'
or take advantage of 'a number of manoeuvres to put the prob-

lems out of mind'. They described it as 'compensations for or distractions from problems of living,' and they specifically mentioned such things as mass media addiction, child-rearing, immersion in work, and, more spectacularly, alcoholism, suicide, and promiscuity. Richardson and Stewart (1977: 824) introduced the term 'muddling through' to the literature of conversion. They proposed that people try to muddle through before dealing with their problem in more dramatic ways: 'Muddling through may well be something of a quiescent state to which people regularly return when more dramatic solutions are not viewed as available.' Richardson and Stewart add a few more examples of the use of a conventional perspective (as put by Lofland and Stark) to solve problems, such as getting divorced, getting married, moving, changing jobs, and affiliating with a religious group.

When dealing with the phenomenon of conversion in older age groups, looking at the moral side of the experience may also offer an explanation. Scholars like Thouless (1979: 104) and Lonergan (1972: 238ff) posit that religious conversion may involve a few types of change: social, moral, and intellectual. Through moral conversion 'swearing Tom', as Thouless calls him, whose conflict was primarily a moral one, changed from an old way of life, one of swearing, to a new way. Yet moral development may not be possible until a higher or more mature state of thinking had occurred. Kohlberg's (1984: 172ff) cognitive-developmental theory of moral reasoning might be of use here. Kohlberg categorised moral development into six stages, and these six stages are grouped into three major levels: (1) the preconventional[9] moral level is the level of most children under 9, some adolescents, and many adult criminal offenders; (2) the conventional level is the level of most adolescents and adults; (3) the postconventional level is reached by a minority of adults and is usually reached only after the age of 20. This level includes such mature concepts as self-chosen direction, a more universal ethical outlook, evaluation of options, and personal ethical principles that move one to ethical decisions. All of these changes require a cognitive conversion in areas of morality. The postconventional individual judges by principle rather than by convention. This perspective is of an individual who has made the moral commitments or holds the standards on which a good or just society must be based (Kohlberg, 1984: 178ff). Movement to a postconventional morality requires specifically adult experi-

65

ences. Therefore, only adults who reach maturity can experience religious conversion with a deeply moral tone. This suggests that adults would be the prime age for moral conversion (Conn, 1985: 513; Gillespie, 1991: 56, 96). In short, Kohlberg implies that conversion of a moral variety demands a certain maturity of thought and cognition for which later ages, possibly at this stage of postconventional morality, are better suited.

To conclude, analysis of the preconversion histories of the converts to Islam suggests that conversion is a complex and gradual process which is prepared by individual conditions over a long period. It is much more than the moral and religious crisis of adolescence. For the vast majority of the subjects interviewed conversions occurred beyond adolescence and were likely to occur in the late twenties. The Eriksonian concept of identity achievement/diffusion, and therefore the moratorium period which may end in young adulthood or adulthood with conversion, and therefore with identity achievement may help us understand conversion at a later age. During moratorium, the converts to Islam made themselves concerned with life's basic questions like one's purpose in life, and questioned the values their own society presented to them. They adopted secular identities letting the religious quest lie asleep at the back of their mind, but eventually searched for a religious alternative. This will be explored in the following chapter.

THREE

CONVERSION PROCESS

'When you do your prayers in the mosque you have physical contact with another human; you touch the man standing next to you. When you meet somebody you shake hands. In British society you don't have any contact apart from girlfriends and things. I think it is a human bond that they miss. Religion in this society doesn't have any place, it is something you do on Sunday.'

Keith, a convert to Islam

A Background Analysis

1 Religion

The converts who participated in this research span a wide range of backgrounds regarding their former beliefs and practices. They were predominantly (nominal) Christians. Fifty one (73%) of the 70 reported that they were raised as Church of England; 12 (17%) were Catholics; 3 (4%) were Methodists; 4 (6%) were Jews (table 3.1). By and large, the sample seems to represent approximately the size of these religious communities in Britain. The approximate community size for these communities throughout whole of UK are: Church of England 26.6 million, Roman Catholics 5.2 million, Methodists 1.5 million, Jews 0.4 million.[1]

Table 3.1   Religion of origin (n=70)

Church of England	51 (73%)
Catholic	12 (17%)
Jewish	4 (6%)
Methodist	3 (4%)

Only 8 (11%) of the 70 reported that they were practising their religion of origin prior to conversion. Thirty two (46%) reported being nominal, weak or disillusioned with their old religion. Sixteen (23%) had no religion or were not interested in religion at all. And 14 (20%) were involved with a religious movement prior to conversion (table 3.2a). (In fact, 20 (29%) were involved in new religious movements, but 6 left these movements long before their conversion). Sufis have a higher record of trying new religious movements. Of the 23 Sufis, 13 (56%) reported previous involvement with new religions, while only 7 (15%) of the 47 non-Sufis reported involvement.[2] All new religions tried by the converts, be it Sufis or non-Sufis, were Eastern religions (table 3.3). Their involvement or commitment to these movements did not seem to have been very strong and did not last a long period of time. Only two reported a long period of membership.

Table 3.2a   Religious affiliation before conversion (n=70)

practising religion of origin	8 (11%)
nominal/weak/disillusioned	32 (46%)
no religion/not interested	16 (23%)
involved with a NRM	14 (20%)

For a significant number (29%) of converts' rejection of the faith of their parents or culture did not imply a rejection of religion in general or loss of belief in God since they proceeded to explore other religious alternatives following their initial rejection of a particular faith. As for 'belief in God', 58 (83%) reported that they believed in God; 9 (13%) lost their belief in God, while 3 (4%) were not sure if they believed or not (table 3.2b).

Table 3.2b   Belief in God prior to conversion (n=70)

believed in God	58 (83%)
lost belief in God	9 (13%)
not sure	3 (4%)

According to previous religious affiliations and belief in God prior to conversion, and what conversion meant for these people in terms of these areas, they may be classified into three groups:

68

Table 3.3   Religion or religious group involved
before conversion other than religion of origin

Buddhism	10 (5)*
Divine Light Mission	3
Hare Krishna	2
Hinduism	3 (2)
Rajneesh	2 (1)
Subud	2 (1)
Taoism	1 (1)
Zen-Buddhism	2
total	20 (29%)

*Numbers in brackets indicate the number of subjects who
were involved with more than one group.

(a) Those who had no religious commitment for a long time or described themselves as nominal in their religion of origin. People who fell into this group formed the vast majority (75%) of the sample. For them conversion meant a religious intensification, not through the religion of childhood, but through a different religion. It was returning to a religious life. So their changes fit the definition of conversion by William James (1962: 194) who defined it as: 'the process, gradual or sudden, by which a self hitherto divided, and consciously wrong, inferior and unhappy, becomes unified and consciously right, superior and happy, in consequence of its firmer hold upon religious realities.' Before conversion, religion for them was this other thing called Christianity or Judaism. Consider the case of Rachel: 'I didn't have a belief in Christianity or any other religion, but I had a belief in God and life after death and I knew there are reasons for our being here.' Laura also lost her belief in her religion, but never doubted the existence of God:

'I never sort of doubted the existence of God. It was rather sort of the doctrinal differences between different thesis, that's what I had to work out. But there was a time when I became extremely disillusioned with Christianity for several reasons. And it was at that time that was sort of fading in my life. I did want something else. I didn't want just to live without a religion. And I think it was around that time I found out about Islam and as one was sort of fading while the other one was growing over a period of a few months.'

(b) Those who described themselves as religious for a long period of time, but became disillusioned later on and were on the brink of losing their belief in their religion prior to conversion. Around 12 percent of the present sample fell into this group. Consider the case of Adam who was brought up as a very strong Catholic. In his teens Adam wanted to become a priest and his ambition was noticed by the local bishop who came out to visit his parents and suggested that he should carry on studying religion. When he was 17, before he went to university, Adam's ambition somewhat faded. He felt very deeply about social issues which was actually a part of wanting to become a priest, because he had some notion of being involved in the 'Third World' and doing missionary work in Africa. At university his life changed. In his first year he felt very insecure and he devoted himself to the football team. His social life was dictated by that, parties and being in the bar most evenings. In his second year Adam changed quite a lot when the Pope paid a visit to England. The Pope's visit gave him a chance to think and he sort of converted to his old faith. Then he went to Rome on an architectural course and stayed in Vatican city for a while. He was much more idealistic at this time and joined different groups in his university town which gave domestic help to the elderly. Yet, Adam admits, since he began university he had come under the influence of socialism due to his idealism for helping the underprivileged, although he has formally joined a socialist group. He then rebelled against his parents' conservatism and had endless arguments with his father about 'how life could be improved without capitalism'. By this stage he had begun to hate the Western way of life for being so entrenched in capitalism and he came to believe that Christianity was an emotional response to life. 'For example,' he said, 'I would go to church on a Sunday and feel very high emotionally, but then I would come away and there wouldn't be anything during the week to keep me going. I didn't have strong guidance. I was looking for something absolute. I felt if there was a God, He wouldn't leave man with the Bible because it was so unclear. I felt that there must be something else more than that.' After his first degree Adam went to a different university to do a diploma in economics. Here there were a lot of Muslims on his maths course. By that time he had stopped practising Christianity and felt very much disillusioned, and therefore was vulnerable to any influence. The Muslim students

70

on the same course had a big impact on him. He was impressed
by them during the fasting month. He said: 'They were fasting
whole days and still doing exams, they did as well as anybody
else . . . They had a very great dignity which I really respected.
Above all, they had a great love for their religion which I had
never had for my faith. Even though I'd loved my faith it was a
purely internal thing. I could never display to other people
because it wasn't really a creed which I could really back up one
hundred percent with my intellect. Muslims seemed to present
this strong force; their hearts loved and their minds believed in
it.' So it was not long before Adam made up his mind to convert
to Islam. His conversion was brought on as a result of his distaste
of capitalism and thereby western way of life rather than his
theological disillusionment with Christianity. He is now among
the few converts in the present sample who have changed the
way they dress, due to their reaction towards the western way
of life.

(c) Those who lost belief in God after rejecting their religion.
For them conversion meant finding God again. Around 13 per-
cent fell into this category. Leonard said: 'When I was much
younger, 13–14, I was very much interested in religion. But when
I went to university I lost my religion all together. I became
totally disillusioned and I shut off all belief in God completely.'
Jimmy portrayed how the life he lived was encouraged by a
'Godless society' which he now strongly condemns:

'I left home when I was 16 and that time I've never known
anything about religion. I was a lovely chap and I helped
everybody, but in terms of religion I was an animal and
barbarian. This sounds incredible, but that is what this
society likes. In this society you can go out and drink ten
pints of beer and half a bottle of whisky and still get up in
the morning to go to work. They think you are a hero. I
wouldn't say I was disillusioned by the society because
I knew it for what it was, I would do all right out of it
and I did. I mean I knew the world exactly what it was,
but as a man of the street I was very aware of what my
society is all about and how to get on in it and how to win.
I was involved with my own gang which was a group of
people who earned money by all means. We also used to
take drugs. If you are a young kid on the street and you

71

don't take drugs, you don't mess about with about three/ four women a month, then nobody is interested to know you. They think there is something wrong with you.'

Jimmy believes that Islam gave him his honour back as a human being. He says that the moral code of Islam whereby he can lead his everyday life, abstaining from drugs, alcohol and illicit sex, has made him a respectable person. Similarly, Jason found that Islam put him back on the right track:

'To me Islam is like finding God again. With Islam I am back in contact directly with God, whereas over the last 20 years I haven't really. It is also reconfirming or strengthening my moral and ethical outlook on life.'

The accounts given by the converts suggest that the effect of religion on society, and the prevalence of religious practices are diminishing. The church seems to be losing its authority over people. A review of the past and present state of Christian religion in Britain and the West examines these ideas.

2 Modern western culture: is it post-Christian?

Until modern times the formative tradition of Western culture has been Christian, but the impact of Christianity on Western culture is no longer what it used to be. The fundamentals of modern western culture, especially in Britain, are said to be post-Christian, because modern culture is gradually losing the marks of that Christianity which brought it into being and shaped it (Gilbert, 1980: ix; Vahanian, 1967: 152, 228). This does not mean that Christianity has become irrelevant, but it has become marginal for many people. To think and act in secular terms and even be indifferent to religion has become the norm. Some members of a post-Christian society continue to see Christianity as indispensable to their lives, but they find themselves in the minority in terms of social life and culture. The relationship between the state and the church in Britain in the past was close (Bossy, 1985: 153). On the eve of Britain's industrialisation and modernisation Anglicanism remained a powerful element in the political, social and legal structures of the society (Gay, 1971: 64ff), but in the twentieth century this close relationship has gradually diminished (Hastings, 1986: 663–4).

The primary historical context of modern British Christianity has been the emergence of an essentially secular culture. Like other societies in the industrial world, the growth of social structures, settlement patterns and life-styles has given birth to a secular culture. The industrial revolution led to the emergence of distinctively 'modern' types of culture and social structure. Human values and attitudes to the world were bound to change in response to this development (Gilbert, 1980: xiv, 22). In the history of secularisation the Reformation played an important role. Protestantism was an important facet of the conditions which hastened the transition from medieval Christendom to the more secular environment of Enlightenment Europe. The Reformation reimposed upon Europeans a distinction between Christianity and culture which resulted in making religiosity a private, voluntary, individual matter. This meant, on the popular front, turning collective Christians into individual ones (Bossy, 1970: 62; Gilbert, 1980: 27).

Modernisation began with industrialisation in the 18th century which provided jobs that meant leaving a rural life for the cities. In the course of these important transitions, the cultural system was transformed too, bringing breakdowns in traditional values and beliefs. These cultural changes can be seen as an inevitable effect of economic growth (Thompson, 1967, 97; Baumeister, 1986: 67). It was then feared that people would lose morality and virtue if Christianity failed, since Christianity was perceived as the source of moral standards (Howe, 1976: 21–2). In the nineteenth century the West and Britain, in particular, witnessed a breakdown in the network of culture, institutions, and tradition that society had used to furnish meaning to individual life. (Clark, 1962: 32–40).

In modern western culture religion has been relegated to the edges of modern consciousness. The social structure has transformed from largely rural to predominantly urban settlement patterns which has resulted in disappearance of traditional community life, the rise of class structures as primary social barriers, and changes in social control, education, and family life (Howe, 1976: 9–10; Gilbert, 1980: 66, 69). Social status in the twentieth century is a blend of education, occupation, and income. Privacy is highly valued. The role of the family, which in the past placed children in adult roles and was the connection between the individual and society has greatly diminished in this regard. As society became more complex, offered choices, and embodied change, the traditional models stopped providing all the answers (Baumeister, 1986: 77, 87, 104). Consequently, the individual in advanced societies became a member of an increasingly secular society (Gilbert, 1980: 107).

To examine the current situation of Christianity in Britain, it is reported that around five percent of the population is explicitly atheist and just over ten percent accept the entire literal truth of the Bible (Martin, 1967: 54). About 76 percent of the nominally Christian adults believe in God, 57 percent in heaven, and 27 percent in hell. Only 23 percent attend church at least once a month, and membership of a church is confined to about 15 percent of adults. Mainstream churches show signs of decline in almost all respects (Beckford, 1991: 182). The 1987/88 edition of the UK Christian handbook reveals a continuing decline in the major Christian churches' active membership with a loss of half a million members in the previous five years. However, there are also instances of religious revivalism. Religion, with its emphasis on personal relationships and transcendent values, still offers fulfilment to people who, in Wilson's terms, experience personal discontents with the increasingly impersonal, large-scale, societally-organised social system (Wilson, 1991, 202).

The decline of religion in Britain has been interpreted by some observers in terms of secularisation. To them secularisation is the dominant feature of contemporary religious change in the West (Wilson, 1976: 85; Martin, 1967: 100). By this they mean a continual reduction in the influence of religion on society and people's lives as a result of the rise of science and technology, the replacement of village life by city life challenging the place and role of religion in society. Wilson sees secularisation as a process of structural change in society. He defines secularisation as a 'process by which religious thinking, practice and institutions lose social significance, and become marginal to the operation of the social system. According to Wilson, as a consequence of secularisation, religion in advanced societies has lost its control over social activities which once it exercised. Various institutional orders of social life (the economy, the polity, juridical institutions, education, etc.) is no more under the control of religion (Wilson, 1991: 196).

The rise of science and technology also brought 'individualism' which became a characteristic of Western civilisation. Religion

may not make sense in the modern world. Therefore, technology's children today may not be all that ready to accept their
parentage, and in a quest for identity they may rebel against
their computerised heritage, against the 'Enlightenment' that
locked them into a rigid objectivism, scientism, and rationalism
(Wright, 1982: 180). In his book, *Identity: Cultural Change and
Struggle for Self*, Baumeister (1986: 145) discusses how individualistic values and collective life came to contradict one another in
the twentieth century West:

> 'The spread of urban, industrial bureaucratic life and devel-
> opment of a consumer economy ... have resulted in the
> 'mass society' with its collective behavior patterns. The
> individual lives in the midst of society and is totally depen-
> dent on it. Society provides the individual with a means of
> livelihood, information, food and clothing, entertainment,
> and so forth. But society refuses to provide a meaning for
> life other than the system of extrinsic rewards (as in earning
> lots of money). If the individual is at all sensitive, he or she
> feels that society is indifferent to his or her fate.'

Sociologists, like Berger (1969: 133) and Wilson (1991: 207),
illustrate that in this process sectors of society and culture are
removed from the domination of religious institutions and symbols, and all forms of social world activities which have previously been motivated by secularisation and religion have
become less and less significant. Eventually, religion lost its connection with the everyday world. It is believed that the present
upsurge of 'new religions' and the explosion of exotic new sects
are themselves a manifestation of this ongoing secularisation.
Nick's perception of present state of religion in Britain seems to
reflect the degree of secularisation of the society:

> 'Islam affects society and it is a stabilising force. This was
> a very important factor in my conversion. I think one of the
> weaknesses of Christianity is that it is prepared to change its
> rules to suit changes in society and, therefore, it is no longer
> a stabilising factor. It follows the secular need. The society
> is secular and the Christians can't keep up. That's why they
> are changing. Now they want to have woman priests and
> homosexuality is no longer a sin. I've always felt that

religion should be a stabilising factor. I think man needs to have rule and order. We are not animals.'

So in Britain religion has become a compartmentalised marginal item in the society which caused the clergy's loss of status and power (Wilson, 1976: 86ff). However, as Martin (1967) points out, the majority of people still retain central Christian beliefs and go to church occasionally. Although committed religious people are a small percentage, there are many more who are nominally Christians, though it probably has little affect on their lives (Argyle and Beit-Hallahmi, 1975: 14–5). Religion has become what people believe, not what they do. One of the interviewees, Alan, gives a critique of English religion which is in tune with these assertions:

'English people, we have this ability to sort of believe in God, but not do anything about it. We are sitting on the fence really as regards to being actually active in the religion and demonstrating our love and worship for Allah. Because in Christianity you don't need to do that. You can just be intellectual about it. It can be all in your head. And you don't really even need to go to church. English people are not very bad to their neighbours, they don't steal things, so they live quite good lives, but they don't actually actively worship Allah which Islam teaches. That is the difference.'

Wilson (1976: 19–21), discussing the effects of secularisation in modern society illustrates how moral control by religion has given way to modern society's mechanical and bureaucratic devices, and how everyday life has been demoralised as human involvement in many areas of activity is replaced by technical controls. Arguing the decreasing role of the church in England Wilson asserts that 'people have what might be called a "post office" conception of the Church, a service facility that is well distributed over the land area of the country to be available when needed.' Keith's perception of this society seems to confirm the points made by Wilson:

'When you do your prayers in the mosque you have physical contact with another human; you touch the man standing next to you. When you meet somebody you shake hands. In British society you don't have any contact apart from girlfriends and things. I think it is a human bond that they miss. Religion in this society doesn't have any place, it is something you do on Sunday.'

Conversion for some of the interviewees meant turning from a secular culture to a non-secular or less secular one. Their accounts concentrated on their attraction to Muslim societies where religion was a fundamental part of the culture. Their attraction to the impact of religion in Muslims' lives was an important factor in their conversion. Therefore, it will be helpful to examine the current situation of the culture of Muslim societies in general and in particular their differences from secularised western societies.

Unlike industrialised Western countries which are said to be living in a post-Christian era, in Muslim countries religion was less eroded by secularisation, and their culture remained Islamic. In his book, *Postmodernism, Reason and Religion*, Gellner writes how secularism could not gain ground in Islamic civilisation:

At the end of the Middle Ages, the old World contained four major civilizations. Of these, three are now, in one measure or another, secularized. Christian doctrine is bow-dlerized by its own theologians, and deep, literal conviction is not conspicuous by its presence. In the Sinic World a secular faith has become formally established and its religious predecessors disavowed. In the Indian World a state and the elite are neutral vis-a-vis what is a pervasive folk religion, even if practices such as astrology continue to be widespread. But in one of four civilizations, the Islamic, the situation is altogether different. (Gellner, 1992: 5–6).

Gellner cites a few reasons why Islamic culture was less secular-ised. *First*, he says, society was endowed with both a fundamental and concrete law, each in its way entrenched, and usable by its members as a yardstick for legitimate government. *Second*, in Islamic culture church/state dualism, which would cause alienation between the community and the state, never emerged. *Third*, in Islam there is a theoretical absence of clergy. No distinct sacramental status separates the preacher and or the leader of the ritual from the laity. Such a person is not a different kind of social being and Muslim theology is in this sense egalitarian (Gellner, 1992: 7–9).

Modernisation in Muslim countries did not culminate in a

widespread religious lukewarmness and secularisation. It may not have eroded religious commitment in general. Although modernisation and secularisation have taken place to varying degrees in Muslim countries (for example, Turkey is more secularised than Algeria) and affected religious practices, the traditional faith remains intact and Islam still exists today as a living culture. Religion has always played a big role in maintaining moral and social solidarity in the community (Rodinson, 1974: 177).

The interviewees' accounts suggest that the oversecularisation led them to seek for an alternative way of life. They believed that Islam gave them a practical means of getting closer to God, living a good life, and getting peace in 'this secular' environment. They became interested in Islam in the first place because they felt that Islam had strong clear values on things they felt concerned about, not just the abuse of environment, but even things like homosexuality. Their revolt was not always directed against religious beliefs, but against certain practices legitimised by religion, such as homosexuality no longer being a sin. Richard expressed how he felt before and how Islam helps him now in this environment:

> 'In this society Islam helps me not to sink into quite deep depression because of the political or economical circumstances. I can see how the earlier saints whether Christian or Muslim could actually progress so high. It gives one a code of conduct which has become virtually lost from contemporaries and younger generations. I think this is a feature of Islam. It requires from people outward manifestation. Unfortunately, Christianity has fallen away so tragically and dramatically. People no longer have the habit. Churches have a huge responsibility in this. And I think if churches had been stronger when I was growing up, may be I wouldn't have become a Muslim. It is certainly significant now that church gives no clear cut lead on moral issues.'

While giving their accounts of their previous life the converts interviewed strongly emphasised that they felt a need for a religion whereby they could orient their everyday life, and they chose Islam because 'it is not a compartmentalised religion confined to certain areas'. Sarah pointed out: 'As an ex-Christian I now see Christianity as just a religion, but Islam, as I understand, is the way you live. It is a different approach. For instance, you can be a Christian and you can do almost everything and you can say you are a Christian happily. But if you are Muslim, it is different, you are restricted in that matter.' They felt that something was missing, and that was the influence of religion in their lives. Before coming to Islam they started criticising the existing culture and began having certain affinities and world views closer to that of Islam which eventually made a possible correlation between their views and Islam, and this facilitated their conversion. The description one convert made is very clear to indicate how these people felt and what they wanted: 'Going to church is like going to McDonalds', said Robert. Alan recollected that he wanted to be restricted in the moral sense rather than being a free man in a free society: 'When I was looking for a faith I met Rajneesh people. They said, "You should come to India and you can do anything you want." That's not anything worthwhile. If you can do anything you want, what is the point of it?'

Some of those who were involved or became interested in new religions, over a quarter (29%) of the sample, were in search of an alternative to the secular way of life with a strong reaction to the materialistic and secularistic perspective of society. Garry, for example, became a Zen-Buddhist in the university when he found that spirituality was lacking in the teaching system. Yet Garry found Zen-Buddhism monastic, not encompassing the social dimension of life. He said: 'It could answer personal questions, but it couldn't answer global questions.' The interviewees were also asked the question: 'Why is it that, you reckon, some people are moving towards new religious movements?' They unanimously agreed that 'people feel spiritually and intellectually unfulfilled, they are fed up with materialistic perspectives of life and they want to escape from the sheer materialism of life.' In fact, what they recounted on new religious movements does not contradict the sociologists' accounts of the decline of liberal Protestantism. They argue that 'the defectors from liberal churches do not embrace secular humanism, but that they may eventually be drawn to a more traditional faith.' (Wallis and Bruce, 1986: 49).

To conclude then, the accounts given by those interviewed suggest that in general they have not achieved a religious identity since society has failed to create a social nexus for strong religious identification. For them, the identity label as Christian or Jew was no more than a passive acceptance of a social convention, and as this label was imposed from outside it did not lead to real ego-involvement.

3 Socio-demographic factors

The converts who participated in this study have a good educational background and qualifications. As table 3. 4a shows, 60 percent had at least a bachelor's degree. Indeed, 20 percent had advanced graduate degrees. They tended to come from the middle class section of the society. 46 (66%) associated themselves with the middle class, while 24 (34%) identified with the working class. Significantly, none came from the upper class (table 3. 4b). They seem to have had a wide range of occupations, from taxi drivers to university lecturers. Many of them appear to have attained successful positions in various professional fields such as teaching, journalism and engineering. 6 were enrolled in higher education, 2 were unemployed, and 6 women preferred to be a housewife to look after their children, although they had good job prospects. Of the 70 converts, 50 (71.4%) are males and 20 (28.6%) are females. As for marital status, 40 people were single at the time of conversion, 23 were married or engaged (14 to Muslims, and 9 to non-Muslims), and 7 were divorcees. It must be emphasised that the rate of female converts to that of males is higher than the present sample indicates. It must also be admitted here that this research covers less female

Table 3.4a   Levels of completed education (n=70)

Less than college	28 (40%)
College (BA/BSc)	28 (40%)
Master degree (MA/MSc)	9 (13%)
PhD	5 (7%)

Table 3.4b   Social class (n=70)

Working class	24 (34%)
Lower middle class	8 (11%)
Middle class	32 (46%)
Upper middle class	6 (9%)
Upper class	0 (0%)

subjects than it should because females were not easy to contact compared to males and they were more reluctant to give an interview especially to a male interviewer than males.

B Immediate antecedents of conversion

A conversion experience does not just happen. It is the result of a complex process. Most studies of conversion have emphasised social and psychological variables to explain why and under what conditions certain individuals are drawn to a movement (Harrison, 1974; Greil 1977; Ebaugh and Vaughn, 1984). These models assume that all converts go through the same, or similar, processes. Both emotional and cognitive factors have been proposed in the socio-psychological literature to account for the experience of religious conversion. As mentioned in the previous chapter the psychodynamic approach purports that converts experience increased emotional upheaval during childhood and in the period preceding conversion. Although some proponents of this psychodynamic approach emphasise the possible integrative and adaptive consequences of this experience, all trace its origin to childhood conflicts which have reemerged before conversion (Salzman, 1953; Christensen, 1963; Allison, 1969). The cognitive approach emphasises the pertinence of cognitive factors in precipitating the change of beliefs conversion entails. According to the cognitive approach conversion is a conscious cognitive quest for clear and comprehensive understanding of reality rather than a struggle with personal stress. Supporters of the cognitive approach have adopted a more humanistic perspective that allows for an acting and conscious human agent. This contrasts with the passive psychodynamic approach. Jung broke dramatically with Freud claiming that religion can often help people integrate their lives. In his book, *Modern Man in Search of a Soul,* Jung presents his 'active agency' view. Likewise, Allport, in *The Individual and His Religion*, supports this view, as Frankl, whose *Man's Search for Meaning* and *The Will to Meaning* involve a rejection of Freudian dominated psychodynamic viewpoints (see Richardson 1985: 166–7). In order to test the presence or absence of emotional turmoil, or personal stress and cognitive or existential crisis, the two-year period preceding conversion was examined. Now these two areas will be analysed respectively.

81

1 Emotional antecedents

Emotional turmoil or conflict that is experienced prior to conversion can arise from various life experiences, which may include the perception of childhood relationships with one's parents and any traumatic events or stressful circumstances. And conversion may occur after periods of emotional confusion and disturbance. Family stress often causes such disturbance. Having reviewed the lives of twelve historic converts like Pascal, Luther, and St Augustine, Krailsheimer (1980) found that most had lives marked by tensions or imbalance in family relationships.

A significant number of the testimonials in the present sample included accounts of troubled lives before entrance into Islam. Nearly half of the sample (48.6%) had preconversion lives which were judged to contain emotional distresses. For them this period of their lives seems to have led them to look for something. For one fifth of the sample the emotional turmoil that had characterised their descriptions of their childhood and adolescence was also apparent in the immediate antecedents to the conversion experience. Their unhappiness was, in most cases, caused by parental marriages which either ended up in divorce or nearly broke up, and they described these as the major trauma of their lives (table 3.5). Because of unhappy or unstable childhood or adolescence, these people described considerable distress during the two-year period prior to conversion.

The perceived instability of the social world is believed to be a necessary condition for conversion (Dollah, 1979: 48–9). The individual takes for granted the reality of the social world around him until something comes to disturb or challenge this assumption. Instability is frequently affected by thought provoking literature, or through new experiences and by finding new alternatives. Separation or isolation of an individual from his fellow man in the social world would also lead to instability of his world view. Death is the most extreme type of separation of an individual from his person of importance. Another example of separation is a broken marriage. A divorced person may lose his identity and meaning in life. His future becomes uncertain. So all these problems make him restless and unhappy about the existing social world. Finally, the world view and particularly his identity in life begins to gradually break down. Thirteen (19%) of the 70 converts involved in this research had divorced or had a broken relationship (8 divorced and 5 had a broken relationship) before conversion, and this caused emotional turmoil and anxiety for a long time. Nine (13%) had had one of their parents die before they were 16 years of age. Five (7%) had had a serious illness or accident that left them either disabled or stricken, and one convert (1.4%) had had the experience of imprisonment for a long time (table 3.5). In 8 cases (11%) the emotional distress was reported as serious, and they sought therapy at some point in their lives. Sufis have a higher record of experiencing a traumatic event in life before conversion. 78 percent of the 23 Sufis reported experiencing a traumatic event in life, as against 53 percent of non-Sufis.[3] Divorce, either that of parents or converts themselves, was the major traumatic event reported by Sufis. This may be an explanation as to why they were particularly affected by the warmth in the Sufi group which they could not find in their home, and as a result they may not have had much hesitation to jump into this newly found 'safe haven'.

Table 3.5   Reported traumatic events* in life before conversion

divorced	8 (11%)
parents divorced	11 (16%)**
parents nearly broke up before the subject was 16 and this caused an unstable childhood	3 (4%)
one of the parents died before the subject was 16	9 (13%)***
serious illness or accident that left the subject either disabled or stricken	5 (7%)
a broken relationship	5 (7%)
imprisonment	1 (1.4%)
total	42 (60%)

*Some experienced more than one event which may be described as traumatic. In this case the event which the subject described as the most important was taken into account.
**One subject was adopted never knowing her parents.
***One subject's mother was killed when the subject was 30 years of age.

It has been suggested that a single emotional 'trauma' or shock may affect an individual and may bring personality change or a conversion experience (Clark, 1958: 215). This does not mean that an emotional turmoil or trauma is enough for conversion or personality change, but that the effective crisis that causes turmoil after the incident could simply cause a process which leads to conversion or personality change. However, the final decision for conversion may depend on intellectual elements. Some cases of the conversions in the present sample seem to apply to the above description. For example, Charlie said that leaving Christianity was an emotional experience, but embracing Islam was an intellectual process. Charlie went through a distressing period when his marriage broke up. Charlie had had a religious upbringing through his father and been to church regularly. In 1973, aged 25, Charlie went to France and became involved with a charity for handicapped children run by Roman Catholics and worked for them for two years. During his stay in France he was only exposed to Roman Catholic belief and he continued attending Roman Catholic Church until 1983. That year Charlie got divorced:

> 'When the marriage broke up it was particularly dirty; a lot of recriminations, a lot of both sides saying they are in the right. And I found that a lot of the Christian values that I've been taught to believe such as "when you marry, you marry for life" weren't put into practice by Christians and my wife committed adultery. I took some action against the man involved which resulted in my going into prison for a year. And my friends, who were Christians, on my side condemned me rather than her and they said divorce was the best thing.'

Then Charlie began looking for ideas and philosophies, some sort of guide, although not necessarily a religion. He read books on Buddhism, Hinduism, and Islam. He said that his choice had been Islam because he had found it not that far from Christian belief. He found the Islamic viewpoint on adultery or marriage law closer to his own views. Now his perception of this society is one of repugnance:

> 'I am critical of Western society in its hypocrisy; the fact that the society claims to subscribe to a set of values, but it doesn't necessarily really follow the logical process of subscribing to those values. For example, in a Christian society that values family, it makes divorce very easy. In a society which values life, it makes abortion very easy. In a society that values so-called freedom of speech, it only seems to value it for the majority. And even ten years ago to say that you were a communist or a Marxist would turn

a lot of antagonism towards you, just as saying today you are a Muslim. There is no such thing as freedom of speech. It is all sorts of hypocrisies.'

The vast majority of the converts who went through emotional distress said that they were grateful to God to have experienced such distressful incidences because it was these events that had sparked them to think about religion. Timothy, who lost his business and had a marriage breakup commented:

'So at the time it was exceedingly traumatic. I'm very grateful to God for this experience because I think then my life really began to forget about God. I was becoming trapped in the material world in the notion of wealth and position and all this sort of thing. So I felt almost as if God said, "That's not what you are born for. That was not the purpose for you." I think He forced me to look at things. That was the time I began to question.'

Lofland and Stark (1965: 864) suggest that a state of acutely-felt tension or frustration is a necessary predisposing condition for conversion. Snow and Phillips' (1980: 433) study of Nichiren Shoshu seems to corroborate this expectation. Their informants characterised their preparticipation life situations in terms of various problems and tensions. Sixty eight percent of their sample, for example, indicated that prior to or at the same time as encountering Nichiren Shoshu they were experiencing one or more spiritual problems, such as meaninglessness, a lack of direction or purpose, or a sense of powerlessness. Snow and Phillips retrospectively categorised five personal problems which were referred to as characterising life situations prior to conversion:

1 Problems coded as 'spiritual' include meaninglessness, lack of direction and purpose, a sense of powerlessness, poor self-image (68%).
2 Problems coded as 'interpersonal' include marital problems, child rearing problems, parental problems, and other relational problems (48%).
3 Problems coded as 'character' include drugs, alcohol, self-centeredness, and various personality problems such as uncontrollable temper (52%).
4 Problems coded as 'material' include unemployment, job dissatisfaction, finances, and school-related problems (43%).

5 Problems coded as 'physical' include headaches, nervousness, chronic illness, obesity, lack of energy, and so on (30%).

When looking through the preconversion period in the present sample to find out how many of Snow and Phillips' categorisations apply, it was apparent that they were present in varying degrees. The first three problems seemed to dominate the last two. Thirty four subjects (48.6%) reported feelings of aimlessness, lack of purpose or direction and meaning, incompleteness, etc. Nineteen (27.1%) reported problems coded as 'interpersonal' including marital, parental and other relational problems. Six (8.6%) reported drug-use, and 7 (10%) reported excessive alcohol use in the two-year period preceding their conversion. Eight (11.4%) reported material problems like unemployment, job dissatisfaction, and school-related problems. Five (7.1%) experienced problems coded as 'physical' like chronic illness or lack of energy.

Though some evidence was found in favour of Snow and Phillips' findings, the material from the sample studied does not strongly support their proposal relating conversion experience to emotional turmoil or personal distress experienced in the immediate preconversion period. Only the finding on problems coded as 'spiritual' seems to lend support to Snow and Phillips' findings. Spiritual crisis in many cases was caused by existential or cognitive questions. These findings, and the general atmosphere of the interviews suggest that conversions did not occur as a direct result of the emotional turmoil or personal distress. It may be associated with conversion, but it is not necessarily a predisposing condition. In the preconvert, there may be an unconscious conflict, and a psychological set, but these factors, alone, in many cases, may not be enough. There must at the same time be an immediate factor which acts as a catalyst. This catalyst is likely to be cognitive and existential questions.

2 Cognitive antecedents

The two-year period preceding conversion was also examined for the presence or absence of a cognitive quest. Cognitive quests which were present tended to be concerned with social, and moral issues, religious doubts, and existential concerns which covered questions like 'what is the meaning and purpose of my life?', 'how does one deal with the fact that one is going to die?', and 'what should one do about one's shortcomings?'

Thirty three (47%) reported preoccupation with cognitive concerns. As stated above 34 (49%) reported feelings of aimlessness, lack of purpose or direction and meaning, incompleteness, etc., which mainly arose out of cognitive and existential concerns. Alan, who described himself as a seeker for the ultimate reality said:

'When I was a young man of 18–19 I was what other people called a "hippie". I didn't need to go out and take life very seriously . . . Later on I started feeling incomplete. I found that I was reading a lot of books about things that suggested a greater reality than all I could see about me. Because what I could see about me was quite small. And I had been doing things and experimenting with mind expanding drugs with which I'd actually seen that there was an awful lot to reality . . . I was aware that there was much much bigger things going on and I wanted to know what those things were.'

Tim was also in search of a religion that would satisfy him cognitively:

'I was looking for a religion and an explanation, a way of life, a philosophy that was explaining and giving meaning to life and answering questions that I felt very fundamental about myself, about existence, about creation, etc. I studied philosophy in the university and this brought me into the domain of religion and belief, knowledge and so on. I think inevitably it is all entwined. I was not satisfied with the answers this society provided . . . I think I struggled on the level of reasoning.'

The stories of some converts to Islam suggest that an active, continuous and relentless search for meaningful answers to questions about the nature of life and death preceded their conversion. They had been asking questions about the meaning and purpose of human life and they had been compelled to reexamine and reevaluate their previous life-styles. These people believe that the cognitive problems that used to bother them are met by Islam because they felt that it offered them 'a philosophy of life; it proclaimed the responsibility of man, a future life, and a day of judgement.' Islamic emphasis on life after death and the Day of Judgement, for example, motivated Janet's conversion:

'When I was at secondary school there was a girl in my class. Her parents were religious. Since my parents didn't talk about religion I used to ask questions to that girl. I wanted to have that faith as she had. I used to have dreams about nothingness after death. You have nothing, nothing and then just sinking in this pit. I thought there must be something after death, there must be life; you can't just die. My mum would say, "We'll just get eaten up by worms, that's it, nothing else." So I used to ask my friend how she had this faith. I wanted to believe in something.'

Janet had this niggling question in her mind over the years and accepted Islam after she was introduced to it by her Muslim friends in the university. Anne's conversion may also be traced back to her concern with life after death which came after she had feelings of guilt due to a 'sinful' and 'troubled' life. Anne was born to a Catholic family in a small town. When she was 18 her parents sent her to university in London, though she felt she was not prepared to stay at the university in London. When she got there she could not believe that 'all the girls were so outrageous, and they all had so many boy friends, and they were all drinking'. Anne became totally caught in this scene, and ended up very unhappy. To block out her unhappiness she drank more and more. Her performance at university was also badly affected. In the end, she was so depressed that she went to a psychotherapist. However, he was unable to help her at all: '. . . because the psychotherapist didn't believe in God and a lot of my problems came from the Catholic Church which was telling me to be good and I couldn't reconcile it with society. And, of course, in Catholicism you just go straight to Hell for some of the things you do wrong and there is nothing you can do about it really.' In a discotheque, Anne met a man whose mother was Italian and his father Turkish. This man was not practising any religion at all, but he suggested that Anne read the Koran. Anne bought a Koran and started reading. When she read the verse which said: 'Things of this world take your attention until you come to the grave' Anne was deeply impressed and thought it was talking about her life. Then she thought she had to find out about life after death and spent a large amount of time reading books on other religions like Buddhism and Hinduism: 'I was reading and I was also talking to everyone to find out why we are here. It was the realisation that we are all going to die which made me feel that I had to find out what this life is about and what happens after death. And I wasn't satisfied with any other religion but Islam.' Towards the end of the interview Anne did not hesitate to blame her parents and the society for her 'troubled' life: 'My parents brought me up to believe in God and then told me to dress up nicely, but threw me into the middle of a corrupt society and expected me to find my own husband which was such a pressure, especially while alcoholism was going around.' As Anne's story shows, many of the converts were discontent with their life-style preceding their conversion and they wanted to change. Anthony's conversion to Islam occurred after a long time of disillusionment with his life-style:

'I used to drink a lot and a lot of parties used to go on. Normally, I imagined I had a very good time, but it was not really that satisfying, and I felt that there must be something much more significant or meaningful, something that could be more satisfying than what I was doing at that stage. My disillusionment with my life-style was growing, and stemming from this I was interested in the big questions of life . . . And perhaps as a result of that I looked at other religions, certainly not with any intention of becoming religious at all, but only really because the questions I was becoming interested in were basically questions that were addressed by religions about who we are and what life was all about, and what kind of purposes we should have in life.'

Questions regarding 'social justice' were also an important motivating factor in some converts' choice of Islam. Ten (14%) converts reported an inclination towards socialism in the two year period preceding their conversion.

Conversion experience, in many cases, was a search for meaning. They reexamined the ground rules dictated by their culture. They were discontented with ambiguities in their life-styles and society, and, therefore, were preoccupied with what was right or wrong, with universal questions of meaning. Their accounts centred on urgent spiritual needs rooted in the particular circumstances of their lives, and they described the fulfilment of these needs as the primary consequence of their conversion. This pattern emerges clearly in the case of Nick whose first contact with Islam came about when he was abroad. Nick was a student nurse and did a casualty course and then went abroad to Libya and Iran, staying a year in both places. His experiences with Muslims abroad were not of any consequence and he had the stereotype of Muslims which he described as 'a hangover from the Crusades'. So he was not too impressed, and it never occurred to him that he would eventually become a Muslim. About a year after he came back from Libya Nick had a serious illness:

> 'The diagnosis wasn't serious, but before it was diagnosed it was expected I had cancer and I knew from my experience that would give me six months to live. So I spent about four days not knowing. That affected, of course, my decision to look for a religion. I was already looking for something by then, but that experience made it more urgent. After the illness, although I knew it wasn't anything that was going to kill me, I realised that you could be killed tomorrow and hoped to gain something after death. Then I thought I should do something. I was working with Christian nurses who wanted to go and work in Africa and be missionaries. I couldn't agree with them at all, but I envied their faith. But I knew that if I followed what they believe, I wouldn't be really truthful because I couldn't accept it. I had a great respect for Buddhism because it is a passive religion, but I didn't really believe in its cosmology. So I knew this wasn't the truth as I perceived it.'

Then Nick went to Kenya through the Red Cross on a famine relief programme as the team leader. He found the scene of famine very disturbing and distressing. This reraised the question of death and the meaning of life in his mind. This time he had a much stronger desire to have a faith. In Nairobi he bought a translation of the Koran and in reading it he felt that it gave the right answer to his existential quest: 'The more I read, the more I felt that I was a Muslim and I took the *shahadah* when I was 30. It wasn't a question of choice like 'Oh, Yes, I will be a Muslim.' I felt 'Oh, Yes, this is what I believe, therefore I am a Muslim.'

Modern Western man appears to be in existential trouble. Many of the great thinkers of recent times believe that as a people

Westerners are beginning to lose a firm hold on their values, their spiritual grounding and meaning for existence. Nick said:

'In the West, we are living in the post-Enlightenment period. We have environmental problems, Aids and so many things, and scientists are not coming up with any solutions. I think the quality of life isn't improving, people are becoming more and more disillusioned, life is becoming more insecure for people. I remember when I went to Iran I was living in a rural community and the most striking thing I noticed was that the people seemed more content. I still feel strongly that the more simple the life, the more content the people. If you look at this society, it is more and more complex, more problems and it is less content.'

What Nick feels regarding discontentment with life in urbanised society has also been a theme for Muslim thinkers in their criticism of modern Western society. In his book, *The Encounter of Man and Nature: The Spiritual Crisis of Modern Man*, S. H. Nasr (1968: 17) writes:

'Today, almost everyone living in the urbanized centres of the Western world feels intuitively a lack of something in life. This is due directly to the creation of an artificial environment from which nature has been excluded to the greatest possible extent. Even the religious man in such circumstances has lost the sense of the spiritual significance of nature. The domain of nature has become a 'thing' devoid of meaning ... Furthermore, even this type of secularised and urbanized existence is itself threatened, through the very domination of nature that has made it possible, so that the crisis brought about through the encounter of man and nature and the application of the modern sciences of nature to technology has become a matter of common concern.'

Viktor Frankl (1988a; 1988b) maintains that in this century man's feeling of despair has become ubiquitous. He refers to this condition as the 'existential vacuum' which is spiritual distress. It is characterised by feelings of emptiness, boredom, valuelessness, and meaninglessness. Frankl believes that people have cognitive needs to perceive wholeness, pattern, purpose, or meaning in the stimuli that confront them. It may, therefore, be concluded

91

that adopting an encompassing religious world view would be a way of meeting this need. Without some moral and evaluative pattern, the world may be experienced as chaotic and meaningless. Jason's account of his experience echoes the existential vacuum described by Frankl:

'The 1960s and 1970s generally were a time when most young people who had any kind of education were looking for an alternative and most of my contemporaries were seriously looking around for a radical alternative, for a new way of being. And I suppose my looking around was prompted by that. I would now interpret it as being a spiritual quest for the ultimate reality. I didn't know what it was, but certainly it was something that everybody was looking for, something more real. Later on, as I progressed some of them have progressed in the direction which they've chosen. They realised what it was. And all the social movements of this age, including social or political, were actually sublimations of the religious urge.'

In 1965 Lofland and Stark argued that a religious problem-solving perspective is a precondition to conversion. By this they meant that the converts' previous cognitive orientations will make them more or less likely to accept the ideology of a particular group. In the following years a number of writers (Baer, 1978; Greil and Rudy, 1984; Richardson, 1985; Gartrell and Shannon, 1985) have argued that this is the case and suggested that predispositions are an important factor to consider in understanding of the conversion process. In short, this view asserts that people join religious movements whose ideologies make sense to them. In his study of conversion to a Pentecostal sect, Heirich (1977: 674–5) challenged explanations of conversions that focus on emotional stress or past socialisation and called for a study of conversion as an existential quest. Heirich suggested that conversion entails a change of explanatory schemes of 'root reality' similar to the gestalt shifts. He concluded that links between the content of a new vision and adherents' prior experiences are crucial: 'the new 'reality' used by converts should speak directly to the problem they have encountered and should explain it more successfully than its earlier competitor.' Greil (1977: 120–1) argued that the search for a new perspective is guided by the individual's 'stock of knowledge' and 'cognitive style'. Thus cognitive theory implies that those whose identities have been spoiled become 'seekers' who search for a perspective that can restore meaning to the world. Batson and Ventis (1982: 82–7), maintained that religious experience involves cognitive restructuring to deal with one or more existential questions. They argued that creative problem-solving may serve as a model for understanding religious experience and distinguished four stages of problem-solving regarding the religious quest: (1) there are persistent but unsuccessful attempts to solve the problem by using the old structure; (2) encountering repeated failures, the person then gives up the active search for solutions; (3) there is a sudden emergence of a new organisation, a switch of gestalt, that enables a different view of the problem and, consequently, its resolution; (4) there is a testing and verification of the new view. The four-stage model, suggested by Batson and Ventis, seems to apply to the case of many converts to Islam, who had been in search for solutions to existential queries. The first stage refers to the 'existential crisis', which fails to find solutions to existential queries. In the second stage, the convert gives up of his quest in despair. In the third, he gains a religious revelation that supplies a sense of resolution. In the final stage, he applies the new vision to behaviour.

Cognitive quests in the two year preceding conversion contained ambiguities in one's belief system which were also in operation. These ambiguities were anchored during adolescence, but revived later in life when one became actively involved in life situations and felt an urge to have a faith, or a need to return to religion. Until this stage of their life these people seemed not to have bothered about religion, but at this stage when these needs became more manifest they requestioned their previous beliefs and as a result they felt confused or they decided to give it up entirely. As the average conversion age for the present sample suggests, their conversion to Islam came after this stage and it was an attempt to reduce cognitive ambiguities. Requestioning some elements of the old belief exposed them to different perspectives closer to that of Islam. John, for example, explained why he chose Islam: 'It was the best way that I had found to express my belief in One God whose presence I had always been aware of.' The ambiguities with regard to their previous religious beliefs, namely Christianity, centred around some basic concepts of Christianity and its theological implications such as Trinity,

Jesus being the Son of God, original sin, atonement theory, and the mediatorship of the clergy. Frederick has always questioned the position of the clergy:

'The priest is like a middle-man between God and people. It was something I didn't like when I used to make confession. You have to go to the priest and say what you did wrong and his role was to absolve you. When I was a teenager I used to think what gives him the right to absolve me. He is a human being.'

Some criticisms also focused on perceived hypocrisy in mainline churches and them having no capacity to lead the people in moral issues. The following written testimony comes from a lady who is not involved in this study:

In order to live in our society we are forced to make compromises with Christianity. And in order to keep up its authority, to survive in this society, the church itself is ever so ready to make compromises. To mention one example only, the church says that sexual relations should start only after a couple is married in the name of God. Yet in the West hardly any man or woman is ready to buy the cat in the bag (i.e. to enter matrimony without having tried out first whether the partners sexually suit each other). A priest will readily absolve a confessor of this sin with one or two prayers. I simply could not accept a church which is ready for compromise in such important matters. I longed for something really perfect as the guide of my life ... Due to these doubts I could not really feel near God even when I was kneeling in the church. (Heeren, 1966: 29).

To conclude, emotional and cognitive concerns seem to be equal in characterising the two year period preceding conversion. Thirty three (47%) of the 70 reported specific concerns that could be designated as cognitive or existential and 34 (49%) reported emotional distress during the two year period prior to conversion. As this finding illustrates, selecting one factor as being relevant and eliminating the other as irrelevant to conversion would be premature. They both seem to be precursors of conversion.

The course that the preconversion period takes in many cases is that the emotional turmoil or personal distress of the individual leads him to a stage where he develops cognitive concerns. For example, Anthony, whose case was presented earlier, was in turmoil because of his life-style and he reached a stage where he started asking questions about the meaning of life. He was looking for a way of shedding his old life-style. He believed that taking up a religion which had a strong and decisive framework towards things that were causing him unhappiness would help him in that direction. To cite another example, Raymond was still feeling distressed when he became a Muslim at the age of 18. This was due to the fact that he had been born illegitimate, and had been brought up without his father. Raymond said: 'When I observed how strong the family structure of Islam was through my Muslim friends in the university, I decided to take up this religion'. Raymond thought that he would not have suffered if his parents had adopted the Islamic way with regard to male-female relationships.

Even in cases where the religious conceptions of Islam or its expression of the ultimate meaning of man's existence were not a primary element leading to its adoption, once the religion had been accepted, new concepts penetrated consciously or unconsciously through religious action. Those who had instability, a turbulent background, and an unstable world view stated that Islam seemed to promise a release from anxiety if they transferred to it. However, they also pronounced that it provided answers as to why they had been in turmoil in the first place.

To sum up, most of the studies on religious conversion, especially those on new religious movements seem to eliminate the cognitive style and give credit to turbulent background. The analysis of converts' preconversion period suggests that cognitive style is a variable, at least it goes hand in hand with emotional style, to be taken into consideration to understand the appeal of particular social and religious movements.

C Conversion motifs (patterns)

In some types of religious conversion belief emerges out of interaction with members of a religious movement (Snow and Phillips, 1980), while in others outcomes of evaluating cognitions such as intellectual satisfaction with an experimental orientation precede it (Straus, 1979: 163). Stark and Bainbridge (1980b: 125–6) purported that religious organisations offer both tangible social and material rewards, as well as rewarding beliefs and ideas. Investigations of religious conversion brought to light several conversion 'patterns' or 'motifs' of the experience. Lofland and Skonovd (1981) offered six types of conversion (intellectual, mystical, experimental, affectional, revivalistic, and coercive) characterising each using five independent elements: (1) degree of social pressure; (2) temporal duration; (3) level of affective arousal; (4) affective tone of conversion experience; and (5) the belief-participation sequence. They characterised each conversion motif by a particular profile in terms of these variables. They also noted that these major types occur at different times and with different frequencies, depending on the social and historical content. Reviewing the Lofland-Skonovd's conversion motifs Robbins (1988: 71) concluded that 'in "advanced" Western society, intellectual and experimental conversions may be increasing while revivalist conversion motifs have declined.' Now the six conversion motifs outlined by Lofland and Skonovd will be reviewed and their applicability to the case of converts to Islam will be examined.

In the first, the **intellectual** mode of conversion, the individual becomes acquainted with alternative ideologies and ways of life by individual, private investigation like reading books, watching television, and other impersonal ways. Though some individuals convert themselves in isolation from any actual interaction with devotees of the respective religion, in intellectual mode the individual is still likely to be socially involved with members of the new religion. However, there is little or no external social pressure, the process does not take long, and a reasonably high level of belief is attained prior to actual conversion.

The second, the **mystical** mode of conversion is characterised by high subjective intensity and trauma. It has alternative names such as 'Damascus Road', 'Pauline', 'evangelical', and 'born again'. The experience can not be expressed in logical and coherent terms. In this conversion mode there is little or no immediate social pressure upon the convert: he is even likely to be alone at the time of the actual event. The critical period of the conversion is quite brief, although a period of stress preceding the critical event may stretch back some days or weeks. The level of emotional arousal is extremely high, and this is followed by active intensification of belief.

In the third, the **experimental** conversion, the potential convert takes an experimental 'show me' attitude and is ready to give the process a try. In this mode, genuine conversion comes later on. First, the prospective convert participates in the group's ritual and organizational activities and learns to act like a convert. It involves relatively low degrees of social pressure to participate since the recruit takes on a 'try it out' posture. The actual transformation of identity, behaviour, and world view takes place over a relatively prolonged period and does not appear to be accompanied by high levels of emotional arousal in most instances. Belief arises out of participation.

In the fourth, the **affectional** mode, personal attachment or strong liking for practising believers is central to the conversion process. Though social pressure is present, it functions more as a 'support' and an attraction, rather than as an 'inducement'. The process is relatively prolonged. Even if the central experience is affection, the ordinary level of emotional arousal seems more in the range of 'medium' intensity, and as in experimental conversions belief arises out of participation.

The fifth, **revivalist** conversion refers to managed or manipulated ecstatic arousal in a group or collective context which has a transforming effect on the individual. The best known revivalist conversion is the style of Billy Graham's meetings. The revivalist style seems to have declined, but new religious movements like the Unification Church or Hare Krishna appear to have resurrected the revivalist experience. In the revivalist conversion motif recruits are overwhelmed initially by waves of intense sentiment orchestrated by the movement. It involves intense social pressure and is of a fairly short duration. There is a high level of affective arousal, and belief comes after participation.

The sixth, **coercive** or brain-washing 'takes place only in extremely rare and special circumstances, but it has been alleged by some to be prevalent among the new religions of the Western world.' The two keys of the coercive motif are the compulsion of an individual and the confession of guilt or acceptance of an ideological system by the individual. Revivalist conversion may provide a setting in which 'social-psychological coercion' may rise. Therefore, there are crossovers between revivalist and coercive conversion. Revivalist and coercive conversion differ in terms of longer duration of the latter, but share the high levels of social pressure and affective arousal, and belief arises out of participation.

97

When Lofland-Skonovd's finding of six conversion patterns is applied to the present sample it indicates that converts to Islam primarily go through three conversion motifs: intellectual, affectional and experimental (table 3. 6). The two motifs, affectional (example and imitation) and intellectual (response to teaching) are significant characteristics. These two motifs seem to have been accompanied by the experimental mode (trying it out). However, mystical and coercive motifs are also found though the latter is extremely rare. Only 3 (4%) converts were judged to have gone through the coercive motif, but in all of these three cases there was an affectional motif involved as well. The revivalist motif in which the individual should be emotionally stimulated at a high level is nonexistent.

Table 3.6   Conversion motifs (patterns)[4]

motifs	total=70	male=50	female=20
intellectual	50 (71%)	38 (76%)	12 (60%)
mystical	10 (14%)	9 (18%)	1 (5%)
experimental	42 (60%)	28 (56%)	14 (70%)
affectional	46 (66%)	28 (56%)	18 (90%)
coercive	3 (4%)	3 (6%)	0 (0%)

The intellectual motif was found in 50 (71%) cases.[5] Other motifs like affectional and experimental have also played a role in their conversion, but these subjects said that their initial scepticism about their previous beliefs, and their intellectual discovery of Islam preceded their conversion. There were, of course, subjects who have gone through a purely intellectual motif, whose main problem has been that of accepting as true the propositions of religion and whose central change has been the acceptance of a system of beliefs. Consider the case of John who came to Islam after discovering the view that Jesus was not divine and he was not crucified. John holds a bachelor's degree in theology and is currently teaching religious studies in secondary school:

'When I was at college I had the advantageous opportunity to learn New Testament Greek. So I could look at various Greek manuscripts. And the reason why that was an advantage was because whatever Bible I picked up there would be several variations to it. And one of the things at that time, although I did not appreciate it, was that the older the manuscript became, the purer it became. The later manuscripts would have bits taken away or bits added. That is quite significant. Because when I was teaching religious studies I was involved in the task of teaching a GCSE O-level group and the course was divided into two. The areas which I was responsible for teaching was the Gospel of Luke and Islam. I did not do any preparatory work on Islam when I was at college. And I decided to do Luke part of the course first because I was very proficient on that area, but when it came to Islam I did not know it at all. I wanted to prepare the course in earnest as a teacher and I decided to study it a bit. And also when I was preparing lessons on the Gospel of Luke I felt that there was so much more to be said about it since there was not any suitable text on Luke. So I said to myself that the task of writing a commentary on the Gospel of Luke would be interesting. I found that was a wonderful experience, because I did a lot of research behind it and I decided to approach it in different ways. I tried to understand what the Gospel says from my point of view, how would I under-stand it as someone who is not already blinkered into understanding it in certain channels. So having borne that in mind I then looked at other interpretations and other sources. Basically, I was applying all of the forms of biblical criticism to the Gospel of Luke. And when I was making cross references to other Gospels I found that the infant narratives in Luke are fairly thin, but in Matthew they are quite extensive, that is the birth and childhood of Jesus. I found that the basic content of Jesus' teaching was superb, highly spiritual, highly inspirational, but when it came to the crucifixion narratives of Luke, in particular, I found that textually they were quite inadequate. For example, the writings of Paul predate that of the Gospel writers in some of the older manuscripts of the Eucharistic statements, that is Jesus' body being the bread and his blood being the wine. There is nothing of his death on the cross being sacrificial. This is Paul's writing, I thought, which was inserted into Luke's writings. And so when I removed all these textual inaccuracies what I found was quite specifically Jesus was not crucified. (I still did not know what Islam is). I found that Jesus was not God as the Christian church teaches. I

99

found that Jesus is the word of God, but not God. (There is a distinction there). I was always hoodwinked into believing that the word is Jesus, therefore the word is God, Jesus is God. But I could find no substance to prove it right. Any link to perhaps Unitarian statements in the Gospel, again, are future additions. And, therefore, highly questionable. So I came to some fundamental conclusions. *One*, about the divinity of Jesus; Jesus was not divine. *Two*, that the crucifixion did not take place.

'And it did not bother me at all. I was happy, I believed in God, I believed what I was doing was right. But what bothered me was when I came to prepare for the course of Islam I bought a translation of the Koran. What I found was shocking. When I started to read it I was specifically interested in verses which relate to Christianity, and it shocked me. I was horrified to read the verses in the Koran about the crucifixion of Jesus, about him being the word of God, but not God. And as a result it made me begin to think: "Well, this is interesting." Because in my findings of the Gospel of Luke, here is this book telling me things which if the Prophet Muhammad were the author of it, how would he know? I know today because I have great access to other sources that he wouldn't have had. One of the biggest accesses, of course, is that I can read and write whereas he couldn't. So what I decided to do, because I knew I had to be honest, was that I had to challenge the Koran in the same way that I did the Gospel of Luke. The Koran was offering this challenge. I decided to write a commentary on the Koran from my limited resources. So I went through it from the beginning verse for verse and bit by bit. One of the things that I found was that when I found a problem I would then begin to find an answer to that problem, whereas in my experience in using the same technique on the Gospel of Luke when I found a problem the answer to that problem brought me further problems. And the more I worked on it, the more I realised that I was handling something that was beyond my means. Then it got to the stage that I realised that I was handling something divine, not a work of human hand. Then I realised that "this is the word of God." So there was only one thing for me, and that is to believe in it, to follow it. And at that

100

stage I had not spoken to any Muslim. So I became Muslim in the absence of a Muslim, just through the study of the Koran.'

The affectional motif was present in 46 (66%) people. Their personal contact with Muslim friends or acquaintances whose opinions or behaviours are valued played a role in their conversion. Emily recollected how she was impressed by the Muslim family that she knew: '... At that time I was seeing this Muslim family and I was watching and listening to what they said and what they did. I was trying to see how they were different. They were very sincere in their faith and they were friendly in this materialistic and selfish society. That really helped towards my reversion.' Raymond talked of the family aspect of Islam:

'My initial contact with Islam came through Muslim friends at the university. I didn't ask them any question about Islam and they rarely mentioned it. It only came up in general conversation. But the family structure attracted me. The women want to be woman, not man, and the men go off to work and the women remain woman in the home. Very nice. Yes, I like this. They don't try to get drunk all night. They have moral values; they don't have sex before marriage with as many people as possible. This is the kind of woman I want to marry. I could see this directly from the way they live their life-styles. You can see the women are not running off with anyone.'

Some were affected by the Islamic concept of brotherhood. Simon said:

'Muslims have a very strong bond because we share an ideology. It is not like, for example, I have a friend and we go to a football match. When the match is over our bond is finished, but with Islam it is everything. Even if we don't like each other as individuals we still have that bond that holds us together.'

The second conversion experience of Malcolm X provides a unique example as to how affection can cause a conversion experience. Malcolm X converted to the heterodox Black Muslim Movement first, but when he visited Mecca for pilgrimage a few

101

years later he gained new insights that led him to realise that Islam transcends the sectarian character of the Black Muslim Movement and thereby converted to the *ummah* (community) of orthodox Islam. He declared his second conversion in a letter from Mecca to his friend back in the United States:

> You may be shocked by these words coming from me. But on this pilgrimage, what I have seen, and experienced, has forced me to re-arrange much of my thought-patterns previously held, and to toss aside some of my previous conclusions . . . Never have I witnessed such sincere hospitality and overwhelming spirit of true brotherhood as is practised by people of all colours and races here in this Holy Land, the home of Abraham, Muhammad, and all the other prophets of the Holy Scriptures. For the past week, I have been utterly speechless and spell-bound by the graciousness I see displayed all around me by people *of all colors* . . . America needs to understand Islam, because this is the one religion that erases from its society the race problem . . . During the past eleven days here in the Muslim world, I have eaten from the same plate, drunk from the same glass, and slept in the same bed (or in the same rug) – while praying to the same God – with fellow Muslims, whose eyes were the bluest of the blue, whose hair was the blondest of the blond, and whose skin was the whitest of the white. And in the *words* and in the *actions* and in the *deeds* of the "white" Muslims, I felt the same sincerity that I felt among the black African Muslims of Nigeria, Sudan, and Ghana. (X, Malcolm, 1964: 340–1, Italics in original; for a discussion over Malcolm X's conversion see Gallagher, 1990).

Denis has had an experience reminiscent of that of Malcolm X, which prompted his interest in Islam. Denis met a couple of Muslim students from South Africa in London and he travelled with them and they became friends. They invited him to go for a holiday in South Africa:

> 'So while I was there they said: "Come and see the mosque!" and I went along. I saw South African and Indian Muslims praying side by side. And I thought this was unusual and strange in South Africa; seeing the races

together like this. So when I came back I got a few books on Islam including the Koran and started reading and wanted to know what it is special about Islam that brings the races together whereas at that time the Christian church was very segregated.'

Some converts were deeply affected and thereby attracted through their visit to Muslim countries. Jason recollected how he was affected by the extent of religious influence in people's lives when he spent sometime in Egypt:

'I did a lot of travelling around Egypt and just talked to the people. What surprised me was the extent to which so many people adhere to religion. It struck me because over here although we are all Christians we don't really adhere to Christian teachings. In Egypt you get into a car and the taxi driver has a copy of the Koran. This was very shocking for someone like myself who lives in a country where people are not that dedicated towards a particular religion.'

Tim talked about how he was affected by Muslims when he saw that they always mentioned the divine names in their daily conversations like *bismillah* (in the name of Allah) before they did things, and *salamalaikum* (peace be upon you) to one another when they met.

Those who were married to a Muslim before their conversion were more likely to go through the affectional conversion motif. Fourteen (20%) were married to a Muslim when they converted. Thirteen of them were judged to have gone through the affectional motif.[6] The affectional motif was also significantly related to gender. Women were more likely to go through affectional motifs than men. Eighteen (90%) women as against 28 (56%) men were judged to have gone through the affectional motif.[7]

No matter what reasons or motivating factors they had for their conversion, the majority went through a period of experimentation during the process. Forty two (60%) came to Islam after studying or spending a considerable amount of time among Muslim friends, families, or in Muslim countries. While some spent sometime in Muslim lands and knew quite a lot about Islam, some had first hand experience of Muslims through their friends over here. As well as getting information and impressions from Muslims and reading about Islam, they also visited mosques, attended meetings and even joined the prayers to see and try it out for themselves. Jason said: ' . . . So through talking to people I learned about the way Muslims live. I already understood about the faith, it wasn't that strange to me when I converted.'

Ten (14%) converts (9 men and 1 woman) reported having a mystical experience before they decided to embrace Islam. Kathleen, who converted one year after she married her Muslim husband had a mystical experience which made her feel 'complete'. Kathleen's husband was not a practising Muslim when they got married, but he turned to religion sometime after their marriage. Until then she was not very much interested in Islam. After her husband changed she felt deep down that she had to change and come to terms with it. But she did not know where to turn; whether she should follow her husband or return to her own religion. One day she went to church and prayed to God saying: 'Look, I am here, tell me what is the truth, guide me, and I promise I will do it.' The answer came the following day:

'I had a very strong dream. I saw myself in the middle of a field. It was very dark and there was so much rain. And I was crying feeling that all the pain in this world was with me. Then I heard a voice that said, "Oh, human beings why are you so bad, making me very sad? I have created you because I love you. Why are you doing this to me?" I woke up finding myself crying. So what happened that night, in my opinion, was I was washed off my sins of the past.'

When Kathleen had this dream it was the time of fasting month of *Ramadan*, and she decided to do the fasting with her husband despite not being a Muslim. The last day of *Ramadan*, Kathleen had another experience which made her decide to become a Muslim:

'I woke up at six o'clock in the morning and I heard the *adhan* (the call for prayer) in X where there is no mosque around. So that was it. I said, 'This is for me, this is a sign.' I woke my husband up and said that I wanted to become a Muslim. That was the happiest time of my life because you feel you've done it, and you are one person, no more conflicts. Because the conflict is constantly within you unless you find God.'

The experience that George had was not of a dream kind. It was an ineffable one. George became a Royal Marine commando in 1965 and his first posting was to the Yemen. He knew nothing about Islam/Muslims. The first thing he learned was that they pray regularly when he saw the workers on the side of the road praying when he was driving to the camp after he had been picked up from the airport. George was employed as a cook in the camp, and became familiar with a Somalian Muslim called Ali Noor who was working with him. George described Ali Noor as a gentle, straight and practising Muslim person liked by all the Marines. He hardly spoke a word of English, and George felt that there was something special about him. George used to sit and watch him praying. He was also reading a book on Islam, which was going around the Marines. During this time a particular incident happened to George:

'There was a beach quite some distance from the camp and I used to go there quite regularly. One day I was down there on my own and I decided to pray as I saw Ali Noor praying. I didn't know any words, but basically I was doing this and asking for guidance to help me over my problem. At that time I was married and my wife was expecting a baby and she was in England, having no parents to look after her. I felt very worried in some way about leaving her behind. And also I had a drinking problem. After praying on the beach I was walking towards the camp and I passed a graveyard and there was a building there and something drew me towards it. There was a small door in the side of the building and I decided to go in. Something made me stop and something came to my mind that I should take my shoes off before I go in. I had never heard of any custom like that before. Something made me do it. When I entered the building there was a sort of square box in the centre of the building. There was Arabic writing around the walls and the room had a very beautiful smell. I sat down for half an hour. And I felt very relaxed and I felt as if all my problems were lifted away from me. And after that I decided to return to the camp. As I walked into the main galley to see if Ali Noor had some tea, Ali Noor walked straight towards me and pushed me towards the wall and said, "For you Islam" and I said, "What is Islam?" He

105

pointed to his heart and said, "Peace!" That was very strange because he never ever preached Islam to anybody.'

Three months later George returned to England and on meeting some Muslims there he became a Muslim at 23. Since that time George has learned the history of the area of his base in the Yemen and it turned out that the building that he had been into was the tomb of a saint. Now George believes that it was the experience which emerged out of his saint's blessing that made him Muslim.

The convert may undergo two or more types of conversion motifs at the same time or at different times during the process leading up to actual conversion. However, an overview of the lifespan and the accounts of conversion experiences give clues about the primary conversion motif. As the conversion accounts presented so far indicate, the pattern of conversion in the present sample in terms of conversion motifs seems to be a mixture of more than one motif. That is to say, the converts appear to have been under the effect of two or three motifs rather than just one. Only a few were judged to have gone through only one motif. To illustrate the fact that they have gone through more than one motif the process that David went through can be examined. Throughout his life, even when he was a child David had always had certain questions like 'Why are we here?'. He said: 'As I got to be in my teens I could see there was a lot of injustices in the world and I was looking for answers.' As an extension of these worries in his youth David was quite active in various socialist groups and also groups concerned with racism or similar issues. But 'quite quickly', David said, he saw the shortcomings in some of the left-wing ideologies and groups:

'For example, I could see the spreading of Marxism and Leninism in countries, say, such as China, was a form of imperialism in the sense that it is a form of dissimulation of Western cultures and Western values which is materialistic amongst people who are Westerners. So I've come to view it as more of a left-wing politics and I gradually changed my view rather than thinking that they were seeking justice in the world. I've come to see it as like a way of expanding the hegemony of Western materialistic thought. Then I gradually drifted away from what was at first a very conventional form of left-wing ideology and I started to

106

read some of the French post-Marxists particularly who extended their criticism to the underlying foundations of Western society. And this in turn led me to read many different authors who concerned themselves with the political and social history of the West who were becoming increasingly critical of Westernism. Particularly there was a group of American anthropologists who were concerned with real value which they termed the 'primitive' and their perception was very much that Western progress was not progress.'

This search for the 'primitive' led David to read the Bible for the first time ever. He was very struck by some of the older books that the Bible had in Genesis. He said:

'I was looking for something more fundamentally human, that's where this thing ties in with "primitive". Because the society we are living in now is very alienated; one human being is very alienated from another. We tend to get to know people through various things, through literature or something else. And I found this directness and this kind of mentality in the Bible. It wasn't really a religious reason that I started to read it. It was because it was simply a very ancient text and I was looking for this directness between human beings. Reading the Bible was like a new world to me because here was the understanding of revelation from God. It was wholly different to what I had experienced before which was a very intellectual and deductive way of looking at things.'

From reading the Bible David started to read the Koran. He began to acknowledge that the words of the Koran were the words of God. He believed that in the Bible there were things which were undoubtedly the word of God, but there were certain things which were unacceptable, and that the Bible had been compiled over a very long period of time. He believed that there was continuity between the revelations sent to Moses, Jesus, and Muhammad. David admitted that this was a big step for him to take because he had been completely irreligious until then. At this stage David did not know any Muslims. Over a period while he was searching he increasingly had the desire to practise the religion, but he did not know how to, because he was so divorced

107

from religion and religious experience. He gradually became more receptive to a way of thought which was religious. His internal inclination towards Islam soon turned into action when he decided to take up Islam when he was visiting a Muslim country as a tourist. At first glance, David's conversion appears to have been purely an intellectual one. Nevertheless, this is only one part of the story, as David concedes. While David had all these intellectual questions in his mind, his marriage was collapsing and in the end his wife left him. After she left David she started living with another man who beat her badly. David had to get involved, sometimes physically, and he was very much caught in the middle, because his daughter had remained with his wife. David described this period of his life as 'dark' and 'period of perpetual crisis' and added that it certainly played a part in his journey to Islam. As well as these intellectual yearnings he desperately wanted to find something, a code of behaviour, to live by. He said: 'As the momentum of events continued to build up, it became increasingly obvious that I was going to become a Muslim to have solidity in life. Anyway, there wasn't really any alternative.' David recollected the time when he decided to convert while visiting a Muslim country. He was sitting in a park looking back over his life and the various chaotic events that had overtaken him. When he had gathered his thoughts he took stock of his life and decided that there was no alternative but to convert to Islam to escape from his past and start a new life.

Poston's (1992: 176) questionnaire study of 72 American and European converts to Islam seems to lend support to the present findings regarding the conversion motifs. For Poston's subjects response to teaching was the chief motivating factor which the overwhelming majority found significant. Fifty four (75%) of Poston's subjects mentioned aspects of the teaching/s of Islam as being instrumental in their decision to convert, while 43 (60%) mentioned specific individuals or groups which had influenced them in their decision.

Sufis seem to be more likely to go through affectional, rather than intellectual motif. 87 percent of the Sufis as against 55 percent of the non-Sufis reported affectional motif.[8] The way the Sufi group is formed; the warm and spiritual atmosphere, and the sense of brotherhood, has the primary role in their conversion. Many Sufis talked of the psychological and emotional relief and comfort which they experienced when they found such an atmosphere in which they felt at home. Sufis also seem to be mystically oriented. 8 (35%) Sufis as against 2 (4%) non-Sufis underwent mystical motif. Since Sufis also have a higher record of reported drug-use[9] before their conversion, this may prove the influence of psychedelic drugs in having a mystical experience. Deutsch (1975: 171) found that virtually all of his 14 subjects who converted to Hinduism had made at least moderate use of LSD and other hallucinogens. His subjects believed that drug-use had influenced their conversion and typically had a "mystical" content such as experiences of unity with others or the cosmos, and revelations of the universal.

Apart from judging the conversion patterns that converts went through, each convert was also asked to identify the most motivating factor for their conversion. As table 3.7 illustrates, response to the teachings of Islam with regard to religious beliefs, moral or social matters, and its spiritual aspect were the most motivating factors.

Table 3.7   Most motivating factor in conversion process (n=70)

Emphasis on brotherhood, community, and friendliness	7 (10%)
Witnessing life of a Muslim and attraction to the culture	7 (10%)
Religious doctrines and teachings	19 (27%)
Moral ethical standards, social matters, and political ideology	19 (27%)
Spiritual, mystical aspect, or inexplicable religious experience	18 (26%)

Self-regarding motives like 'wanting the approval of others' and 'social pressure and urging' are not the case for the converts to Islam. However, there may be some cases where a non-Muslim partner might have felt psychological pressure from their Muslim partner for conversion to Islam, though none described such a pressure. Interpersonal bonds, including marriage, and social relationships seem to have played a significant role in the conversion process. Now these issues and the conversion process model for the present sample comparing with Lofland-Stark's process model will be examined.

D *Social influence and the conversion process model*

1 The convert as a social type

Social influence theories suggest that the range of perspectives used by close associates affects the persuasiveness of a new view of reality. Increased contact with a devout follower of the new faith increases the likelihood of conversion (Ullman, 1989: 81). Nevertheless, an individual must already be oriented towards a religious quest at the time of social contact (Heirich, 1977: 673). If the individual is not already a religious seeker, or if he is attached to a religion, such contact may not be sufficient for conversion.

Studies of conversion on new religious movements seem to have applied two theoretical approaches in order to ascertain what is most influential in the conversion process. The *first* is the **deprivation-ideological** appeal point of view (Balch and Taylor, 1977; Anthony, et al, 1977; Richardson and Stewart, 1977; Baer, 1978) which hypothesises that people are deprived (socially, psychologically, physically, etc.) and ideologically predisposed to accept a cult or a sect's message. This approach claims that people do not join a group unless something has bothered them, and thus cults and sects tend to recruit people who suffer from some variety of deprivation. Lofland and Stark (1965: 864), for example, hypothesised that people must experience enduring and acutely felt tensions before they will join a cult. The *second* approach may be called the **social networks** point of view (Stark and Bainbridge, 1980a; Snow and Machalek, 1983; Long and Hadden, 1983) which emphasises that interpersonal bonds between members of a group and potential recruits are the essential element in the process. The first approach claims that groups reward the members and make deprivations more bearable. The second approach puts interpersonal relations at the centre of the recruitment process and argues that membership spreads through social networks. The 'social network' theory does not completely deny deprivation theory. It states that deprivations and social problems are facilitating factors of conversion, but the crucial step in joining a group is the development of strong social ties with group members (see Stark and Bainbridge, 1980a: 1380).

Although both approaches emphasise the different nature of elements and factors in the conversion process there is nothing contradictory about them. Even those who question the centrality of deprivation admit that it must at least be included as a condition 'enabling' or 'facilitating' conversion. This research suggests that both seem obvious requirements of any adequate theory. As the accounts of the interviewees portray, the potential convert may have ethical, psychic, or social deprivation in their background and at the same time they may have a social relationship with a Muslim associate. The study of conversion to Ananda Marga by Nordquist (1978: 87), in fact, lends support to the proposition that both approaches are important. Nordquist's questionnaire study of 28 Ananda members revealed that they were overwhelmingly characterised by 'social withdrawal or introversion' prior to joining Ananda. Presumably, one of the deprivations that caused these people to seek a religious answer was social isolation. Yet, Nordquist also found out that an overall majority of the converts reported that 'fellowship with other devotees' was an important factor in keeping them in Ananda.

The converts involved in this study entered into the fold of Islam by various means and for a variety of reasons. Some accepted it after studying it for a long time, and some entered it in order to be able to marry a Muslim, or after marrying a Muslim. Whatever the reasons and purposes of their choice to convert, it seldom emerged without human contact. All but 9 converts had been in contact with Muslims in one way or another for a long period of time before they made their decision. Their conversion was a result of interpersonal relationships with Muslims.

The interviewees were asked how they first made contact with Islam, whether any family members, a spouse or friends belonged to Islam, or if any other means like literature or travel to a Muslim country was applicable (table 3.8). Sixteen (23%) people's first contact with Islam was through literature. Michael's first contact came about when he was doing a part time course in art and architecture. Part of the course involved Islamic art, and that set him off reading introductory books on Islam and also books on Islamic spirituality. Literature here also covered reading the Koran. Tracy, whose marriage was on the verge of break-up when she read the Koran, was impressed by the verses concerning woman:

'It was the Koran that really made me Muslim. The verses

related to woman, the way it speaks of woman as having the same right as man in marriage struck me. It says: "man and woman were created equal with different roles". It is not necessary for a woman to put up with a bad marriage. Because Islam says that "both of you should be equally happy". Both have equal responsibility and he should treat you with respect.'

The overwhelming majority of the converts speak of a gradual process involving conversation with Muslims, reading of the Koran, and/or other Islamic literature, and in some cases journeying to Muslim lands. Sixteen (23%) people were first introduced to Islam when they travelled to a Muslim country. Twenty six (37%) reported they first learned about Islam through conversations with Muslims. Ten (14%) came into contact with Islam through male-female relationships, (this included 3 female converts who followed their English husband's conversion), while 2 had one of their family members or relatives converted to Islam.

Table 3.8   First contact with Islam (n=70)

Travel to a Muslim country	16 (23%)
Conversation with a Muslim/s	26 (37%)
Reading literature	16 (23%)
Male-female relationship	10 (14%)
Family members or relatives	2 (3%)

In some cases infatuation occurs after a more or less chance meeting. The individual meets someone who seems to be a reasonable person and he later finds out that his friend has different ideas. Upon discussing these ideas and related issues further with his friend he comes to the view that they seem pretty reasonable. Sometimes new perspectives come to those who were not even searching for them, and sometimes conversion is experienced via new acquaintances and as the general acceptance of the beliefs of these acquaintances. Alan and his wife came to Islam after they observed a new neighbour:

'A couple moved to a farm just near where we were and we got to know them very well. The man was a wimp and the wife tried to dominate the man. And the man went to London and stayed there for sometime. When he came back he was Muslim. He came back a man. He was no longer a wimp. Islam changed him. He had come back a man with purpose. And his wife followed him into Islam. . . . We noticed Islam in this man and we were convinced by him.'

However, since adult identity is very reluctant to change, the mere presence of direct or indirect forms of social influence is hardly enough in conversional change. The convert is hardly a passive recipient of social manipulation. As Alan reported above, converts' accounts show that their conversion was not a result of manipulation or of group influence, but the influence of an individual Muslim or the possibility that the religion may provide the opportunity of a new start in life.

Conversions do not come in a flash. Long months of study and reasoning are necessary with the help of Muslim friends in most cases. With different people it can take varying lengths of time, according to the individual, and sometimes the person's age. The accounts of the converts suggest that younger people arrived much more quickly at the decision to convert than older people did. The majority of the converts made a calculated decision, consciously taking into account all the relevant details. They expended a great deal of time on weighing up the relative importance of all the pros and cons. Erick said: 'During the process I would describe myself as unsure, confused about some questions. It sort of evolved naturally. I was not to commit myself till I was sure and perfectly satisfied.' The converts gradually began practising Islam, in ways such as abstaining from pork and alcohol, learning ritual prayers and thinking like a Muslim about the events going on around them. Nevertheless, the process preceding conversion sometimes involves scepticism. Anthony had some doubts, though he was motivated by the rationality of Islam:

'Everything made sense and was reasonable, everything added up, but there were one or two aspects of Islam which I couldn't quite understand at first. They were not fundamentally contradictory problems, they were problems which might have been correct or might have been wrong and so I took the attitude on these issues to accept them and believe them perhaps in the future . . . Of course, I can understand these much better now.'

In sum, the accounts of the converts suggest that social relationship played a significant role in the conversion process. Contact with Muslims was a key element in their conversion.

2 Conversion through marriage

After the immigration of Muslims in 1950s the marriage rate between Muslims and native British people began to increase throughout Britain. The rate of conversions to Islam also began to increase. It has long been established that marital status bears a strong relationship to the religious belief and practices of the individual (Argyle and Beit-Hallahmi, 1975: 51). Many studies on religious conversion have shown that spouses are often instrumental in inducing the individual to convert (Salisbury, 1969; Mayer, 1987). For some converts involved in this research, marrying a spouse in the new faith seems to have been the primary motivation for their conversion. Perspectives are maintained by social relationships; an individual's perspectives are likely to change when his social relationships change (Shibutani, 1955: 567). The conversion process then becomes a process of coming to accept the opinions of one's significant others who in this case are Muslims.

Fourteen (20%) of the present sample were married or engaged (5 engaged) to a Muslim at the time of conversion. Of the 14, nine were female and five male. Five people (4 men and 1 woman) converted before marriage in order to be able to marry their future spouse. Nine (8 women and 1 man) converted after marriage. Three of the women followed their English husband's conversion to Islam, as Helen said: 'My husband decided and I went along with him'. Some candidates, however, are motivated by the desire to marry a Muslim rather than by conviction, as Jason admitted: 'To be honest, I'm not quite sure which came first; my attraction to the girl, or my attraction to Islam. I think they moved along with each other because we talked about Islam a lot.' Though the initial impetus for conversion comes from the desire to marry a Muslim partner it may later on develop as a sincere desire to embrace Islam. Martyn met his future wife in Egypt and they tentatively decided to get married. Martyn realised that there was no way a non-Muslim man could marry a Muslim woman, and that there was no way a Muslim woman could leave the country without the permission of her guardian.

Yet he did not want to become a Muslim on paper because he believed that religion was something meaningful in itself rather than just a way of getting something else. He then came back to England and decided to study Islam. Fiona also converted for the sake of marriage, but now she feels a strong Muslim: 'My first contact with a Muslim came about when I coincidentally met my first husband in Italy where we were both on holiday. He was an Egyptian staying in London and he was not practising Islam at all. And through him I had contact with several Muslims. Some months after we first met we got married and I became Muslim in name for the sake of marriage.' Fiona is now divorced from her Muslim husband, but she regards herself a better Muslim than her ex-husband.

This research does not claim to ascertain the scale of conversion to Islam in Britain for the sake of marriage. However, it seems that there are people whose primary motive was to marry a Muslim. The account of an English man I encountered, who is not involved in this research, demonstrates that this is sometimes the case. During one of my visits to the *Islamic Circle* led by Yusuf Islam in the Islamic Cultural Centre in London I noticed that an English man, who was apparently not Muslim, joined the circle and had a conversation with Yusuf Islam afterwards. I approached the man, and we talked. He was a Middle East correspondent for a well-known American paper, and it turned out that he had fallen in love with an Egyptian journalist whom he described as gorgeously beautiful. He was a born-again Christian, but he wanted to convert to Islam in order to be able to marry this Egyptian lady. I asked him if she was worth the conversion to Islam. His reply left no room for doubt: 'She is worth more than that!'

Conversion overcomes the differences in religion, but does it really eliminate the differences of heritage and tradition between husband and wife in an intermarriage? Is conversion necessary to eliminate those differences? Since intermarried converts live in Britain, generally not within a Muslim community, their attachment with Islamic tradition and heritage seems to be limited. Therefore, there is no social necessity for conversion of the non-Muslim spouse in order to become an integrated part of the community. The answer to this question also lies in the nature of Islam which welcomes any heritage or tradition unless it clashes with the doctrines of Islam and its way of life.

115

Mixed marriages in some degree represent a confrontation of two religious systems. In a study of the conversion phenomenon in mixed marriages between Protestants and Catholics, Salisbury (1969: 125–9) examined three areas; religious identification, sex roles, and social status, which seem influential in religious conversion in mixed marriages. Religious identification is more important for the Catholic spouse than Protestant, as the Catholic religious system is tighter and more closely integrated than the Protestant religious system. So given this fact, Salisbury found Protestant spouses convert to their partner's faith at a higher rate than Catholics. Secondly, he found that because of the females' traditionally subordinate role, they convert more frequently than their husbands. Thirdly, females are more likely to convert to the husband's faith if the husband has professional social status.

Salisbury's first two findings apply to the present research in the cases where converts married Muslims. However, his third finding seems less relevant, since only one convert's spouse had a better social status than them at the time of conversion. Islam is one of the strictest religions in the world concerning mixed marriage. It does not tolerate mixed marriage, with the exception that a Muslim man can marry a Christian or a Jew. Muslim women are not allowed to do so as it is normative and traditional that the man should be the head of the house. So in order that a Muslim woman may marry a non-Muslim man, be he a Christian or not, he must convert to Islam. The Islamic religious system seems to be a tighter system than that of Christianity, and powerful sanctions operate to hold the Muslim husband to his religious affiliation. So given a mixed marriage, the Muslim husband is more constrained than his non-Muslim wife regarding religious conversion. The Muslim husband's community is less likely to tolerate his conversion to another religion. Religious identification is an important feature of Muslim social relations and an important source of social location. This reality may play a significant role in conversion experiences as a result of mixed marriages between Muslims and Christians. The family-in-law and the new Muslim social environment of the non-Muslim wife may expect her to convert. Therefore she may look upon conversion as a necessary means of achieving complete social identification with her husband. Furthermore, women are socialised towards 'expressive' and 'socio-emotional' roles more than men, and religious behaviour and attitudes are clearly in the 'expressive' and 'socio-emotional' areas. This may lead to the Christian wife to decide that a religiously homogeneous and harmonious family is the highest state of religious expression and that conversion is therefore the highest family duty.

Prior to conversion the partner may not be committed to a religion. Of the 14 converts, who were married or engaged to a Muslim at the time of conversion, only one reported practising their religion of origin prior to conversion. One was involved with a new religious movement. Two reported that they identified themselves with no religion, while 10 reported themselves as being nominal or weak in their religion. One partner's conversion to the religion of the other sometimes may simply be for the sake of marriage and children. On the part of the non-Muslim partner there might be a perceived need for family stability or religious homogeneity later in the marriage as the children pass from infancy to childhood. Sarah's description of the process of her conversion hardly touches upon the meaning or the truth revealed in her new faith: 'I've never converted to Islam formally. I just assumed it when my children reached the age of education. I started taking them to the mosque for classes in order that they may learn their religion. Then I assumed it and took the *shahadah*.' The interviewees who converted through marriage stated that their Muslim partners took Islam more seriously than the interviewees did their religion. It is quite understandable that when a Muslim partner has a strong commitment, and the non-Muslim partner has a relatively weaker commitment, there is a strong probability that the latter will convert.

Those who converted after their marriage expressed the view that through living with Muslims and by studying and discussing various religious problems with them they were acquainted with the rationality and truth of Islam. Debbie said: 'People probably would say that I changed my religion for my husband. But this is a real joke. This is nothing to do with my husband.' Sheila's account was similar to that of Debbie:

'After getting married I kept studying Islam. So gradually I was turning to it. He just brought books to me and I liked to read them. He didn't make me Muslim, it came totally from me. If he made me, I wouldn't. People don't understand, especially when you say you are married to a Muslim. They say, 'Oh, yeah, it's your husband then." I can't understand because I know lots of them who are married and they haven't turned to it.'

In the case of some women converts, further examination of their background reveals how actively they participated in converting themselves. Joining the new faith clearly held great rewards for these women, who might have otherwise lost the only stable relationship they had. These women were alienated from their family and had had a fragile and unstable identity throughout their adolescence and early adulthood. Conversion for them meant regaining their identity, and achieving total separation from their parents. Such a case is present in Barbara's story. Barbara was born to a Roman Catholic family in London, with an Irish father and an English mother. When she was young she perceived her parents and Roman Catholics around her 'hypocrites'. She said: 'You go to the church, you sit there and be nice to each other. As soon as they get out the priest would be out in the pub along with my dad and along with everyone else's dad. And mums would go out on the street. I used to feel so sorry for them.' She described her childhood as extremely unhappy because her parents always wanted to leave each other 'fighting like cats and dogs'. Because of her father, as a child Barbara vowed never to marry an Irish man or a Catholic. Her distaste grew further and she refused to make her confirmation although she was always sent to catholic schools. After she left secondary school she never cared about religion. However, she said, she 'loved God and believed that Jesus existed'. After she completely dissociated herself with her parents' religion Barbara felt in her heart there was something missing. She said: 'It sounds weird, but it is true. When you lose your religion yet you are still looking for something. But I wasn't actively going out and looking for something and I didn't try any other religion before.' By that stage Hare Krishna people who ran a restaurant next to where Barbara was working had tried to convert her, but Barbara did not find anything interesting in them. When 18, Barbara met her present husband who used to work in the shop nearby:

'I didn't know he was Muslim until he mentioned his name. He liked me because I used to dress like a hermit and he kept asking me to go out, but I wouldn't go out with him. I was very happy as I was. But he kept pushing and pushing.

118

Eventually, I said, "Yes," and I took my little sister with me to put him off. And we went into just the cafe beside. But he just liked me more because I took my sister with me. I couldn't believe it. If it was English or something they wouldn't like it. But I found out in Islam it is good to bring someone along. And the next time we went out I found out how nice he was and I really liked him. And we soon decided to get married. I know it sounds weird, but it's true. I did it out of something in me. Anyway, we got married and we didn't talk about religion. He didn't drink and smoke or anything like that. And I didn't touch alcohol after I met him.'

Six months after their marriage Barbara converted to Islam. She described the most motivating factor for her conversion as what she saw in her husband: 'When I saw how good and how kind he was ... Even if I cooked something and he didn't like it, okay, he wouldn't eat it all, but he would eat a bit of it. He cared about you. I think that comes from Islam.' Barbara is now married for two years and she seems to be very happy. She said that her parents were getting a divorce and she thanked God that she would not have to face what her parents were facing.

To conclude then, it has become clear that contact with a follower of the new faith increases the likelihood of conversion and is instrumental in the process. In general, conversions in the present sample did not occur without contacting a Muslim. However, it must be emphasised that converts were already oriented towards a religious quest and were intellectually satisfied with what was offered to them.

3 Certain processes involved in the conversion experiences of the current group of converts

Lofland and Stark (1965) presented an influential model of conversion based on their study of a Doomsday Cult (pseudonym for Unification Church) which may be viewed as the beginning of sociological and social psychological studies of new religious movements. They described seven conditions emanating from the immediate circumstances of the person's life and the group process as determining conversion to deviant perspectives. According to them, for conversion, a person must (1) experience

119

enduring, acutely felt tensions; (2) within a religious problem-solving perspective; (3) which leads him to define himself as a religious seeker; (4) encountering the [cult] at a turning point in life; (5) wherein an affective bond is formed or (preexists) with one or more converts; (6) where extra-cult attachments are absent or neutralised; and (7) where if he is to become a deployable agent, he is exposed to intensive interaction.

Critics disagree on the importance and sequential ordering of the seven steps in the Lofland-Stark model, but there seems to be widespread agreement on the necessity of two elements in the model; these are cult affective bonds and intensive interaction with group members.[10]

Of the seven steps of Lofland-Stark's process model, some seem to be applicable to the present sample while others do not. More than anything else, Lofland and Stark's research related to this study in that their investigation included individuals who had 'relinquished a more widely-held perspective for an unknown . . . and, often, socially devalued one'. Such a description would seem to be applicable to the present sample, for they have indeed rejected a more widely-held perspective offered to them by their society and have instead adopted Islam, which is relatively unknown in the West and perceived by some to be socially inferior. Now the relevance of Lofland-Stark's seven step process model to the present sample will be examined.

The first process, experiencing acute tensions prior to conversion, is discernible in only a few accounts. This, however, may be due to the fact that the converts were, because of their age, beyond the stresses which normally accompany adolescence and the integration struggle. These individuals had resolved this struggle by rejecting the religion or culture in which they were raised and entering a 'spiritual moratorium' period.

The second process, thinking in terms of a religious problem-solving perspective, seems to be true of the present sample in as far as they sought a religious solution to questions of ultimate significance.

The third process, seekership, can not be seen as a necessary predisposing factor, though it seems to define some cases. While the present sample contains 20 converts who were involved in new religious movements after rejecting religion of origin and defined themselves as 'religious seeker', it also consists of men and women who converted for the sake of marriage. While some converts spent a substantial period in active searching between the rejection of the old religion and acceptance of the new, others did not bother about it. This dimension of the Lofland-Stark model may be applicable to the present sample in the sense that many of them (47%) had cognitive concerns, and the vast majority described themselves as being nominal in their religion. However, in a later paper Lofland (1977b) suggested that perhaps 'religious seekership' dimension of their model is not as important as originally thought, since 'people not previously religious at all have joined' movements like the Unification Church 'in noticeable numbers' since the late sixties. Snow and Phillips' (1980: 438) findings corroborate Lofland's later observation. The vast majority of their sample (78 percent against 22 percent) were not seekers in the sense of searching for some satisfactory system of religious meaning.

The fourth process, encountering the [cult] at a turning point in life seems to be applicable to those who converted through marriage, and to a few subjects who experienced conversion after moving into a big city. However, this process does not seem to be applicable to many since conversions, in general, came about when they had already developed a settled life-style.

The fifth factor, called the formation of affective bonds, seems to be of crucial importance. The majority reported being influenced by a Muslim friend or an acquaintance who had nurtured them along the way. This friendship did not serve as a recruitment mechanism, but simply as human contact. Here, it may be hypothesised that it is highly unlikely that one will convert to Islam without some form of contact with an adherent of Islam. However, it must be emphasised that the converts' previous dispositions strongly influenced their selection of friends and, hence, their choice of perspective.

The sixth process, the absence of neutralisation of extra-cult attachments does not seem to be the experiences of converts to Islam in general.

The seventh factor, intensive participation in the activities of the group, does not appear to have been an important factor, although a substantial number of the converts said that they had occasionally started practising some articles of Islam.

It may be concluded then that Lofland and Stark's paradigm of conversion to a minority religious belief is only partially applicable to the present sample. It cannot be claimed that Lofland-

Stark's model is a general model of conversion applicable to all groups. Austin (1977: 283), for example, examined the applicability of Lofland-Stark's model to 'born-again' Christians and concluded that 'most (stages) can be rejected as necessary determinants of conversion. Indeed, all seven conditions were not satisfied by even one subject.' However, Lofland-Stark's model has often been treated as if it was a general model of the conversion process by researchers studying groups of a more varied (in ideology, organisation, and public reaction) form than that of Lofland and Stark. Lofland, in a later paper (1977b: 816) made it clear that Stark and himself did not claim their model to be valid for conversion to other movements. The material in this research suggests that there is no one process model that can account for all cases of conversion. This study agrees with the investigators (Richardson and Stewart, 1977: 820; Snow and Phillips, 1980: 444; Greil and Rudy, 1984: 318) of religious conversion in that the conversion process may well be different in different kinds of groups. Furthermore, since Lofland and Stark, some investigators of conversion to NRMs have tended to focus on the group as the unit of analysis rather than the individual and have seen conversion as a one event phenomenon, in that people who join a particular group have the same background characteristics, join for the same reasons and experience the same changes. In fact, as the analysis of converts' background involved in this study illustrates, this is not always so. They varied in their background, their reasons, and their conversion patterns.

However, in the light of the present findings certain processes seem to be common within the current group of converts to Islam as follows: (1) Religious conversion is more likely to occur if the individual deems the religion of origin and values presented to him by his parents or society as irrelevant to his current life. As a consequence, he enters a sort of 'spiritual moratorium' that may last some years. At the end of this period the person must still experience disillusionment with society at large and still define himself as nominal in his religion. During this period he may have either cognitive concerns, sometimes causing him to seek answers from other religions, or emotional distress arising from personal problems such as divorce which may cause him to contemplate the possibility that religion could be the answer to his problems. Apparently, because of his nominal level of belief and previous rejection of the family the person must rule out the possibility of returning to the 'old' religion. To move back to the religion of childhood may mean the tacit approval of the family which he does not wish to do. Thus he is prevented from a return to his religion of origin and must continue to look elsewhere. In this way he is sensitive to other possibilities. By the end of the first stage, he must have in his background experience that renders him in some way sensitive to the message of Islam. (2) At this stage the presence of other significant Muslims is important since it is often Muslim individuals who make Islam available. The potential convert encounters Islam through social relationships (this could be through preexisting ties like marriage or chance encounters), and mass media or any other available sources of information. 'Affective ties' to Muslims, though not always necessary, are usually developed. The individual is affected by the example of the Muslim/s or the atmosphere as he perceives it, and at the same time he may question the truth of the Islam. (3) The individual may go through a preparational period. Before he announces himself as a convert little by little he may play the role of convert by learning some practices of Islam, and a life-style which becomes a part of him as he takes on a new definition of his own individuality and personality. He may explore its suitability and try it out. It is important to note that the potential convert seems to test out the new faith experimentally, rather than embracing it without thought. The decision is therefore characterised as being intellectual which is the end result of a deliberate choice made after careful examination and consideration rather than emotional.

It is concluded that religious conversion does not emerge out of a single influence, but out of the mutual interaction of various forces that make a person sensitive to conversion. This study does not deny other approaches to religious conversion, since both the motivational model focusing on predispositions and the activistic approach pointing out the role of the subject appear to have value. The pattern that emerges from this research is that people decide to play roles and get involved in new beliefs and practices with a more thoroughgoing acceptance of beliefs occurring later in the process. The model presented here is implicitly activist in orientation, because of its stress on the decision to become involved in the role. The present finding regarding the experimental motif (60%) which stresses the activistic view of conversion shows that one cannot avoid the part

123

played by the convert. One also has to realise that conversion is a social phenomenon, with affection and emotional ties playing key roles in the affirmative decision. Therefore, it is suggested that the conversion experience is gradual in nature and therefore encompasses the whole process of change in its definition. It is the product of a long and protracted process. It includes a reorientation of the personality system and involves change in the constellation of religious beliefs and practices, as it will be presented in the next chapter.

FOUR

POSTCONVERSION

'My father did not speak to me for two years. He was too angry, which is really quite strange because he doesn't have any belief. But he explained it to me two years later that he is a great royalist and he felt that by taking Islam I'd slighted the Queen and slighted being British. And that offended him very much.'

Rachel, a convert to Islam

The new being

Religion is a very effective context for identity as it is generally accompanied by moral systems which support identity by establishing basic values of right and wrong, good and bad, and by regulating interpersonal conduct (Baumeister, 1986: 248; Shafranske, 1992: 167), or at least it is one of the subidentites among others of which an individual's identity is made up (Beit-Hallahmi, 1989: 101). Modern Western society may produce identity problems because it has relegated religion to a minor role and therefore abandoned the context of religion for identity. It is in this context that the conversion experience provided the converts to Islam with an identity.

Religious conversion is defined as a definite break with one's former identity such that the past and the present are antithetical in some important respects. Investigators of conversion seem virtually unanimous that conversion involves a radical change in one's identity, beliefs, ideas, values, and personality (Travisano, 1970: 600; Snow and Machalek, 1983: 264; Barker and Currie, 1985: 305; Gillespie, 1991: 67).

Conversion from one religion to another means changes that

involve large areas of personality, and these vary according to the religion itself. Parrucci (1968: 145) defines conversion as 'a reorientation of the personality system involving a change in the constellation of religious beliefs and/or practices.' The extent of personality reorientation involved is determined by two factors: the degree of commitment to the new socioreligious ideology engendered in the convert, and the degree of similarity between pre and postconversion identity. With regard to the first, Lofland and Stark (1965) have drawn a distinction between 'verbal converts', who maintained limited involvement in the new religion, and 'total converts', who exhibit their commitment through regular and active involvement. The magnitude of personality change affected by religious conversion is also determined by the level of similarity between preexistent and postconversion self-definition. Parrucci (1968: 146) differentiates conversions that require a major transformation in basic religious identity (e.g., Catholic to Buddhist) and those that involve changes in emphasis, but not major identity restructuring (e.g., Presbyterian to Methodist). Singer (1980: 171) terms these respectively 'interfaith' and 'intra-faith' conversions. Likewise, Travisano (1970) separates mere alterations in faith commitment from true conversion referring to intra-faith and inter-faith conversion. Here, we are concerned with inter-faith conversion.

Gillespie (1991: 73), dealing with the experience of religious conversion in general, distinguished three aspects of the identity issue. *First*, the obvious organisational affiliation of the conversional change provides a new sense of belonging and acceptance. *Second*, religious conversion may provide a sense of personal identity and it challenges the person to reorganise himself on a deep level of consciousness. *Third*, religious conversion provides a sense of cosmic identity.

Along both structural and subjective dimensions of religious change, the interviewees reported an identity change of greater magnitude. 'Why did I have to become a Muslim if I was not going to change?', one convert said. The converts said that this had emerged naturally. One convert pointed at the grass blossoming on the edge of the pavement (while we were walking together) and metaphorically related his conversion to this grass, saying 'it is natural, you cannot stop it.' All the converts laid stress on the achievement of convert status/identity and experienced a profound change not only in beliefs but also in practices and life-style, though changes in the latter varied between individuals.

With conversion the purpose and meaning of life take on major importance for the convert. The decision to change forms the basis which enables him to view life from a different perspective. The change caused by conversion fundamentally transformed their conception of the world and changed the converts' perception of the universe of discourse in which their meanings were understood. Thus becoming a Muslim resulted in a change of identity at both a personal and a pubic level. They committed themselves to reshaping their lives. Their purposes in life became clear on a very personal level. Simon said: 'My actions are now for God and I have a reason to live. I understand Islam as an ideology, not just as a religion of praying, etc. Islam encompasses the whole of your life and every action you do.' Kevin said:

'I sort of felt that life has become manageable. All my life had always seemed like events and everyone else were always one step ahead of me and I could never catch up with them. It feels like now that I am in control of my life in a way. Whereas before it had always seemed like somehow there was always something I was missing. I do not now exactly what it was. But now it brings everything into equilibrium and balance. That is the best thing about it.'

The majority of the converts did not report going through any postconversion depression. This may be explained by the fact that the conversion process had taken a long time, during which the individuals weighed the pros and cons of their conversion. However, for some converts the transition took an especially lengthy period of time. These converts went through a critical period, they still had some doubts and relapses occurred periodically. 'I had for quite some months trouble in saying God because I didn't believe in it before', Keith said. But in the end they 'took the plunge', as one interviewee described it. Five (7%) converts reported going through a transition period in which they attempted to do the things they had been doing in the past which were unacceptable in Islam. They did not feel confident that they could fulfil the demands that Islam required. Nick, for example, felt that it demanded a lot: 'I sometimes wished that I had belief in the Christian religion or even Buddhism because they are easier to live, not so demanding, but I knew if I did that, I wouldn't be truthful because I believed in Islam.'

Religious groups require their new members to change their formal identity by adopting a new name which is a way of fostering higher involvement through external identity symbols and stronger identification with the group (Beit-Hallahmi, 1989: 101). One of the first thing that the converts to Islam seem to do is to take a new Islamic name. It is almost always done when the convert takes the *shahadah* in front of others. It is suggested s/he takes a name although this is not required unless the existing name has a bad meaning. Of the 70 converts, 57 (81%) now bear an Islamic name while 13 (19%) do not. Most of those who have taken an Islamic name use their new name within the Muslim community while they use their old name in their daily life in the society. Only 4 (6%) people have changed their name legally and they use it in all of their interactions. Some of those who did not take an Islamic name expressed that by keeping their name they are able 'to show people that it is possible to be both English and Muslim'. Most of those who took an Islamic name preferred the common names in Judeo-Christian and Islamic tradition or names similar to their Christian names, such as Maryam for Mary and Dawud for David.

It has been proposed that converts tend to denounce preconversion life as sinful and immoral (Ullman, 1989: 15) and they tend to exaggerate their preconversion 'sufferings' or 'sins' so as to glorify their present salvation (Heirich, 1977). However, only 12 (17%) of the converts involved in the present study regarded themselves as sinful in the past. Twenty five (36%) subjects regarded their conversion as fulfilling. The rest described their preconversion life as purposeless, ignorant, or in the wrong direction. Twelve (17%) said that their lives had been purposeless. Eight (11%) described them as lost, 6 (8%) said that they had been ignorant while 7 (10%) said that their lives had been going in the wrong direction. Some see their previous life, despite its frivolity of possible detrimental effects on them, as the process which led them to conversion. They believe that if they had not destroyed themselves completely, they would have been unable to rebuild and shape themselves again. Peter was one of them: 'My former life was necessary because everything that has gone before has brought me to this point. Therefore, if I hadn't had my previous life, then I may not have reached this point.' The converts felt that they were cleansed from all the dregs of the past. They felt that by accepting Islam they were wiped clean of their former sins and the 'bad deeds' they had committed. It is, in fact, the Islamic precept that made them feel that way. According to Islam once one is converted, he is cleansed of his previous sins.

1 Change: beliefs, practices and habits

Inter-faith conversion is primarily concerned with changes in the contents of faith. The converts involved in this study, by the act of pronouncing the *shahadah*, accepted the oneness of God, and the Prophet Muhammad as His last messenger. The idea of Jesus being God or the Son of God was dropped and the doctrine of the Trinity was refused. Jesus was accepted as one of the Prophets in the line before the Prophet Muhammad, and He did not die on the cross but was lifted to heaven. Converts now believe that Jesus' and Muhammad's mission was in essence the same. As one convert said 'by accepting Islam Jesus' dream of *one flock and one shepherd* is fulfilled in Islam.' For them, Islam meant finding the end of the line started by the Prophet Abraham, not rejection of the Judeo-Christian tradition. Alan said: 'Isa (our master Jesus) and Abraham and Moses and Muhammad, going all the way back through are all connected.' Conversion for them did not mean a total renunciation of their former religious tradition, and they even found what they had learned from their previous religion helpful in understanding Islam. Mike said that his previous experience with Christianity had been very helpful: 'I've never had a great deal of problem with the moral teaching of Islam because so much of it was very similar with Christianity.' They see that their conversion has achieved a culmination in Islam, and express no hostility or anger towards those who practise Christianity or Judaism.

In terms of religious practices, converts expressed that they did not in general find them difficult. Since they went through a preparational period before their conversion, when they formally accepted Islam their commitment to some practices occurred naturally. However, no matter how much they felt they were prepared to commit themselves, some aspects still remained hard to digest and observe, since Islam brought a lot of restrictions to them. But in general, they committed themselves to observing these restrictions. Simon said: 'I had come into Islam which put a lot of restrictions on my life, to things what I used to do before. But I was still happy, I've done this because it would change my life.' A few people became Muslims without going through any preparational period, and had little knowledge of Islam and Islamic teachings. They had to learn, for example, how to pray in Arabic, although some said they prayed in English for a time. In learning the elements of Islam, and committing themselves to the new faith some were very eager and dynamic, while others took it more gradually. Adam said: 'Prayers were the first thing I really wanted to devote myself to. Because it seemed to me it is the thing which I'd missed in my life.' Helen, on the other hand, reported that it took her quite some time to start praying regularly.

Thirty four (49%) converts reported that they now observe five daily prayers. Thirty six (51%) do not practise five daily prayers regularly, although they think they should. Nineteen (27%) reported that they do not observe fasting properly in *Ramadan*, but that they fast for a few days, while 51 (73%) said they observe the fast for the whole month.

The converts interviewed seem to initially practise the 'don'ts' rather than the 'do's' of Islam. They are more likely to abstain from pork, alcohol, and sex outside marriage, rather than observing prayers and fast. Bernard said: 'I stopped drinking straightaway, it wasn't very difficult, but prayer came a year after that.' Perhaps this may be explained by the fact that many were social drinkers or stopped drinking before their conversion. Some were already not eating pork because they were vegetarian. Others may have been observing the moral aspects of their former religion. All converts now observe the Islamic diet regarding pork. All but 6 people reported that they did not drink alcohol. Charlie is one of those who still drinks occasionally:

> 'I would very very occasionally have one glass of beer even now. It is out of habit more than anything else. It is a cultural thing, I would think. You associate having a long day's working with coming off the hills and going into a pub and having a glass of beer, and not to do it you would feel as if the day is not quite complete. So drinking has virtually gone, but not completely gone.'

For some, conversion facilitated identity change, enabling them to give up some personal habits such as drunkenness and drugs. Six (9%) converts who reported drug-use prior to conversion and 7 (10%) converts who reported excessive alcohol use prior to conversion do not use drugs or drink alcohol at all any more.

Regarding dress, it presented difficulty for women rather than men, because in Islam, due to her physical nature the woman is required to cover her body and hair. Of the 20 women, 14 (70%) wear a scarf (5 do not wear it tight under the neck), while 6 (30%) do not wear it. But all the women wear long sleeves and a high neck, and skirts below the knees. Wearing a scarf proved difficult to get used to. Diana could not wear it for a long time because she felt embarrassed with it. Rebecca does not see a scarf as necessary and she concentrates on changing herself 'inside'. She also finds wearing a scarf difficult because she is English:

> 'If you are English and you are brought up in this country and then you become a Muslim, you have to try and find your own way of doing things because you continue to be English. The whole thing of a code of behaviour or a code of dress would be at the back of my mind whatever I was trying to do. So it is not enough simply to start wearing a veil because essentially what you are trying to do is change yourself inside. So I feel for myself I have to go, to some extent, by the accepted norms of the society I live in. So what is regarded as modest dress (long sleeves and a high neck and the skirt under knees), would be the sort of standards I would set for myself. I mean I don't wear a scarf when I am out. Because basically, I don't feel comfortable. That might change as time goes on, but I don't really want to draw attention to myself.'

Of the 50 men, only 3 (6%) changed their dress completely. They wear robes and a turban. They are of the opinion that the Muslim man should distinguish himself from non-Muslims. All of those who are involved in Sufism and around half of the others wear a beard now. But this is not necessarily a thing brought about by conversion, since some had beards before conversion and some would have grown them even if they had not become Muslim. Of the 50 male converts, 16 (32%) had circumcision after their conversion, while 24 (48%) did not. Ten (20%) were circumcised when they were a child, either due to coming from a Jewish background or for hygienic reasons.

So regarding former habits and practices, the present sample covers people who gave up former habits and took the new practices immediately, and people who still keep some of their former habits. It consists of people who bet occasionally although they know it is forbidden in their new religion, and people who even avoid using the expression 'I bet you!' because it is a kind of gambling. Thus it may be concluded that change of the values and habits, etc. which one inherits from the past do not come automatically. The interviewees see their conversion as a continuing process, rather than a cut off point. However, a question which may be raised here is whether converts are more committed than life-long Muslims. To answer this question, there is unfortunately no available data, and the answer very much depends on personal piety. But to express a personal view it may be said that they seem to be more committed and take their religion more seriously than many life-long Muslims. This observation lends support to Beit-Hallahmi's (1989: 100) proposition who, in the light of psychological theories distinguished two different kinds of religious involvement: 'One is the low-involvement religion, the religion of identity, learned within the family of origin and having little emotional significance; and the other is the high-involvement religion, often the religion of converts, who learned it outside their family of origin and invest much emotional energy in it.'

2 Maintenance and socialisation

The maintenance of a new identity requires a structure to make it workable and commitment flourishes in that structure. Conversion is also described as a process of resocialisation with distinctive ideas and values. A new language and a life-style become a part of the convert as he takes on a new definition of his own identity and personality and of the social context in which he participates (Wilson, 1982: 119). Commitment following conversion often forms a sociological bond in a community. After conversion it matters a great deal how the new community provides for the ongoing sponsorship of the new convert. In this case, sponsorship can be seen as the way a person or community provides affirmation, encouragement, guidance and models for a person's ongoing growth and development (Fowler, 1981: 286–7). Most of the interviewees reported that they had received this sponsorship from the Muslim community around them. They were welcomed by Muslims with great sympathy in the sense that they embraced Islam willingly.

The person who wants to remain converted must engineer his social life in accordance with his purpose. This may require the individual to disassociate himself from previous associates or groups that constituted the plausibility structure of his past religious reality while he associates himself with those who sponsor him in his new religious reality. As Berger and Luckman (1971: 177) pointed out: 'To have a conversion experience is nothing much. The real thing is to be able to keep on taking it seriously; to retain a sense of its plausibility. This is where the religious community comes in. It provides the indispensable plausibility structure for the new identity.' Likewise, Meadow and Kahoe (1984: 108) emphasised that some of the success of a healthy conversion, versus an unhealthy, regressive conversion experience lies in the quality of later contacts with adherents of the new faith. Long and Hadden (1983: 8), in their study of Moonies, suggested that conversion is understandable as an instance of a more general process of socialisation, rather than being a qualitatively unique phenomenon which requires concept-specific explanation.

Nearly all writers who use the term identity imply that identity establishes *what* and *where* the person is in social terms. When one has a new identity in the shape of a social object, by the acknowledgement of participation in social relations he establishes an identity for both himself and others to facilitate meaningful interaction. The convert reflects at great length on his change. He and all others see his change as monumental, and he is identified by himself and others as a new or different person (Travisano, 1970: 597, 602). Greil and Rudy (1984: 317) categorised the new religious movements in the West into two types on the basis of the differences among the groups in terms of the converts' social roles. *Type one* includes groups which, like the Unification Church, Hare Krishna and Divine Light Mission, are stigmatised and involve a radical discontinuity of social roles. *Type two* includes groups, like Crusade House, the Levites and Nichiren Shoshu, which are not stigmatised and which do not sponsor a drastic transformation of social roles. Seekership and neutralisation of extra-cult attachments seem to be prerequisites for conversion in the context of the former, but not in the context of the latter. Regarding the social roles, the converts to Islam fall into the second type of group. They still regard themselves as members of their society and they do not favour isolation. On the contrary, they are fully conscious and aware of their own local environment as well as the universal aspects of the faith they have adopted. Most still keep their previous names, jobs, etc. More importantly, they see no contradiction between being Muslim and English/British and living in this society. However, many do not make their new identity central to all interactions in society, while they do make it central in their interactions within the Muslim community.

So far, it is clear that there must be social conditions for a successfully maintained religious conversion and this social base is essential so that the convert can get continuous confirmation and recognition from other individuals. Marriage seems to be the most important agent of this social condition in many cases, since the great majority of converts who were not married at the time of their conversion married Muslims after conversion, feeling that they would fail in their duties if they married non-Muslims. Forty eight (68%) are married or engaged now (only one is engaged). All but one who married after conversion have Muslim partners. Fifteen (21%) people married converts. (4 convert couples were involved in this study). Almost all who were not married stated that their future partner should be a Muslim. Only 4 (5.7%) said that the religion of a prospective partner was not important.

3 Cultural transition

It has been said that when Christianity began to spread through the Roman Empire, the greater concern was of Christianity becoming pagan, rather than of the Roman Empire becoming Christian (Sharma, 1985: 124). A similar concern is relevant to native-British converts to Islam. Will they westernise Islam or will they become Islamised and assimilated into the culture of Muslims around them? Will they go through a cultural transition? The answers to these questions vary according to the changes each convert has experienced. Some converts have formally changed their names, the way they dress, their attitudes and values, while there are converts who have not changed their dress, nor even taken an Islamic name, and who still keep some of their previous habits and values. A crucial point needs to be emphasised here. Converting to Islam does not necessarily mean excluding being English or British. Elements of Christian religious traditions can be found in the life-style of a convert unless it absolutely contradicts Islam. To give but one example, some converts stated that they celebrate Christmas on the grounds that it is the birthday of Prophet Isa (Jesus), and they exchange presents with their family at Christmas. The converts studied tried to find a practical way of adopting Islam in Britain on their own level in order to fit in and live in this society. As Janet stated:

> 'I did everything with confidence. If you haven't got confidence in doing things while people tell you that you mustn't do this and this, then you realise in time you can't live like that. It has to be practical in Britain as well. So you find your own level at the end and you fit in. You actually find that balance. Because you can not be so strict as you wouldn't be able to live here.'

Most of the converts seem not to have changed culturally. They have not wiped out their culture completely, even though they have undergone some cultural changes over the years. They do not feel that by becoming Muslim they have been 'Arabised' or 'Pakistanised'. They feel that they are still English/British and see no conflict between cultures before one becoming Muslim and afterwards. They feel that it is just as valid to be a British Muslim as being a Nigerian Muslim or an Egyptian Muslim. Richard said:

> 'Islam is a religion that overlays the culture. The religion which gave rise to the British culture is, of course, Christianity. And a particular style of Christianity is not actually incompatible with Islam. The thing which helped this culture evolve is in itself quite akin to Islam, therefore, Islam and European culture should be able to sit quite comfortably. Islam and Europe are so closely connected over the last thousand years. Simply by following British culture and adopting the religion of Islam there wouldn't be any conflict. I am proud of being an English man. Being a Pakistani or whatever wouldn't necessarily bring me any closer to Islam.'

135

Steve expressed that it is an advantage to have access to both Islamic and Western culture, since he is able to take what is good from both. However, the convert sometimes faces the problems of being between two cultures. Ibrahim Hewitt (1990), a convert to Islam, observed that the 'two-headed syndrome' often afflicts new Muslims, as he writes:

> 'We all experience it sometimes – you walk into a mosque and every head turns slowly and blatantly to stare at you, suspicion oozing towards you. After checking your files, you realise that they are not looking at a fellow Muslim, they are looking at a white man who has been introduced on the Asian ghetto.'

Instead of associating with a specific Muslim community, the converts had a feeling of belonging to the greater Muslim community and the universal brotherhood. They did not feel at ease with the culture or tradition of Muslim communities around them. They stated that some elements of different ethnic communities had been inserted into Islam and regarded as part of it. Therefore, they tried to understand Islam differently from Muslims of other ethnic backgrounds and bring an inquisitive mind to their new fellows' cultural understanding of Islam and break some of the un-Islamic practices and attitudes prevailing in the Muslim community. They felt that Muslims confused culture with their religion. Anthony said: 'Many born-Muslims will have particular ideas of Islam which perhaps reflect cultural traditions or conservatism or things rather than Islam itself.'

In response to the question 'Would you wish you had been born into a Muslim family or in a Muslim country?', 51 (73%) converts said 'No', while only 19 (27%) said 'Yes'. All of those who gave a positive answer were people who had suffered before conversion, having experienced traumatic events like parental divorce or had a divorce themselves. They felt that they would not have suffered if they had been brought up as Muslims. Most of those who did not wish to have been born into a Muslim family or in a Muslim country said that if that had been the case they would not be able to see the difference between Islam and the culture adopted by Muslims. Some did not wish to have been born into a Muslim family, since they found conversion itself to have been a wonderful experience, and they had had a terrific voyage of discovery which people born into a Muslim family hadn't have. Others had a feeling of pride in themselves for coming to Islam after 'seeing, tasting and rejecting everything'. So they saw themselves as understanding Islam better than life-long Muslims, because their Islam is mixed with non-Islamic culture.

4 Relations with parents, ex-friends and society

Converting to Islam in a non-Muslim society may mean social suicide and boycott for some converts. But sometimes objections raised by the family and friends of the converts tended to make them more determined to carry on their new life. One convert said that he had decided to adopt an Islamic name legally to make it clear to his friends (who thought he would grow out of it) that he had taken up Islam in earnest. Here, it must be emphasised that hearing others talk about oneself or even receiving postconversion reaction may provide the convert with a convert status and an identity which serves to enhance the ongoing processes of self-definition as a successful convert.

The reaction of converts' parents to their conversion seems to vary in proportion to their social status, being less in the lower class and greater in the middle class. According to the converts' perception of their parents' attitude towards their conversion, their parents may be classified into three types: (1) those who were hostile or extremely unhappy about it. They felt that their son/daughter had turned their back on everything they had given them. Thirteen (19%) converts' parents were judged to fall into this group. The type of reaction varied. Some treated their son/daughter's acceptance of Islam as a 'social death'. Anne's mother, who was a strong Catholic, told her she would be 'like she was dead' to her. Rachel's father did not speak to her for two years: 'He was too angry, which is really quite strange because he doesn't have any belief. But he explained it to me two years later that he is a great royalist and he felt that by taking Islam I'd slighted the Queen and slighted being British. And that offended him very much.' Type (2); those who were more or less indifferent to it. Twenty two (31%) converts' parents did not take it badly, or showed little or no interest in knowing about it. Some were not delighted, and felt socially ashamed of their son/daughter, but they let their son/daughter continue with what they wanted. Fiona's father was a bit cynical about it and her mother did not say much at all, but she said to Fiona that she was taking a step back to the Middle Ages when she started wearing a scarf. Two female converts reported that their parents opposed them marrying a Muslim after their conversion, though they were not upset by their conversion in the beginning. Type (3); those who welcomed their son/daughter's decision. Ten (14%) converts' parents fall into this group. They were pleased that their son/daughter had found something they could relate to. Henry said that his parents perceived that Islam had changed him for the better and could not really say anything about it. When Nigel, who was a violent and aggressive person, told his mother that he had become Muslim and he would respect her from then on as Islam demanded him to do so, his mother responded to him saying: 'Why didn't you become Muslim before then?' Some of the parents in this category had some worries about their son/daughter's conversion initially, but soon they, like Alex's parents became more positive: 'They were very worried. But having spent a week at home they saw I was still normal, healthy and not doing anything crazy or not dressing differently, and they stopped worrying.' The parents in this category seemed to have appreciation of, or an interest in, their son/daughter's new choice. In fact, two converts reported that they had got their mothers converted to Islam sometime after their conversion.

Seventeen (24%) converts did not have the opportunity to see the reactions of their parents, since some had lost their parents before conversion, and others were/are not in touch with them. They were ostensibly free of any ties with their parents. Charlie said: 'The sort of relationship I have with my parents is that we correspond once or twice a year. And you don't talk about your conversion in your letters.' Eight (11%) people did not tell their parents that they had converted. They felt that they had to keep their conversion secret for a time. No matter how strongly and negatively the interviewees' parents reacted, in all cases, they reported, there has been either partial or complete reconciliation at a later date. They now have an improved relationship, or at least an understanding with their parents.

Four (6%) converts (all male) were married to Christians when they converted. One convert's wife died four years ago and he had no problems in his marriage regarding his conversion. Another got a divorce 14 years after his conversion, but this was nothing to do with the conversion. The other two are still married to Christians. One has no problems in his marriage concerning his conversion, while the other's (Victor) marriage was slightly affected. Victor said: 'The only problem after conversion was my family, the opposition from my son and wife. They are very religious Christians. My wife reads her Bible more loudly since I have become a Muslim, trying to make me angry. It slightly affects our relationship, but not dramatically.'

Converts' accounts describe their friends' reactions to conversion in a number of ways. They infrequently refer to the generation of hostility between themselves and former friends because of conversion. In Nigel's case this hostility manifested itself on others' tendencies to ridicule the convert. Nigel's friends at work started calling him 'messiah'. In most cases, however, there was no hostility, and friendship died out gradually, and it was the ex-friends who cut off relationship rather than the convert. But in other cases the converts themselves wanted this relationship cut off as they felt they would not be able to maintain their new identity. Some converts still keep their relationship with their friends and they received no aggression or hostility and found their friends respected their new choice.

Converts' perception of a greater society, or their relation to it varies according to their immediate environment. A person is more likely to know and be known by neighbours in smaller places. The small-town dwellers care more what their neighbours do and say; as the saying goes, 'everybody's business is everybody's business in a small town' (Batson and Ventis, 1982: 46). However, wherever the converts live they may experience tension within the environment, because by conversion they have moved from social acceptability to social unacceptability. They may still go through great turmoil and concern, especially if their parents are strong in their faith, or if they are greatly concerned about their respectability in their environment. Converts who live in Muslim populated parts of the country may experience less stress than those who live in the areas where Muslims are almost non-existent. Charles used to work in a city where he could relate to Muslims, but due to redundancy he was forced to move back to his home town where there are no Muslims, and now he feels that it is like a foreign place to him.

Converts reported that in general they keep a low profile. They do not talk to non-Muslims about Islam, or why they embraced

Islam unless they are asked to do so. However, Four (6%) reported that they were able to 'help some people come to Islam.' On the other hand, they seem to be more active within the Muslim community. Eleven (16%) people work, paid or voluntarily, for Islamic organisations. Some were given jobs because they were English. Four (6%) give talks on Islam in meetings organised by Muslim organisations. Five (7%) are involved with various activities like teaching in local Muslim communities.

To conclude, it has been found that an individual cannot completely forget the previous meaning of his social world even after transition (Dollah, 1979: 77). The present research, by and large, confirms this finding. Change requires a process of resocialisation. It is more difficult than the process of socialisation in the previous world because it is affected by the existing meaning in individual self. An individual tends to reshape or modify the world view when he enters the new province of meaning. Sometimes he tries to reinterpret the past province of meaning and then reshape it. For some of the converts in the present sample transition to the new province of world view is not necessarily accompanied by a complete change of social world. That is to say, resocialisation may never be completed for some converts.

Although the lives of the individuals studied here changed markedly as a result of their conversion experience, and in adopting new beliefs and life-styles, one may still question whether these changes entailed a transformation of the self. With regard to the change of the self the approach presented by William James (1945: 176) may be an explanation. James distinguished two aspects of the self as object and subject; the 'me' and the 'I'. The former is the self as known, or the 'empirical ego' being everything the person calls his/hers, including the material self (body and possessions), the social selves (roles, relations, and interpersonal traits), and the spiritual self (thoughts, beliefs and values, psychological mechanisms). The latter, on the other hand, refers to 'pure ego' as knower, which is present in all of the person's experience and which constitutes experience and is therefore elusive and difficult to examine. Following James' explanation, this research has focused on the study of the 'me' leaving the 'I' to philosophical inquiry. Evidence has been found that for most converts important components of the 'me' changed in consequence of conversion. However, conversion brought different consequences for each individual, not in the content of

140

their new belief system, but in degree of commitment. Some made their religious commitment a total way of life by adopting all aspects and rituals of the new faith, whereas others avoided some of them. In sum, most of those interviewed reported changed outlooks, and feelings of purpose. Changes were seen to be ongoing, but related to the cultural context of Britain. Preconversion social ties had not been severed.

FIVE

CONVERSION THROUGH SUFISM

'For me *dhikr* is a method of purification. It is like during the day you build up all these things during the working life; it is like going into a room which is full of people who are smoking and you cannot smell in that smoke and you need to be washed of that smoke. Working in the world is very much like that, we pick up things. And I feel that *dhikr* is a method of cleaning that smell of the world away.'

George, a convert to Islam

A Sufism: the agent of Islam

Sufism is believed to have been the principle agent in attracting non-Muslims to Islam throughout history (Levtzion, 1979: 17). This seems also to be true for conversion of Westerners to Islam in our time (Gerholm, 1988: 264–5). Twenty three (33%) of the 70 who were interviewed for this study came to Islam through Sufism or are currently involved in Sufism. In this chapter the conversion experiences of the Sufi converts as well as the two Sufi groups, Shayhk Nazim and Abd al-Qadir as-Sufi (al-Murabit), will be investigated. Before moving on to the Sufis' experiences, Sufism in the West and in Britain will be described.

Sufism has always been an important concept in the West. It is widely believed that in Europe and America the spiritual nature and mystical vision of esoteric Sufism accounted for the success of Islam. There are tens of Sufi groups in Europe, Britain and the United States (Haddad and Lummis, 1987: 22, 171). In some cases, immigrants affiliated to Sufi orders brought over their own brand of Sufism. In other cases, groups sprang up as part of the recent interest in Asian religions, and they were able

142

to attract many converts to Islam (Shah, 1980: 21; Yusuf, 1989: 82). Apart from the Sufi groups there are also Sufic organisations and centres studying Sufism and disseminating information about it. Among them are *The Mawlana Centre* and *The Society for Sufi Studies* in London, and *Muhyiddin Ibn al-Arabi Society* in Oxford.

Hundreds of people in the modern Western world, while claiming to be Sufis, maintain that Sufism is independent of any particular religion (Lings, 1981: 16). In Britain there are those who believe that Sufism is not confined solely to Islam. Irina Tweedie, for example, a Soviet born mystic teacher, based in Willesden Green, North London, believes that she is a Sufi but not a Muslim and asserts that Sufism and Islam do not necessarily go hand in hand.[1] *Subud*[2] is another Sufi-like movement known to thousands in the West, but it is not considered within the boundaries of Islam by authorities (see Shah, 1980: 21) on Islamic Sufism on the basis that in its current presentation it has diverted from the original Islamic Sufi teaching though its procedure is mainly based upon *Naqshbandiyyah-Qadiriyyah* methods.

The stories of some contemporary European intellectuals as to how Sufism attracted them are quite well-known throughout the Muslim world. Among them the French philosopher René Guénon, English mystic Martin Lings, and Swiss intellectuals Frithjof Schuon and Titus Burckhardt may be cited. They sought in the Muslim East a model for a life of wisdom, a contact with supra-sensory realities and also with ancestral secrets handed down by a long line of initiates (Rodinson, 1988: 73). On a more popular level Sufism attracts many young people, often with a background in left-wing politics.[3]

Nicholson (1963: 2), in his book, *The Mystics of Islam*, writes: 'If Judaism, Christianity and Islam have something in common in spite of their deep dogmatic differences, the spiritual content of that common element can best be appreciated in Jewish, Christian and Islamic mysticism, which bears equal testimony to that ever-deepening experience of the soul when the spiritual worshippers, whether he be a follower of Moses or Jesus or Muhammad, turns whole-heartedly to God.' Why would then someone, say, from the Christian tradition, take an interest in Sufism? Though all the great types of mysticism have something in common, each is marked by peculiar characteristics resulting from the circumstances in which it arose and flourished. Sufis regard Jesus as their exemplary *par excellence*. Sufi writings have abundant literature containing references to teaching of Jesus and other Prophets. For example, the famous Sufi Rumi in his *Mathnawi*, retells the tales of the prophets. Jesus is one of his favourites (Renard, 1987: 55). He does not raise the doctrinal matters which cause conflict between Muslims and Christians, but what the life and deeds of Jesus bring to mind about the believer's relationship with God. So this kind of approach taken by Sufis is immensely significant in the sense that a potential convert from a Christian background feels at home when he finds out that the sort of themes with which he is familiar are also of great importance to Sufis.

B Sufism and new religious movements (NRMs) in the West

Since the 1970s new religious groups have gained widespread attraction in the western world. It is estimated that from several hundred thousand to as many as several million young people have joined these groups in America alone (Rochford, et al, 1989: 57). As well as the groups emerging from the Judeo-Christian tradition, Westerners have also shown enthusiasm for the religious movements brought from the East. In his study of Eastern religions in America Cox (1979: 10) describes how these movements are springing up:

> Within twenty blocks of the intersection of Massachusetts Avenue and Boylston Street, forty or fifty different neo-Oriental religious movements thrive. A few blocks west stands the Zen center.... In the other direction, in the basement of a hospitable Episcopal church, the Sufi dancers meet twice a week to twist and turn like legendary whirling dervishes in a ritual circle dance, chanting verses from the Korán, the Muslim Holy book, in atonal Arabic. A few blocks to the northeast is the Ananda Marga center... a few blocks to the south the headquarters of the Hare Krishnas ... The clean-shaven followers of the young guru Maharaj Ji's Divine Light Mission have a meeting place ten blocks southeast.

Britain also has been a fruitful country for the new religious movements (hereafter referred to as NRMs). At least 400 new religions are reported to have emerged in Britain since 1945 (Clarke, 1984: 2). In 1985 Stark listed 153 cult movements operating in England. The rate Stark found for England and Wales is 3.2 cult movements per million population, which is substantially higher than the American rate 2.3. Stark also found that in Europe, Britain has also the highest number of Indian and Eastern cult centres and communities totalling 146 (England and Wales). This finding may be evidence for the weakness of conventional faith in Britain and a sign of the greater degree of the secularisation of Britain compared to other European countries, as Stark (1985: 334) found considerable evidence that cults abound in the most secularised parts of Europe.

Some of the Sufi groups in the West, as Cox reported above, are treated as NRMs. During this study evidence was found that there are considerable similarities between conversion to Islam through Sufism and new religions, but by no means all. Furthermore evidence was also found that those who converted to Islam through Sufism have usually tried some other Eastern religions. Therefore before drawing the similarities and differences between Sufi groups and new religions it is useful to classify the NRMs in order to see where these Sufi movements stand in comparison.

In his study of NRMs Wallis (1984) classifies the new religions into three types regarding their 'orientations to the world' as world-rejecting, world-affirming, and world-accommodating. The **world-rejecting** movements are much more recognisably religious than the world-affirming type. Their rejection of the world covers secular institutions. They reject the conventional distinction between a secular and a religious realm. They have a clear conception of God and a set of moral demands. Krishna Consciousness and The Unification Church can be cited among others. The world-rejecting sects require a life of service to the guru or prophet and to others who likewise follow him. Long hours of proselytising on the street or disturbing the movement's literature or unpaid domestic duties for leaders or other members and devotional ritual before the deities are characteristics of this type of religion.

On a philosophical level Sufism may be regarded as world-rejecting as it sees no reality other than God. But this theory is not applied in the sense of denying the world, except for extreme cases of some mystics in early Islam. Sufism may rather be

145

described as otherworldly oriented rather than this worldly. The communal life-style which is characteristic of world-rejecting movements is not visible in Sufism, and it is not a characteristic of the Sufis in Britain except for the early days of the movement of Abd al-Qadir as-Sufi (al-Murabit) in the seventies. The devotional ritual before the deities and proselytisation have no place in Sufism. However, a collective identity is fostered by various means, as in some of the world-rejecting religions, including a common mode of dress and appearance such as having beard.

The **world-affirming** new religions cover groups such as Transcendental Meditation and Nichiren Shoshu. The style of this type of movement lacks most of the features traditionally associated with religion. It may not have any developed theology or ethics, and it may have no church or collective ritual of worship. This type of movement claims to possess the means to enable people to unlock their physical, mental and spiritual potential without the need to withdraw from the world, means which are readily available to virtually everyone who learns the technique or principle provided. In world-affirming movements, the social order is not viewed as entirely unjust, nor society as having departed from God as in the world-rejecting case. The beliefs of these movements are essentially individualistic.

The form of dhikr in Sufism is almost equivalent to meditation and some sort of chanting or reciting certain words found in the world-affirming religions. The Sufi groups differ in that members are required to be of a certain religion, namely Islam, practised in the member's daily life whereas this is not necessary in world-affirming new religions. Sufism shares some literature with this type of religion such as self-realisation and self-liberation. It differs also in recognition of the fact that, although world-affirming movements pursue transcendental goals they lay little or no stress on the idea of God or transcendent spiritual entities, nor do they normally engage in worship.

The **world-accommodating** new religions draw a distinction between the spiritual and the worldly. Religion is not construed as a primarily social matter; rather it provides stimulation to personal, interior life. It has relatively few implications for how that life should be lived, except that it should be lived in a more religiously inspired fashion. They feel something lacking in the spiritual lives of people. Their protest is not so much against

146

the world or society, but against prevailing religious institutions in the West. Neo-Pentecostalism, or the Charismatic Renewal Movement are examples of world-accommodating new religions.

Sufism seems to share with world-accommodating new religions a dissatisfaction with mainstream prevailing religious institutions. Wallis asserts that *Subud* falls into this category. Sufism also seems to share with this type of religion a recognition of the fact that there is an experimental element to the spiritual life and the spiritual dimension of life is not to be neglected.

As Cox (1979: 11) asks what has provoked this, especially Oriental religious revival? Who are the people who are involved in it? Why have they left either some more conventional Christian or Jewish form of religious life, or no religious life at all, to become seekers in these new spiritual movements? These questions about new religions are also applicable to conversion to Islam, particularly through Sufism in the West where spirituality weakened and people began to look beyond the borders of the West for guidance embarking upon the search for an individual experience of the transcendent, and upon self-discovery.

For many of the NRMs which came into being in the 20th century West, economic and political frustration have obviously played an important part. Some people rejected dominant values and life-styles by joining a group as an act of protest against the structure and culture of their society (Wallis, 1984: 48). There has been a general sense of dissatisfaction with (the) existing religion, either because it has reached a formalistic state, or because it no longer provides the answers to people's questions (Holm, 1977: 78). In contrast to the scientific culture and psychology of the West, Eastern introspective (mystical) disciplines have focused on meaning and purpose by employing a strategy in which the use of intellect is not central to the process of investigation. Oversecularisation has deprived human life of its spiritual significance. Life was departmentalised into different compartments, religious and secular, spiritual and material. Devoid of spiritual goals many people, especially youth turned from traditional religion and explored a radical alternative (Melton, 1985: 292; Tipton, 1982: 177). The extreme descent into materialism and secularisation resulted in a reaction towards a spiritual and ethical life, as one of the Sufi converts, Jane, remarked rather soberly:

147

'There is a lot of confusion in our culture because it is based on material values. Although the church and Christianity exists formally, it doesn't have any answers to present-day questions that satisfy people. It hasn't got much spirituality.'

One of the interview questions was 'Why do you think people tend to join new religions in the West?' They agreed on the fact that 'more people are becoming increasingly fed up with the materialistic type of life.' So it is evident that they turned in the hope of finding resources which may help revive what has been lost and correct the deep psychic and spiritual imbalances of the West. In spite of overall material development the condition of man remains unsettled. The Age of Reason proclaimed that man's intellect would solve everything. Today, the more that people think, the less seems to be the value of the intellect itself. These facts, as Wilson (1976: 99, 104–8) puts, 'have opened the door to ... many a cult.' So it is claimed by so many that the NRMs have developed as attempts to grapple with the consequences of rationalisation (Cox, 1979: 100).

Although there are great differences among these movements, a notable feature of many of them is their appeal to mysticism. They offer direct experience of God, or union with God, or Ultimate Reality; and the accounts of the converts to these movements indicate that they were attracted by the promise of mystical experience (Jantzen, 1990: 10). Apart from mystical experience, several elements common to new religions may be identified.[4] They are: (1) Moral norms and judgement; (2) refusal of intellectual approach to religion; (3) surrender on the part of the disciple; (4) authority (charisma) on the part of the guru or master; (5) suspension of doubt and criticism; (6) emphasis on the millenium; and (7) missionary dimension. With some differences in their application, these elements are to be found in Sufism, as it will be illustrated below. For instance, a 'missionary dimension' exists in Sufism, but not in the sense of carrying out an organised recruitment programme as understood by many new religions.

Sufism shares more with Eastern religious movements than it shares with other new religions regarding its mystical inclination and philosophical structure. Cultivating a deeper relationship with God through spiritual practice and surrender is common to both most Eastern NRMs and Sufism. Along this path one needs a spiritual guide to come closer to God. The final sacrifice in Divine Light Mission, for example, is 'mortification of the ego' (Downton, 1980: 383). As in Sufism, it is believed that the ego is the chief obstacle to peace. Like Sufism, in many Eastern religious movements spiritual training is believed to increase feelings of self-regard and self-confidence, while it reduces the sense of guilt for one's misdeeds, negative feelings, and desires through the process of becoming emotionally detached from the negative features of the ego (Downton, 1980: 389). In most Eastern religious movements there are techniques or practices corresponding to dhikr derived from ancient traditions, such as special breathing and certain forms of yoga and meditation. Sufism and some new religions set certain rules and guidelines for any member involved which bring about the disciplining of everyday life. To cite an example, there are basic rules of conduct which all members must observe in Hare Krishna such as no gambling, no intoxicants, and no illicit sex (Enroth, 1977: 21). The rules are also absolute basics in Sufism.

Resemblance between Sufis and NRMs' members with regard to their background

The observations and interviews with Sufis disclosed that they share a similar background with people involved in NRMs to a certain extent. Some of the best-known characteristics of the membership of the NRMs are that they tend to consist largely of middle-class youth (Johnson, 1977: 40; Barker, 1989: 14), predominantly male and usually unmarried (Barker, 1984: 206, 234). These generalisations seem to apply to the Sufi converts interviewed. However, the average age of conversion tends to be late twenties for Sufis (the average conversion age is 28.6). Among the Sufi converts there is a preponderance of people from middle class backgrounds with 70 percent against 30 percent from working class backgrounds. Of the 23 Sufi converts involved in this study, 14 (61%) were single, and 9 (39%) were married or divorced at the time of conversion.

There are more significant similarities regarding the backgrounds of people who joined new religions and that of Sufis in terms of their psychological state such as previous involvement in therapy, preinvolvement feelings of anxiety and discouragement about life, and past experience with drugs and alcohol. Using drugs, before commitment to NRMs, is characterised of many movements. It is found that persons who have used marijuana or LSD three or more times are twice as likely to have become participants in NRMs than persons who have either never used these drugs or used them less intensely (Bird and Reimer, 1983: 228). Rochford, et al (1989: 67), studying 214 Hare Krishna members found that only 13 percent of the devotees reported no previous use of drugs or alcohol; 80 percent had previously used marijuana, and 62 percent had taken hallucinogens such as LSD. Of the 23 Sufis, 15 (65.2%) reported use of drugs such as marijuana and hallucinogens like LSD when they were younger or prior to conversion.[5] One of the young Sufi interviewees who recently became Muslim and gave up taking drugs said: 'I encourage young people to smoke cannabis and take acid because a lot of converts used to be hippies, and used to take a lot of acid. Acid puts you in a different world and into a different situation.' By this statement he meant that those who take drugs are more likely to convert and he hoped for conversion of more people. As for the use of alcohol, 12 (52%) Sufis reported previous excessive use of alcohol. George was an alcohol addict beset by despair, and eager for a solution, as he pointed out:

> 'I realised that I had a drinking problem and I got to a stage where I was laying a bottle of rum under the bed and picking up the bottle and drinking in the morning before I even got out of the bed. So I remember going to see the priest to seek help and the first thing he did was to offer me a drink. So I thought I don't think I would have got any help from him.'

The rate of previous drug-use seems to be higher among members of Eastern religious movements such as Hare Krishna, Divine Light Mission, Meher Baba, and Ananda Marga than it is for others (Rochford, et al, 1989; Galanter and Buckley, 1978; Nordquist, 1978). It is, therefore, often discussed whether 'the tide of Eastern spirituality in the seventies was the successor of the psychedelic upsurge of the sixties?' Many of the young devotees involved in these movements studied by Cox (1979: 32) believed that it was, and offered their own experience as evidence. Investigators of new religions concluded that the

150

explosion of movements, therapies and cults reflects the 'crises of meaning' of the sixties and the revolt against technical solutions and utilitarian individualism (Bellah, 1976: 341; Anthony and Robbins, 1982: 217). As Downton (1980: 384) argued, through psychedelic experiences, spiritual frames of reference changed for many of these young people. Then they were attracted to Eastern spiritual beliefs and began experimenting with meditation, chanting and yoga as spiritual practices, for they had been spiritually awakened through their use of drugs. So psychedelic experiences were replaced by meditation-like experiences which takes the form of dhikr in Sufism. The accounts of the Sufi subjects on their experiences with drugs substantiate the above presentation. Alan said:

> 'When I was a young man of 18–19 I was what other people called a "hippie". I didn't need to go out and take life very seriously . . . Incompleteness was something that I felt . . . I found that I was reading a lot about things that suggested a greater reality than all I could see about me because what I could see about me was quite small. And I had been experimenting with mind-expanding drugs through which I had actually been seeing that there was an awful lot to Reality, there was much more than at first glance. There was much bigger things going on than I was aware of, and I wanted to know what those things were.'

Alan now feels that he knows the 'Reality', and the answers to life's basic questions:

> 'Islam has given me absolute hope, hope of Reality. I know what "Reality" is. I know the answers that all the mystics are always talking about. What greater mystery is there to know than Allah? I know the answer to the question "what is the meaning of life?", we had come from Allah and we are going back to Allah. So what more do I need to know? We are created beings. That's what our purpose is. Otherwise if we didn't believe that, there would be no purpose, we would be just an extraordinary accident like a lot of people think. I know we are not that.'

As it is often argued by the investigators of the NRMs, the use of drugs by young people joining new religions means some degree of alienation from the dominant culture and attraction to alternative forms of consciousness, life-styles, and belief systems. The same research by Rochford, et al (1989) revealed that 48 percent of the Hare Krishna members admitted to feeling 'discouraged and/or anxious abut life' prior to becoming a Krishna devotee. More than a third reported taking part in therapy, or participating in psychological groups and movements. Studies on other new religions such as the Unification Church and the Divine Light Mission testify to the findings on Hare Krishna (Deutsch, 1975; Galanter and Buckley, 1978). The interviews with Sufis revealed that 6 (26%) reported participating in therapy, or taking part in psychological groups prior to their conversion. 16 (69%) Sufis acknowledged that they had feelings such as incompleteness, aimlessness, purposelessness and unworthiness.

Most investigators, irrespective of the religious group that they have studied, agree that religious conversions may be psychologically beneficial (Allison, 1969; Galanter, 1982; Ullman, 1988). Rochford, et al (1989) reviewed 10 different studies of cults, finding evidence of psychological impairment among members in order to assess the claims that brain-washing techniques used by these groups have pathological consequences resulting in members being unable to freely leave the cult. They particularly examined two points: (1) whether the psychological impairment found was an outcome of cult involvement or a condition which appears to have predated cult participation; and (2) what, if any, influence did the cult have in either further promoting psychological disorder or relieving symptoms and overall levels of impairment? Of the 10 studies reviewed, seven suggested that the symptoms uncovered were attributable to causes which predated cult involvement. Two argued that the presence of symptoms may be the result of both preinvolvement influences and cult indoctrination practices. Only one study openly argued that cult involvement was the direct cause of disturbance found among members. The same seven studies also found evidence that involvement with these cults reduced preexisting symptoms and increased the sense of well-being. Two studies concluded that involvement reduces preexisting symptoms, but causes other sources of disorder. Only one study, again, revealed that involvement caused psychological impairment (Rochford, et al, 1989: 71).

The present findings on Sufis lend support to the conclusion reached by the majority of the researchers on two points investigated by Rochford, et al. *First*, the majority of the Sufi subjects reported previous psychological disturbances such as depression, meaninglessness, and distress resulting from family problems or other factors, as will be discussed later at length. *Second*, they reported that these predating symptoms were reduced and their psychological well-being improved following involvement in the Sufi group. However, these findings and conclusions do not explain conversion exhaustively, for there are those, though not many, who were satisfied with their previous life, and were in good mental and physical health. They may have felt a sense of incompleteness in the society, but discontentment with their station in life or with the values of the society had not crystallised sufficiently to instigate their journey to Sufism.

The people recruited to the cults were mostly social isolates, people whose prime deprivation was precisely a lack of social ties (Stark and Bainbridge, 1980a: 1380). So when they joined a cult these people did not have social bonds that could have prevented them from doing so. Many Sufi subjects reported that they suffered from the same malaise; they lacked family ties or friends, whereas in many non-Sufi converts' cases their parents severely rejected them upon their conversion to Islam and were upset with them for some time before coming to terms with it. Snow, et al (1980) examining previous social networks among ashram members found that a very small percentage of them had been deeply involved with what they were doing in the larger society. Though most of the Sufi subjects had finished their formal or higher education and had jobs before they found Sufism only a few reported career aspirations that would have kept them at their jobs. Even though they were in their mid-twenties they were still going through a 'psycho-social moratorium' normally associated with adolescence (Erikson, 1968: 128–35, 242; Snow *et al.*, 1980), as Freddie reported:

'In my early adulthood I went through a bit of a difficult period of lacking a sense of identity. Being unsure of myself and lacking a sense of purpose and direction. That was from 16 to 25. I was very politically involved about 8 to 10 years with socialists. That, I suppose, was to do with looking for answers through politics trying to change this world and thereby trying to change my life.'

When people join a religious group they first change their

behaviour by adopting a new role. The changes may be sweeping, but they are not necessarily supported by conviction. The boundless faith of a true believer usually develops only after lengthy involvement. Some members go for months without ever resolving their doubts, yet they may still appear fully committed because outwardly they are acting the way they are supposed to act (Balch, 1980: 143; Lofland and Stark, 1965: 874). One Sufi admitted that it took him five years to internalise the beliefs. The following account by William, a follower of Shaykh Nazim, describes how he felt in early days of his involvement:

> 'It is like you dive into the water for the first time trusting you will be brought up again. You don't know whether you are going to come up or not although you have seen other people diving and coming up. I have dived and I have come out again. That's how it is. You take the plunge.'

Members of new religions see their previous life as a spiritual journey and attribute their 'enlightenment' to spiritual powers and give theological answers such as 'Krishna called me here', 'It was my karma' (Cox, 1979: 95), 'God gave me a clear sign', or 'God had been guiding me throughout my life, preparing me for membership' (Barker, 1984: 255). The Sufi subjects' attributions are not of a different nature to recruits of new religions: 'My heart', 'Allah has guided me', and 'Shaykh's guidance' were some of the answers given.

Conclusion

One wonders 'Why Sufism attracted these people?' 'Why many of them did not settle in one of these religions and went on to Sufism?' To answer these questions it is worthwhile to review the above presentation emphasising why people get attracted to a counter-culture in the western world. As Burfoot (1983: 148–53) discussed, an individual who is attracted to a counter-culture may go through the triple-process of differentiation, disenchantment, and alienation in western industrialised societies, which in the end separates the individual from the society. At the end of **differentiation** process individuals become isolated in private and they may not relate to the rest of the society. Personal satisfaction and meaning within the existing social framework may no longer be possible. Differentiation produces a fragmentation of meaning which results in a vast number of interpretations of the world and since there is no overall system that unifies these multiple meanings, exposure to multiple world views is experienced as an overload of information. This, in turn, can produce chronic cognitive dissonance. Then comes the stage of **disenchantment** where the 'irrational' elements of meaning have been displaced from social action as a result of an increase in bureaucratisation, or rationalisation. In the bureaucratic system relationships are not between feeling people, but between functional rational offices. The individual hardly gains personal meaning from these roles and social actors in a bureaucratic world become disenchanted. **Alienation** is the last stage where the tie between the individual and the society is broken. The individual may not be able to pull the self and society back together into a meaningful whole and the maintenance of identity within that social system may become impossible. However, once the individual has transcended the constraints of society, this lack of commitment may lead him to seek a new identity outside that social system. It is at this point that NRMs arise and flourish, giving new identity and meaning to individuals. The life stories of the Sufis interviewed disclosed that most of them have gone through this triple-process at the end of which they found themselves looking for satisfaction from a counter-culture.

The members gained by Sufism in the West are, to some extent, casualties from the failure and disintegration of the NRMs, particularly, as Robbins, *et al.* (1978: 101) call it, from 'monistic movements'. People who are drawn into Sufism are most likely to be from the group of people who have been progressively seeking to master spiritual and/or physical disciplines in order to achieve a state of enlightenment and self-harmony. To achieve this end they got involved in Eastern religions that emphasise 'inner' practices as a force for the transformation of the individual, by means of which a true moral agency becomes possible. However, they discovered the view that no such world will ever be found and religious maturity meant learning to live in the complex world. The Sufi converts expressed that it had been at this point that Sufism accompanied with Islam had come into the picture which offered them an overall system, a way of life based on moral and ethical values, as the Sufi master Shaykh Nazim expresses:

'I have met so many people here in the West who have delved deeply into the great traditions of the East. They have acquired wisdom through seeking it. They have read, travelled, listened and learned. The attraction for everything Oriental is a Divine inspiration in the hearts of western people ... But as for Westerners who are attracted to the Orient, and often subject themselves to great hardships to travel to those countries, to Tibet and India, and receive wisdom to take back with them, most are in danger of losing all they gained. Why? Because they bring back loose pearls. If a lady buys pearls, does she carry them loose in her pocket, or does she string them on a strong thread? People seek wisdom and are so happy with what they have gained, but all the time the pearls are falling out of the hole in their pockets, because the pearls are not yet bound in a thread. What is the thread I am referring to? Wisdom pearls may only be kept with a strong faith and method. So many people have overlooked this necessity. If you have the thread, one by one you may obtain the pearls and string them.'

The thread that Shaykh Nazim talks about refers to Islam to which the path of Sufism is married. The Sufi interviewees believe that it is this path which gives them fulfilment and makes life meaningful, as Alan expressed: 'I know the answer to the question "What is the meaning of life?". What more do I need to know?'

To conclude, as elucidated above there are social, psychological and religious preconditions out of which NRMs in the West developed, Sufism is no exception to this conclusion. NRMs in the West, as Sharma (1985: 123) puts, are filling the sense of spiritual emptiness, which is an area relatively neglected by Christianity. Conversion to Islam through Sufism can be understood in these terms taking into account that by joining Sufi groups, in the first place, people are rejecting Western culture rather than the traditional religion which is part of its culture. Needless to say, when the conventional or the existing old religions no longer provide satisfaction to many, new faiths will move into the gap. Nonetheless, one must be wary of any conclusion that implies Sufism is growing relative to other new religious groups as there are no available records of members joining or leaving. It is not known how many so far joined in, stayed in or left. What is known is that the Sufi groups claim that a few hundred Westerners have been drawn into their movement. Shaykh Nazim affirms that they were 'less than the number of the fingers of two hands', while Abd al-Qadir's men were not more than a few when they started in the early seventies.

C The group of Shaykh Nazim

In Britain there are some English converts to Islam who associate themselves with Shaykh Nazim and claim to have entered Islam through the works of the Shaykh. Shaykh Nazim is a graduate of chemistry, around the age of 70, and a prominent figure within the *Naqshbandiyyah Tariqah* (order). He is a Turkish-Cypriot, settled in North Cyprus and regularly visits Britain. The data on converts involved in Shaykh Nazim's group is based on the observations, conversations and formal interviews with 17 converts currently involved in the group.

1 Mission in Britain

Shaykh Nazim has been regularly visiting Britain for the month of *Ramadan* to stay around two months since 1973.[6] During his visit he mainly stays in London, but occasionally goes to other places for talks. During *Ramadan* when Shaykh Nazim is in London around 50 German[7] followers and some others from other European countries and America come to London. The Shaykh normally joins these people in the mosque everyday after the late noon prayer until late night. He has conversations with them and answers their questions ranging from the topic of 'abortion' to the 'position of Jesus in Islam'. With these people present Peckam Mosque witnesses prayer services every night, and *dhikr* ceremonies performed by a big crowd on Friday nights led by the Shaykh. After his stay in Britain he normally makes his way to Europe where he has European followers as well as lifelong Muslims. Among others Germany, France, Spain and Switzerland can be mentioned. He bears the label of 'international' for he has disciples scattered around the world. He is always welcomed by some Indian-oriented NRMs in the West. He is sometimes invited to their centres to deliver lectures. Ananda Marga Centre in North London is one of them. He once stayed for three days in the Babaji Centre in Switzerland to deliver talks in 1985 and his talks in the Babaji Centre were published under the title of *Secrets Behind the Secrets*.

The policy of the Shaykh travelling around the world and visiting his disciples, especially those in the West, is very much significant in the sense that he exercises the tradition of shaykh's visitation of disciples very widely and effectively. Shaykh Nazim explains why he comes to the West: 'I have been trained to heal spiritual ailments from a side and with methods not known in these countries, and so I have been sent by spiritual centres to look after the Western countries.' In fact, it was Shaykh Nazim's master, Shaykh Daghistani, who ordered him to go and spread the 'light of Islam' into European countries on the grounds that Western people are going to be soldiers of the *'Mahdi's army'*, and that in the western/European hearts there is a very delicate veil and if that veil is taken away, immediately the light will come to their hearts and they will come to Islam.[8]

When the Shaykh is in Britain the group's activities reach its zenith. While he is away his followers are separated into sub-groups, according to geographical location and gender. One of the subgroups is mainly made up of British converts. They regularly meet to do dhikr on Friday nights. Dhikr, as the Sufi interviewees describe, seems exotic and something different worth trying for the new comer. One convent expressed how he felt when he first joined a dhikr meeting:

'I arrived and I was shown a place to sit down. And around 20 men came in, some of them quite old with big white beards and they all greeted each other and sat down as the lights turned off. And they started repeating some words which, I knew later, praise the Prophet Muhammad. And at this stage I closed my eyes and it was absolutely dynamic. I couldn't believe it.'

2 Initiation to the group

In order to enter Shaykh Nazim's group, or any other Sufi group in general, the candidate must somehow make contact with a Sufi or books on Sufism, probably on some ordinary basis. It is usually the case that the individual is taken to dhikr ceremonies by a friend or acquaintance or he might be given the

158

address of the place and invited to attend a dhikr ceremony. In the first days the potential convert is regarded as a visitor who is interested in Sufism. It is noticeable that the potential convert for some time is in a position of uncertainty with respect to his role behaviour until he learns and comes to accept the norms of the group. In the beginning the potential convert sits quietly and appreciates the sounds and rhythms. Thereafter he receives explanations of the different elements of the dhikr and doctrines of Sufism. Along the path, believe the Sufi converts, they get blessing. Such a convert is Robert who tells of his receipt of blessing: 'I believe that a shaykh is able to transmit something, the *barakah*, which in itself is helpful in this process.'

In the course of his participation in the Sufi meetings it is always suggested that the potential convert should meet the Shaykh when he is in Britain. It is usually the case that the potential convert spends at least a few months in the group before meeting the Shaykh and taking the *shahadah*. When he meets the Shaykh he psychologically feels that he should take *bay'ah* declaring him as his spiritual master. In the *bay'ah* ceremony a circle is convened and the candidate is brought from the antechamber by his sponsor and introduced to the Shaykh. He bows and kisses the hands of the Shaykh. Then after saying the *shahadah* he is conferred a Muslim name by the Shaykh. With the *shahadah* he takes the final act and he is regarded as a Muslim. He is now called by his new name and made to feel that he is a Muslim as well as being a Sufi.

3 Dhikr and the belief of lower-self

There are different methods of performing dhikr. The one Shaykh Nazim's group practise is to sit and repeat the words by closing the eyes. The participants chant in a loud voice which gradually increases in tempo and involves the rapid inhalation and exhalation of breath. Chanting is always related to God, to his attributes, and the Prophet Muhammad. Among the words selected for recitation are 'there is no god but Allah', and '*hoo*'.[9] Religious music is not employed in *Naqshbandiyyah* during dhikr as it is in some other Sufi orders. As for listening to or playing music Shaykh Nazim makes a distinction between divinely inspired music and the 'satanic music', as he calls it, 'of the discotheque which is sexually arousing'. He does not declare music to be categorically evil, but warns that through its misuse it may become the main channel for evil to appear. He recognises that many Westerners are obsessed with music, and thus he does not discourage people from listening to or playing music, but urges them to be wary of 'evil music' (Sheikh Nazim, 1983–1984: 61).

The dhikr meetings, in addition to the ritual importance, are the crucial means for social interaction among the members; communion, commitment and the sense of sharing something with others are accomplished. With the dhikr, members assert, they sense a great peace and this sensation gives them relief and freedom and makes them feel better. They account that it brings them closer to God. Leonard said: 'It is an experience, how can you explain it. You need to drink tea to know what it tastes like. I get the taste and remember that one is always in His presence. I feel very much closeness to God and a lot of love.' George has a different feeling:

> 'For me it is a method of purification. It is like during the day you build up all these things during the working life; it is like going into a room which is full of people who are smoking and you cannot smell in that smoke and you need to be washed of that smoke. Working in the world is very much like that, we pick up things. And I feel that dhikr is a method of cleaning that smell of the world away.'

The theme of lower-self (nafs/ego) is the bedrock of Shaykh Nazim's teaching and he always touches upon it in his talks. It is based on man having both a soul (ruh) from the heavens and ego from the earth. Man is perfect when these two are met in the right way by the soul having complete authority in a man's heart. Then there is a flow of divine energy (love, mercy, etc.) from the heavens, through man's heart to the beings of the earth so that man becomes the agent of the heavens on the earth and God's Will comes into being through man. (Sheikh Nazim, nd: 20ff). According to this theory there is an ongoing antagonism between one's soul and ego. It is believed that through dhikr the soul overcomes the ego. Here soul represents heavenly or spiritual tendencies while ego represents worldly ambitions; all bad characteristics and desires. Shaykh Nazim always encourages people to overcome the ego: 'Ego is either your horse or you are the horse of ego. If you overcome your ego, you can reach heaven by riding on it.' (Sheikh Nazim, 1987: 55). His teaching on 'ego' seems to be one of the essential elements appealing to converts. George recollected a story of the Shaykh on ego which he liked most:

'We went to Windsor Safari Park with Shaykh Nazim and some of the brothers. There was a big fenced area and we went to the fence. There was a warning notice there that when you actually enter this area not to open your windows or doors. We were driving around looking at the lions and they were looking at us. Then the Shaykh said, "There is one thing in man which is far more dangerous than those lions, and that is the ego. And it is like if we had opened the window or the door and one of those lions had jumped into the car, it would have been much easier to regain that situation than it would from the ego because the ego is more ferocious than the lion." '

4 Basic teachings of the Shaykh which play a major role in attracting converts and some features of the group

Shaykh Nazim always emphasises that people of this century, particularly western people have become much more material-istically oriented and that the influence of religion in people's lives is diminishing. By and large, the approach taken by Shaykh Nazim towards other great religions of the world is not a hostile one. To him mankind is one extended family sharing many characteristics; among them a great spiritual power hidden within our being (Sheikh Nazim, 1986: 62), and only the spiritual way of religions can find out this hidden power. He shows the significance and value of every revealed form as well as the necessity to follow and accept a religious tradition in its totality which enables man to reach that Unity which in itself is formless. More specifically for Islam, he shows its 'intermediate position' between Judaism, Christianity and the traditions of Asia. In this sense Sufism presented by the Shaykh seems to be a vehicle for an attempt to present something of cosmic importance to man-kind. He says: 'You obey God whether through Judaism, Christ-ianity or Islam . . . Allah Almighty rewards people according to their intentions. If a person is sincere and has good intentions, he will be rewarded by his Lord, no matter what his religion

161

may be. Don't hold your Lord's mercy any less than this.' (Sheikh Nazim, 1986: 57). As he holds these views he is welcomed by some Christians and Jews in Britain. Once he addressed an audience of different religions at the London School of Economics[10] organised by the Islamic Society in collaboration with the chaplain and a rabbi from the same college.

In his talks and conversations with people around he always makes jokes. He adorns his talks with teaching stories of the great Sufis of Islamic history which makes the atmosphere lively. The secret which significantly lies behind his success in attracting converts seems to be his making Islam easy. He believes that the differences in the conditions faced by converts should not be ignored (Sheikh Nazim, 1985–1986: 95) and that Westerners should be given concessions and not be loaded down with instructions on the full level of worship, fasting, etc., required of a fully responsible Muslim.

Open-hearted tolerance and understanding towards new comers are always in operation in the group. Shaykh Nazim's approach is flexible and he speaks to each in accordance with their understanding. He never makes criticism or comments on what they do and he is meticulous not to put Westerners off. Freddie remembered how he enjoyed the attitude of the Shaykh after his conversion: 'When I became Muslim he told me to relax and take it easy, and not to blow my mind to become a devout Muslim overnight. That was a very important lesson for me in a way not to expect too much of myself very quickly.'

The appearance of women in dhikr gatherings and activities is another significant aspect of the group. The women participate in dhikr ceremonies sometimes in a separate place, sometimes in the same place situated at a relative distance to the men's circle. This is quite important for the converts who come from a Christian background where they got used to cosex presence in church. Nonetheless, there is a noticeable preponderance of men, be it converts or otherwise, in the group. It is difficult to be precise about the percentage of the women involved in the group as there is no membership figure available, but the impression is formed that the present sample which consists of 5 (29%) females as against 12 males from Shaykh Nazim's group more or less represents the proportion of women in the group.

As for the way the male members dress, the Shaykh forms the prototype, with his robe, turban, and beard. The turban makes the Sufis more distinctive than other Muslims, be it converts or otherwise. The Shaykh is very much in favour of his followers and other Muslims wearing turbans. Almost all of the converts in the group wear the turban and sometimes the robe during dhikr and prayers in the mosque or in their homes, but not outdoors, for, they claim, people would stare at them if they were to do so, as people are unfamiliar with it. Only two of our 17 subjects involved in Shaykh Nazim's group reported that they wear the turban and the robe all the time. What is more significant about the dress of the group is that the nationalities of the members are usually distinguishable from the colours of their turbans. In general, Germans wear purple, English wear green, and black members wear red turbans. Green and white are commonly worn by all nationalities; e.g. one can see a black member wear a green turban, but none of the Germans would wear a red turban.

5 Leader-member relations

In Sufic orders obedience to one's shaykh has always been the distinctive mark of the follower. What the shaykh says or does, even though it may seem inconsistent or even incomprehensible, is believed to have a meaning or a secret. Obedience to the Shaykh in the group of Shaykh Nazim is almost a must. It is believed that through obedience, the Shaykh will take one up and his secrets will go from his heart to that of his follower. Living in a non-Muslim country and being away from the Shaykh seems to make little difference to the actions of the follower. Those who are away from him are also believed to get benefits from him. When the Shaykh is in Cyprus some followers travel to Cyprus to visit and stay with him for a while.

Shaykh Nazim is the central figure who determines spiritual and structural guidelines and is the ultimate source of authority as well as being the supreme role model for his followers. He has got charisma and meets the definition of the charismatic leader by Weber (1968: 241ff). According to Weber the charismatic leader is treated as endowed with supernatural, superhuman or at least specially exceptional powers or qualities. In addition to possession of endowments, Wallis and Bruce (1986: 107) add to the definition of the charismatic authority the 'legitimacy to command, rebuke, praise or prescribe for others'. The

Shaykh also meets this additional definition. There is the sense of loyalty towards the Shaykh, which is both submissive and unquestioning.

Downton (1973: 222) in his *Rebel Leadership* argues that charismatic relationship develops through a psychological exchange of affection, encouragement and security on the part of the leader for deference and affection on the part of the follower. However, Downton believes that many significant matters about the charismatic relationship can be explained by psychological means. To answer the question of how a charismatic relationship arises between a leader and his followers Downtown uses Freudian theory (Freud, 1937: 195ff), and interprets the submission of the follower to the leader as conflicts between 'id, ego and super ego', which tend to be aggravated by social changes that tax the capabilities of ego. He argues that the followers are suffering intolerable levels of anxiety or 'inadequate identity' resolved through recourse to a charismatic leader who 'becomes a parental figure to be obeyed during periods of stress' (Downton, 1973: 225). He finds a reversion to infantile patterns of behaviour, in which anxious followers regress to a state of submissiveness before a father figure. Downton infers too, much about the psychological condition of the people from disturbed social circumstances in which charismatic leaders characteristically find a role. Nevertheless, the fact that charisma often arises as a result of social disruption does not involve that those who follow such a leader possess either inadequate identities or suffer intolerable levels of anxiety (see Wallis and Bruce, 1986: 130–1). The theory of Downton may well be applicable to the cases of some Sufi subjects, but it is not evident that one can generalise the theory for all. Furthermore one has to take into consideration that the charismatic qualities which the Shaykh is personally perceived to have, played an important role only in a few people's cases. By and large, they learn to see Shaykh Nazim as charismatic figure towards the end of the process or when the process is completed.

In a later paper Downton (1980: 386) argues why people follow the unconventional spiritual leaders or gurus, which seems more applicable to the Sufi converts. He puts forward the hypothesis that people who have ideal goals end up having feelings of inadequacy and a sense of personal futility which lead them to psychological receptivity to the appeals of spiritual leaders. At first, they hope for enlightenment through personal effort, but they become disappointed as they cannot manage it on their own. When they face the mysteries of the spiritual world and their goals for the future their will seems inadequate. Feeling incapable of changing themselves or understanding the spiritual mysteries they had discovered, many become ready to accept a spiritual teacher for guidance. Then they search for a spiritual leader to follow and a spiritual community to join. Remember Alan's description of himself (quoted above) when he was young: 'incompleteness was something that I felt . . . I was reading a lot about things that suggested a greater reality than all I could see about me because what I could see about me was quite small . . . and I wanted to know what those things were.' The hypothesis of Downton confirms the psychological theory, put forward by Starbuck (1911) at the turn of the century, which claims that there is a collapse of the will prior to sudden conversion, a sense of personal futility which becomes so unbearable that the person simply gives up. It is at this point that the conversion experience is thought to occur.

In the eyes of followers a shaykh travels a particular path and reaches a certain level of closeness to God and, as they describe it, he becomes a 'friend of God'. And through that closeness he is viewed as a bridge for his followers. The true shaykh is believed to have the power to 'break the habits' of creation if he wants, but he would only do so in exceptional circumstances and as the result of an explicit divine command (Chittick, 1989: 265). So one of the most common indicators of being a shaykh is the ability to perform some miraculous acts (karamat). The crucial point here is that it is the disciples, rather than the shaykh himself, who, generally create this quality for their shaykh and reproduce it in case of any necessity. This is also true of the group of Shaykh Nazim. The members all agree in affirming the belief in the miracles of the Shaykh and in that he has spiritual power. One of the very staunch disciples explains how he feels about the Shaykh's spiritual power: ' . . . To speak about the Shaykh is very difficult because you cannot talk about unlimited things by limited words. He is unlimited, we are limited. We cannot express. Whatever you express is not true.' Some of the converts involved in the group reported that they were very much influenced by the spirituality of the Shaykh at first sight.

Norman recounted his meeting with Shaykh Nazim ten years ago:

'I was lucky enough to be working with a man who I had known for a long time and I had a special feeling about him, but he had taken Islam and he had become a follower of Shaykh Nazim . . . I had my Zen master and he had his shaykh. So I used to talk about my trip to Japan and Zen and he was talking about Shaykh Nazim and Islam. And I became interested in what he was saying about the Shaykh and I felt certain things very strongly about him. Then what happened was he said, "Why don't you meet Shaykh Nazim?" And I said, "I'd like to", because I was impressed by what he said about him. And it was ironic because I've travelled round the world; I've seen the Philippines, the psychic surgeons making operations with their hands and living in a Zen monastery in Japan and all these different exotic cultures, but in the end he said, "Come to Peckham Mosque in London and meet Shaykh Nazim." I decided I would go. And as I was driving I remember getting very excited with a tremendous feeling of anticipation in a very nice way I had not really felt before, a powerful and a kind of high feeling. And I remember going inside the mosque and Shaykh Nazim wasn't there and there were only a few people; going inside and sitting down and feeling very excited. And I remember when he came in at the far end I had a tremendous feeling, my heart was like it was going to explode. And when I was introduced to him by an American brother I was very impressed by him and I couldn't take my eyes off him. I never had met anyone like him at all.'

During the interviews some accounted that the Shaykh made several predictions about the future. Some of these, according to them, came about and some did not. However, this did not shake their devotion to him. George recalled:

'I remember him saying many years ago: "Don't take any notice of peace talks!" At that time there was nothing like this, this was about 6–7 years ago. And we asked him, "What peace talks?", and he said, "You will see. They will not be as they seem to be." '

166

The 'peace talks' was apparently referring to the 'Middle-East peace talks' after the Gulf War according to George. Several converts unanimously said that the Shaykh, a couple of years ago, had predicted that 'the Berlin Wall will come down and Germany will be reunited.' These predictions are believed by the followers to have come about. However, in the 1980s Shaykh Nazim has said things like 'the Third World War is round the corner; and it will start by Russia attacking Turkey and as Turkey is part of NATO it will respond. And after that *Mahdi* (the Saviour) and *Dajjal* (the false Messiah or Antichrist) and then Isa (Jesus) will appear successively.' One of the books by Shaykh Nazim (1987: 140–4), which includes his talks in 1986, confirms the accounts of the informants. Seemingly his prediction regarding the Third World War by Russia attacking Turkey has not taken place so far, but his authority remained unquestioned by the followers and their loyalty to him still seems undiminished. When asked how she felt about this Third World War issue after the dissolution of the Soviet Union Rachel said: 'I understand him, it is a teaching method, it does make you act together and work on yourself if you think time is running out.'

Some of the converts on the contrary, do not pay any attention to the issue of Shaykh Nazim's predictions, miracles, and some sort of rumours going around. They purport that it is the people's perception of the Shaykh which causes trouble. For them God chooses some people and those people may break the bounds of existence, but, they think, it is not so important if it happens. To them a shaykh is to teach people how to come closer to God and help people purify themselves. They believe that some people tend to interpret things in a way which is to their advantage and these people misunderstand the Shaykh. Such a convert is Richard, who is one of the oldest converts in the group:

'A lot of things are being said by people who are around him in ignorance. A lot of them have no substance. It is quite remarkable that one can be present at one of his talks and find that people who have been there also have completely misunderstood what he has said. They give a wrong meaning to it, whether converts or otherwise. So they are treating him as some cults treat their leaders making them into little gods and they talk about them in various sorts of extravagant ways. They can't see their

167

shaykhs as they need to see them. A shaykh can reach a high spiritual level and one can see and feel the power when it comes out from the shaykh. They have reached a high spiritual level, and to that extent they are holy men as well as being spiritual guides. But this is a far cry from the extravagant things that people claim for Shaykh Nazim or shaykhs. It is the same phenomenon, I think, that made Jesus Christ into God. Shaykh Nazim may say things jokingly, but they take it deadly seriously. This is because of the big crowd during *Ramadan* which contains people from different backgrounds. I remember from 1974 onwards there were only a few of us, about half a dozen converts, and we were all aching from laughing so much because he was telling these jokes. And he was very humorous, just like the Prophet. It was very simple, innocent humour, but very funny. And he teaches in the same way all the time. Now sitting in the mosque during *Ramadan* and he would be cracking jokes and the people who have been there longest will snigger or giggle, even laugh, but the others if you turn round and look at them, they are deadly serious.'

6 Psychotherapeutic treatment

It is evident that religion has the potential for therapeutic experience and that religious conversion and thereby membership in a group provides the convert with psychological benefits in the form of conflict resolution and identity formation (Bragan, 1977: 177; Brown, 1987: 160). Deutsch (1975: 166), for example, studying a group of converts to Hinduism concluded that on involvement with the guru and a new 'family' they experienced increased well-being and periods of bliss. In this sense, for some people the group of the Shaykh seems to be playing a vital role as the generic therapeutic agent through interpersonal intimacy. The potential convert arrives at the group full of apprehension and doubts of his self-worth, but at the same time he hopes for relief. Within the group individuals feel secure. There is noticeable solidarity between the members. Through relationship with this newly found group of caring people, unconditional acceptance, and lavish love from them boost the potential's self-esteem. His sense of self-worth is heightened by becoming the focus of the group's attention.

The case of Kevin, who has now been involved with Shaykh Nazim's group for 7 years, sets an example on how social identification with a group can help people overcome their depression and make life bearable for them. Kevin was born in a working class home where religion was never discussed. In his twenties Kevin felt that he did not fit into this society and did not accept the usual social values such as working which eventually led him to join, what he calls, an anarchist group where he wanted to get rid of any kind of social conditioning. By doing so he thought he found freedom, peace and happiness and started experimenting with marijuana and LSD. When 26 Kevin became disillusioned with anarchism coming to the conclusion that 'it will not go anywhere', and he developed an interest in a sort of Buddhism through the philosophy of a macrobiotic diet which he described as 'it was almost making your religion out of diet'. He felt that man had become artificial and if he could return to natural living like growing his own food and living on basic things, then the problems of the world would be eradicated.

Having been involved with macrobiotics Kevin had a girl friend who was also involved with macrobiotics. He got her pregnant and she chose to have an abortion against Kevin's wishes. Kevin felt that it had destroyed the love between them, and they drifted apart. Then he felt upset and depressed for quite a while drifting aimlessly through life looking for something, not knowing what it was. He was still interested in macrobiotics for a few years, but he did anything he came across and then he became interested in New Age philosophies. As an extension of his involvement with New Age thinking, he went to live in California because he thought 'all the cults are here'. He also thought that if he went to another country and started again, he could have a better life. There he met a girl and they lived together for two years, and got married. But it did not work out and she took up with another 'guy'. Losing two girl friends one after another led Kevin to involvement with a Rajneesh group which denounces sex and advises celibacy. Yet Kevin was still not happy. After staying three years in California he felt even more rootless than he did in England. So he decided to come back to London in 1982 when he was 34: 'I could never understand what used to bother me. It seemed to me all these other people seemed to be finding things, but I did not. Life generally did not seem to have any kind of purpose.'

169

When he came back he took interest in Buddhist meditation, but still did not depart from New Age. He also started going to church feeling that perhaps the best thing for him to do would be to go back to his original tradition since he was a Westerner. But he soon felt it was a kind of class activity, 'a middle class thing'. Kevin now concedes that perhaps he was deluding himself by being an eclectic, but he felt:

'To me it did not really seem to matter what people believe as long as it worked. That would have been sufficient. If I had found something that worked even if the beliefs had been absurd, I would have accepted it. I was looking for something that worked, something that gives you integration and strength. That was what I was looking for. Whatever it was I did not care what kind of mad beliefs. But if it worked as far as I was concerned that must be true because it works.'

Three years after his return from California he happened to meet a convert follower of Shaykh Nazim who invited him to a Sufi meeting. Kevin was curious and he thought he would go. It was a dhikr ceremony and he felt the atmosphere was very peaceful. He also enjoyed the food served afterwards and thought 'It is even worth coming here just for the food' and decided to go along: 'It seemed like better than any other thing. I was going to because I was always going all the time from one thing to another. I was looking for something. I did not know what it was. And then I kept going every Friday night and just started to understand a bit more about it.' The same night when he first went to the dhikr meeting Kevin had a dream which tells how strongly he was craving to overcome his problems:

'In the dream I was Muslim and I went to a house. And there was a room with some people in it. And I felt that I had these problems in this room and I sorted out the problems. I felt or I knew that I was a Muslim and I was the only one who was Muslim in the house. Other people in the room seemed to be in confusion whereas I was not because I was a Muslim. That was the dream, but it was very clear. It was not vague or weird. When I woke up I thought about it and I said, "I don't have any intention of being Muslim. Come on, I am not going to be a Muslim!" '

Kevin was also attracted to the friendliness of the people in the group:

'I liked people to talk to. They seemed nice people. The feeling was very good. If I had any questions, they were willing to talk to me about things. I just started to get interested in Islam. They were not trying to convert me. They were not saying I should become a Muslim. They just suggested that I meet the Shaykh when he comes.'

When the Shaykh came in four months time Kevin accepted him as his master and took the *shahadah* then. He found an identity in the group; a sense of belonging, brotherhood, and a group of people he can relate to. As his involvement with the group and his relationship with the Shaykh improved Kevin gradually felt that life has become manageable.

By time the converts in question seem to have overcome their problems depending on their assimilation of the group code and standard of behaviour such as no smoking, no alcohol, etc. In this sense, the Shaykh plays the role of a psychotherapist. In fact there are some converts as well as lifelong Muslims around the Shaykh who may be suffering from psychological disturbances. The Shaykh keeps them close to himself and he has been able to help some of them.

The present observation is congruous with observations in clinical psychiatry which confirms that many patients with depressive disorders experience relief via a religious experience (Cavenar and Spaulding, 1977: 210). It is observable that those who were emotionally disturbed before their conversions seem more able to accept themselves and show signs of being able to cope more effectively with their own problems and the pressures of living in society. In this sense, the group of Shaykh Nazim serves a therapeutic function for people because it represents mediating structures which offer the opportunity for close face to face relationships with people who share a collective sense of belonging. However, Sufis regard their system as being far in advance of modern psychiatrists because it goes beyond the conceptual and technical limits of psychology (Deikman, 1979: 195). Furthermore the group offers a holistic self-concept whereby the member can perceive his various actions and experiences as integrated under a single system.

Shaykh Nazim believes that he moves beyond the compass of

psychotherapists in that he has a deeper goal than self awareness and development; he has the goal of achieving self awareness and realisation on the basis of Sufic principle that 'he who truly knows himself (the self) knows God', for every divine quality is reflected in man. He explains what sort of therapeutic methods he has for depression and behavioural abnormalities. He asserts that superficial conditioning causes behaviour abnormalities and depression, etc., and one's environment can affect one's development, but there is the divinely ordained personality in everyone which is always sound and intact which he calls the 'dye of Allah'. The essence is ever the same manifestation of Divine Perfection – like indelible ink that can be covered but never removed. Shaykh Nazim believes that the things which cover this essence (coats of cheap paint, as he calls them) may be removed and this is, he says, what he does with his followers. In this sense, he calls himself as psychiatrist and accuses most psychiatrists of not trying to remove those coats of paint, but only applying a new coat over the old one and making their patients estranged even more from that original Divine coat (Sheikh Nazim, 1986: 36–7). His job, as he defines it, is to remove all the paint and lay bare the original 'dye of Allah' which pertains to the Divine essence, the original spiritual personality.

The main causes of depression, the Shaykh believes, is the 'effect of memory' upon people. He says: 'When we recall such painful events, a fire roars out of control through our hearts. Then we arrive at a gaping hole in our hearts. Our present life becomes a bridge between the past and the future, between two terrible visions: haunting memories and anxiety-filled anticipation of the future. Those memories will persist as memories, but faith may effectively neutralise their painful effects. He who has been absorbed in the love of God may feel himself to have made a new beginning and to have left painful memories far behind.' (Sheikh Nazim, 1986: 51). At this point the Shaykh offers 'love for God', which is, in fact, what the Sufi way can be described by, in order to have the convert or new comer forget about the events of the past which were painful or traumatic for him. Shaykh Nazim also recognises 'hopelessness' as the cause of depression. Here, he opens a new world to the hopeless. He says: 'We, as servants of a great God, have no right to be hopeless. The Lord may change everything in a second. He whose faith is strong will never doubt that his Lord ultimately intends good for him in this life and the next, and he will be patient through adversity, looking for the Lord's promised respite.' (Sheikh Nazim, 1986: 52–3).

Conclusion

People who seek to fulfil some social or psychological need may find satisfaction through joining some groups, as they often provide emotional stability and security. Accordingly the group of Shaykh Nazim offers one a new social identity and provides the individual with companionship and a sense of belonging that he failed to attain within the larger society. In that society he was not living in intimate relations that firmly bound him with others due to the state of modern urban life in which traditional mediating structures between the individual and the larger society, such as the family and the neighbourhood does no longer exist. This process was further accelerated by the past events which most of the converts experienced like family disorders as well as coming from a background where religion had little/no meaning in life at all. Of course this does not explain the whole issue of conversion through Sufism. There is also the dimension of spiritual seekership in a substantial number of converts' case. It seems that they were mostly attracted by the spiritual teaching of the Shaykh and Sufism. As the Shaykh himself claims Western people are attracted to his movement because they are in need for peace in themselves just as a hungry person looks for a place selling food: 'He looks for a restaurant or a Wimpy shop, etc. He does not ask if it is a Christian shop, or a Jewish shop, or a Muslim restaurant. If he is hungry, he seeks not to die by hunger. He looks and takes where he finds.' Here, the individual takes spirituality as the new answer and develops the belief that the spiritual realm holds the key to the resolution of his problems and the society's social problems. So it is observable that the shift is not only about one's departure from Christianity to Islam, but it is also about one's withdrawal from secular to sacred, as the following account from a convert shows:

'Our hearts can feel, can recognise the bright light of goodness coming out of our respected and beloved Shaykh Nazim. In the midst of growing dark waves of modern way

173

of living he is like a lighthouse showing the way to the only worthwhile place to go to: back to our source, back to Allah. He is a living example of the highest quality which a human being can reach: holiness.' (see Sheikh Nazim, 1987: introduction).

In addition to these characteristics, the problem-solving perspective of the group is another stage of the converts' experience. This is an important phase of the process since it focuses on the individual's rational evaluation of the group or the teaching of the Shaykh. Here, the potential convert assesses the group's orientation to change in terms of his private values, goals, and needs and then makes his choice. At the end of the process he feels that he has been provided with a world-view and a perspective on life.

On the part of the Shaykh there are two further factors in people's attraction to his movement. *Firstly*, Shaykh Nazim prefers not to attack Christianity. If he did so, many would not feel at ease with him in the first place. A conversation following a question between Shaykh Nazim and one of his followers elucidates his soft approach towards Christianity. The question was asked in a meeting where a Christian audience was also present. It reads:

> The follower: 'Could you tell us, please, Christianity says Jesus was crucified, and in Islam he was not crucified, can you?'
> Shaykh Nazim: 'Are you a Muslim?'
> The follower: 'Yes.'
> Shaykh Nazim: 'Keep your belief. They are Christians and they keep their beliefs. No need for discussion. Don't touch the beliefs of people . . . The important thing is that if your beliefs are taking you to the Lord, it is all right. If your car is running all right, what am I saying? Am I saying, "Come down and come to my car?" No! But if it is broken, I may say, "Oh, welcome! Come to my car. I will give you a lift." It is a point that 1400 years of discussion has never solved. Therefore we do not disturb people through their beliefs and we speak to our distinguished audience as all of us brothers from one common origin. And we do not make a difference, but we only talk on

the main subjects for every religion. What was their main purpose? To allow mankind to reach their Lord.'[11]

Secondly, the Shaykh does not call for withdrawal from the society or being in conflict with others. He asks his followers to make an impression on others through exemplary tolerance and kindness and not to make conflict with anyone through bad manners. At this point he does not favour disintegration with the wider society and asks his followers to stay in the society discouraging them from establishing entirely separate communities (Sheikh Nazim, 1982–1983: 60).

D The Group of Abd al-Qadir as-Sufi (al-Murabit)

In Britain a Scottish man, Ian Dallas, a writer and actor, who became Muslim in 1967 and was named Abd al-Qadir as-Sufi, started a Sufic/Islamic movement in the early seventies. Since his embracing Islam Abd al-Qadir has been working to form a disciplined organisation which seemed to have had success. Having founded his mission in Britain he travelled constantly, and made *da'wah* all over Europe and America, and even beyond. He later branched into South Africa (Hogg, 1990), Nigeria, Malaysia, Indonesia, and the Arab world (el-Affendi, 1988: 51).

The information and the data on the group of Abd al-Qadir were collected through formal interviews with one present, and five ex-members involved with the group. The sources on the group also cover materials such as Abd al-Qadir's books and tape-cassettes, the group's Journal, *Islam*, which did not last long, and leaflets/booklets by the group. Apart from one, the present members involved with the group refused to give a formal interview on their conversion experience, but they were helpful in providing relevant information on the current mission and activities of the group.

1 History and membership

Ian Dallas was plagued with the same disillusionment that beset the generation of the sixties, who lost hope in the western culture. His story with Islam and Sufism began in the mid-sixties when he bought a Persian miniature and discovered an inscription of the name of the famous Sufi Abd al-Qadir al-Jilani (d. 1166) on

175

its back. Then he travelled to Muslim countries and embraced Islam in Marrakesh in 1967 taking the name of Abd al-Qadir when he was initiated by a Sufi shaykh. In 1968 he met Shaykh ibn Habib al-Darqawi in Meknes, Morocco, who appointed Abd al-Qadir as a *muqaddam* (representative or section head) of the *Darqawiyyah Tariqah*, a branch of *Shadhiliyyah*, giving him the name of as-Sufi and ordered him to call people to Islam (Clarke, 1983: 13).

Soon after Abd al-Qadir started his mission a group of British and American Muslims formed around him. In 1975–6 they squatted in a derelict row of houses in Bristol Gardens, West London, and formed a small community there. They were around 20–30 people, mostly singles with a few couples or families. They were mostly people who had taken drugs before. The whole street was taken over by tens of people in green turbans and Moroccan robes. They lived a romantic life which answered the needs of the disillusioned youth fleeing the West's materialistic culture. In fact, he used to accept in his circle groups of 'seekers' from every walk of life, without making accepting Islam a condition. He would only later tell them that there can be no way forward without Islam (el-Affendi, 1988: 51). As interviewees who were involved in his early group recount, Sufism appealed to them in the first place and they were driven into Islam by the uneasiness they felt in their culture, not because Islam was 'true' or the 'best' religion. 'It was actually a sort of Islamised version of new left politics and philosophy. And it had much more to do with students' revolution in Paris and stuff like that', said an early participant. William described how he felt before he met this group of people:

'In 1974 I met some English-American Muslims living like a community in London. They were following the Sufi path . . . Leading up to that stage I was sometimes looking for something; sometimes just enjoying myself as well as working. I was playing Rock and Roll, smoking things; sometimes I was trying to be serious about life . . . I thought the society I grew up in was too materialistic and I was . . . And the way I experienced it after meeting with these new Muslims there was not any other way to go. It was the way suddenly I experienced. So I just had to take the step and I had to put my trust in it. Then within two-three months I became Muslim when I was 26.'

176

The friendly atmosphere of the group attracted many people like Henry. Henry had come from countryside to London and had been feeling lonely when he happened to meet them:

'Initially when I went to their meeting what attracted me most was people were so welcoming. Undoubtedly, that was one of the strongest thing in my conversion because as one who has been used to a quite warm environment in my home I found London very very different and from that point of view one of the big things was just a good company of the people who were morally much more interesting than most of the people I had been dealing with. I think it was probably 4–5 months since I started going to their meetings and at the end of which time I said to myself, 'there isn't really anyway I am going to understand any more of what people are really talking about unless I practise it with them.' And at that time I didn't have any conception of what I was taking on. And I said, 'Can I become Muslim?' and they said, 'Yes, of course.' That was in 1972.'

Then Abd al-Qadir began to act like a shaykh. He was to be obeyed, not to be questioned. He ordered his community to shun all aspects of modern life. For a few months in the mid-seventies western dress was not allowed; the community was forbidden to use electricity and given the alternative of wood fires and oil lamps. By doing so the whole rejectionist stance towards western culture was becoming fulfilled. Moreover, in later years he banned his followers from sending their children to school, for he believed education to be the main instrument of indoctrination and assimilation into *kafir* (infidel) society.

With the death of Abd al-Qadir's master Shaykh al-Habib in 1971 Abd al-Qadir had the chance of supplying all guidance himself. Nevertheless, for several years he called himself a *muqaddam*, not a Shaykh. His books were published under the name of Abd al-Qadir. To some he added the title *ad-Darqawi*, the *tariqah* of his shaykh al-Habib. In the mid-seventies he began to search for a new shaykh. In 1976, he said: 'We found none to whom we could entrust our noble followers.' In late 1976 he travelled to Libya to see Shaykh Muhammad al-Fayturi from the *Alawiyyah Tariqah*, who allegedly declared him the shaykh of both *Alawiyyah* and *Darqawiyyah*, which were supposed to be unified under him (el-Affendi, 1988: 54). The book entitled *The*

177

Darqawi Way (1979: 322) published by Diwan Press, the publishing arm of the movement, includes Abd al-Qadir's name as the unifying shaykh of the *Darqawiyyah* and *Alawiyyah*, as successor of the Moroccan shaykh ibn al-Habib and Libyan shaykh al-Fayturi.

His community was growing, and he was becoming famous throughout the Muslim world, and his writings were being translated into the different languages Muslims speak. And by the late 1970s his thinking had changed to activism. During the summer of 1976, the group held mid-day prayers in Hyde Park on weekends, with the aim of drawing people's attention to Islam. At the end of 1976 Abd al-Qadir wanted his followers to move into the countryside, Norfolk, to set up a self-sufficient Muslim village[12] of believers 'to create a complete social nexus in which Islam can flourish on the grounds that the environment of the existing society was inimical to the survival of the true Islam, and that Islam cannot be reduced to an hour's religious education for children.' The aim of such a community would be to demonstrate the 'noble morality of Islam' both to the English people disenchanted with materialism and to Muslims in Britain who are now anxious to recover the full Islam that they lost when they left their countries.[13] Yet they were unable to find adequate funding from the Muslim world for this self-sufficient village project. However, they bought Wood Daling Hall, an old mansion just outside Norwich, which they renovated and made their home and centre. It was called the *Darqawi Institute* and from there they published a journal called *Islam* of which the first issue came out in June 1976.

With the establishment of this *Darqawi Institute* tensions began to occur. As the group expanded and included men, women and children, which reached to a peak of around 200 families, their needs grew, and this unplanned life was no longer adequate. There was also some dissatisfaction with Abd al-Qadir's domineering style (el-Affendi, 1988: 53). He had asked people to leave their businesses and go away on some errands. In practice this was inapplicable to many members' circumstances. Alan recollected how he felt then:

'I've seen he said things which are not right. For instance, one time he told us all that we must all sell our cars and we must rent a Cherokee, and we must all share it. When he said that I knew that there was no way I was gonna get rid of my car. Why should I? I need a car. So if I listened to what he says I would have been doing myself such a grave disservice. This is just one example out of many. A few around him did sell their cars, but none of the rest of us did. He just said he didn't like cars, but he was always wanting lifts here and there.'

Moreover, Abd al-Qadir, with the help of donations from the Muslim world, lived and travelled comfortably (el-Affendi, 1988: 54). This led to bitter criticism and later Abd al-Qadir decided that most people should leave Wood Daling Hall. So the theory and the practice were in contrast. One of the subjects, who lived in Norwich at the time and was slightly involved with the group recollected how the community was then known in Norwich by the surrounding society:

'It was hopeless. It never really even worked. It was absolutely awful, it was a big huge building that was really falling down. They kept the women in a terrible state; they hardly ate anything; they just left them to themselves. They were trying to live in the country, but they had no idea. The whole place was completely mad . . . You can't just sort of move into a great big huge house in the country. They became a joke in the vicinity.'

These contradictions finally led to a crisis in the community. It was apparently caused by the idea of avoiding the society in the first place. As an ex-devotee of Abd al-Qadir conceded, 'they were here to transform their lives within the society, but they did not even relate to the actual Muslim community, let alone British society in general.' The crisis was delayed by progressive concessions that were made to the harsh realities of life. First, people were allowed to use electricity and modern technological products. Then the Moroccan dress was thought to be a hindrance in delivering the message to the people around. So the robe was dropped, but the green turban was kept. (The turban too was dropped in turn later. They now wear the robe and the turban only when they do dhikr). And finally, the ban on sending children to school was lifted (el-Affendi, 1988: 56). Though the bans were dropped in practice some of them are still held in theory even now and seem to have impressed some members of

179

the movement extremely. To cite an example, I remember how one of the members refused to have his picture taken on the basis that the camera is a technological product which does not reflect the genuine nature of man.

Then the group split into factions and the whole affair of setting up a community disintegrated. After these problems in Norwich, Abd al-Qadir emigrated to Granada, Spain, where a small community affiliated to him has been formed there since the mid-seventies (el-Affendi, 1988: 56). He stayed in Spain until he moved to Scotland in 1994, but had close contact with those remaining members of his community in Britain and occasionally came to Britain to deliver conferences. Such a conference entitled 'Islam Against the New World Order' was given by him in March 1991, in the aftermath of the Gulf War in Regents College, London. While in Spain he appointed a new *amir* (leader) for Britain and paying allegiance to the appointed *amir* was a prerequisite to being a member. The group still seems to be active. They organise lectures, conferences, Sufic days and dhikr ceremonies for non-Muslims, and more significantly they are still able to draw some converts into Islam.

Now there are around 15 families and 10 single followers of Abd al-Qadir in Norwich, who are all active in making da'wah, in addition to those living in other parts of Britain. According to the ex-members the people who left Abd al-Qadir still remain Muslim and they scattered around the country where they found job opportunities, such as London where many returned. Only one or two people left Islam when they left him. These people, who left Abd al-Qadir, but remained Muslim, do not regret their involvement with him. On the contrary, they are grateful to him for that he introduced them to Islam, but also state that they drifted away from him since his views have gone extreme and his authoritarian personality invoked many problems as Bernard reported: 'We didn't get on well because I felt he was sort of a manipulative man.'

2 The two phases of the movement

The development of Abd al-Qadir's movement presents two significant periods. First he was a Sufi and his call was primarily based on Sufism. Islam was playing a secondary role. As the early group members reported, association was not being made with Islam directly. Esoteric teaching of Sufism was the primary appealing element in drawing people to the group. In the latter period, Islam, combined with Sufism, emphasising the outward form of religion (*shari'ah*) became the cardinal objective of the movement. In both periods the existing society in Britain or western society was not acceptable. However, in the former period Abd al-Qadir took a rejectionist stance favouring isolation from the environment. In the latter, he preferred to work within the society. Propagating Islam as a solution to the problems of 'diseased' western culture and using the channel of social networks became the method of the group. Dropping the Moroccan robe and the turban, and putting the problems facing British people in their daily life today, such as usury, unemployment and family breakdown on their agenda were the signs of this alteration. In the former period Abd al-Qadir took the name of as-Sufi whereas he later called himself *al-Murabit* and the movement, *The Murabitun: European Muslim Movement*, to signify this new orientation. Bit by bit Abd al-Qadir distanced himself from traditional Sufi quietism and became more outspoken and he took the model of *Medina* to mean the following of *Maliki* school (as-Sufi, 1981: 55). He proposed revitalising Sufism, and restoring the *shari'ah* according to the *Maliki* school. He came to the conclusion that *Sufism* and *shari'ah* should go hand in hand.

Taking the new name of *al-Murabit* is significant in the sense that it refers to a movement started in 1029 by a Moroccan Muslim scholar, Abd allah ibn Yasin whose followers rapidly grew in spiritual stature and in numbers and the movement began the first flowering of Islam in Spain (Thomson, 1989: 191). Thus it will be useful to analyse the term to realise the nature of the current nature of Abd al-Qadir's movement. The term *murabit* (literally 'the tied one') is an Arabic term which in North Africa signified pious Muslims who established themselves in tribal territories when the region was not yet thoroughly Islamised. They constituted the 'tie' between Islam and the tribes surrounding them. The term is now used as 'marabout' and has accumulated a baggage of misinterpretation over the years, although it is derived from *murabit*, which means 'the pious one' (Eickelman, 1981: 289). *Ribat* means a fort on the frontier of Islam. The performance of garrison duty at the frontiers of *dar al-Islam* ('the abode of faith') was viewed as a pious duty from the time of Omar (d. 644). Those who performed this duty of vigilance and defence in later Islam were called *al-Murabitun* (the 'ones bound to religious duty'). This became the name of the movement of the al-Moravid – the Spanish name of the dynasty derived from the term *murabit*. The institution of the *ribat* mingled military service with religious observance and some forts (*ribats*) became in time the meeting places of Sufis, and *murabits* had the reputation for engaging in constant dhikr in addition to five daily prayers when they were not fighting jihad (Thomson, 1989). In the *ribat* model the following five principles should be activated: (a) A group of Muslims must enclose themselves in the *ribat* or intensive training; (b) they must study and recite the Koran until they are used to handling it. They must be able to recognise the pure *huda* (guidance) and not to follow *kafir* models; (c) they must practice dhikr of Allah and watch the night in *muraqabah* (vigilance). Intensity of dhikr is a prerequisite for battle; (d) they must be trained in combat; (e) when the training in these elements is complete, the individual then goes into solitary retreat. During this time if Allah wills, his inner eye is opened and he is freed from fear of creation and lack of provision. With this five-part scheme complete the men of *ribat* (murabitun) will be the men ready to fight the infidel society. They will not only oppose *kufr* (the state of being infidel) but also be inwardly and outwardly equipped to establish an Islamic society according to the *Medina* pattern (as-Sufi, 1978: 40).

So in the later years of his mission Abd al-Qadir decided that the time has come to apply the *ribat* model. He felt they should equip themselves to act on their beliefs. He studied Islam to show people that Islam is a political reality as well as doing dhikr or engaging in worship (as-Sufi, 1978: 37). Now he defines his group *Murabitun* as Muslims who manned outposts, training, studying and then went out to spread the message of Islam. In its present form the movement seems to be determined to confront the many and urgent economic, ecological and social problems facing the world today and to find solutions for them. Therefore the nature of Abd al-Qadir's movement now very much differs from those classical Sufi definitions since it is concerned with this worldliness rather than otherworldliness. In an attempt to put their message across the *Murabitun* members in Norwich set up an organisation called P.A.I.D. (People Against Interest Debt).[14] The aim of the organisation is said to let people know that the interest economy is 'a new form of slavery.' The common factor to current problems facing people in Britain such as inflation, unemployment, mortgage repossession, debt, and family breakdown is usury.[15] The issues they discuss are not confined to politics or economics, but covers social issues such as Aids, intoxication, drug-use, and the rise of crime.

3 Islam: a European phenomenon

One of the most distinguishing features of Abd al-Qadir's mission is that it is a movement which predominantly consists of converts. It was started, led and developed by them, having only a few lifelong Muslims involved. It has been founded in Britain and moved to Spain drawing Spanish converts into Islam. Abd al-Qadir's departure from Britain to Spain was not a coincidence. Abd al-Qadir claims that Islam was/is not an oriental phenomenon, but it had in fact become a European phenomenon in Spain. According to him the closest model of the *Medina* model of the Prophet was right there in Granada and Cordoba. That is why he has a vision for Europe called 'from Islam to Islam' with the objective of marrying the culture of Islam with western culture. He believes that Islam lies at the core of western thought. For example, the writings of a Spanish Muslim philosopher Ibn Rusd were translated into Latin and Hebrew and these Latin translations of Ibn Rusd, he claims, became the foundation of Western thought.[16] Abd al-Qadir makes it clear that they stand for the Islamisation of the West, that is to bring Islam into the West, 'not to make everybody a Pakistani or an Egyptian, but to allow the natural genius of the people to express itself.'

Due to these ideas of Abd al-Qadir the movement can be labelled as 'European' in terms of geographical origin and centre. In spite of his rejection of western culture, Abd al-Qadir has always wanted to promote an Islam which will attract western people. And one can easily notice the sense of Europeanism within the group. They are not enthusiastic to mingle or associate with lifelong Muslims from the subcontinent or Arab world since they believe that it is good for non-Muslims not to associate Islam with Arabs or Pakistanis. When this association is made, they say, non-Muslims will think of Islam as a cultural thing, the religion of Arabs or whatever. In the West, in their view, the true nature of Islam is obscured by its false identification with the life-style of Arab and Asian nations, and their modern state-controlled religion.[17] A typical illustration of this disposition is that if they convene a meeting specifically for non-Muslims, they do not want lifelong Muslims to attend those meetings. This stance towards lifelong Muslims from the subcontinent or the Arab world has always been felt by some Muslims in touch with the group, and even by some converts interviewed. It was labelled as 'racial superiority' by Alan who made a bitter criticism: 'I have seen a very distinct racial superiority that comes over. I really don't know why. They seem to reject all the traditional things of Islam.' Abd al-Qadir primarily seeks conversion of British or Europeans to Islam. In his talk in Regent's College, London, in March 1991 he explicitly expressed: 'Our job is to make this country Muslim. Our religion orders us to go out and give people good news.'

Having analysed the development of the *Murabitun* movement we may now move on to explore Abd al-Qadir's teaching and his criticism of western civilisation since disillusionment with it is usually a prerequisite in most conversion cases to Islam through his movement.

4 Teachings

Abd al-Qadir's current teaching is based on the dichotomy of *haqiqah* and *shari'ah*. A man of *haqiqah* defends Islam as a spiritual reality having inner meaning and permitting inner knowledge in the heart about the Divine Creator, while a man of *shari'ah* fulfils the parameters of a social nexus that is permitted within a Muslim community in accordance with the divinely ordained teaching of the revelation of the Koran (as-Sufi, 1978: 9). In this sense the Sufi type that Abd al-Qadir tries to form is the one who has an ideology of a very pure form of Islam which exists in a man of both *haqiqah* and *shari'ah*: a man who has goals of the traditional *jihad* and fights against wrong actions to build a world which is purified by faith (as-Sufi, 1979b: 42–3). Having defined Sufism as 'the journey of the slave to the King' he asserts that Sufism and Islam are inseparable. The whole Islam makes someone a Sufi, he says. Equally, one cannot have any sort of inward spirituality unless one is utterly involved in politics. The inward and the outward are inseparable and the outward is political as well. So Abd al-Qadir names it 'psycho-politics'.[18] It means one cannot change the society unless he changes the self.

184

Sufism, as he understands, is not turning away from the world. The *tariqahs* are not a 'passive force' which are detached from the world, but are dynamic and aggressive (as-Sufi, 1979b: 40). He believes that the *shari'ah* cannot be divided so that some is accepted and the rest rejected, and that in Muslim lands the whole 'political zone' of *shari'ah* has been abolished (as-Sufi, 1978: 12). The teaching of Abd al-Qadir regarding the Muslim world illustrates why his movement turned out to be a European Muslim movement. He refuses to take a Muslim or Islamic model from the Muslim world, but the *Medina* model established in the early years of Islam, claiming that it was later on developed in Spain under the Muslim rule.

As for his analysis related to western culture, he traces the origin of modern western culture to the Jacobins, and defines it as 'structuralism', the 'anti-biological', therefore, 'anti-human' tendency towards 'mathematising, rigidifying', and 'structuralising' man as a 'social-biological reality'. In his writings and talks he endeavours to elucidate that western civilisation has no future. He shows that in the early 20th century the theory of structuralism reached its fullness: 'Marx became foremost spokesman of its economic theory. Freud became the pivotal figure of a movement to structure the nature of the self, psychiatry. Lévi-Strauss provided the deep in-back theory both to situate the past and indicate the future of man with his structuralist anthropology.' All these theories, Abd al-Qadir puts, imprison man in the social structure, the structure of self, language, and human exchanges (as-Sufi, 1976: 4; 1978: 7). Therefore sciences like sociology, psychology and anthropology, he says, are the enemies of Islam in their current forms. In fact, having given the description of Islamic psychology he identifies psychology with Sufism (as-Sufi, 1979b: 46). He believes that the collapse of civilised existence and the present polarity of state tyranny and personal psychosis have placed the human condition in jeopardy: 'There has never been a more vulnerable community than the current civilisation' (as-Sufi, 1982: 1, 12). 'It is a goalless society without direction, like a mouse which chases its own tail in terror, turning on itself.' (as-Sufi, 1978: 18). Modern man in the West, he declares, is now in agony which is the consequence of the development of industrial society:

Schizophrenia – split identity – was the insanity of the

185

industrial culture. Autism is the insanity of the current society – that is, the human creature has been reduced to an automaton, to a totally conditioned machine. The autistic child echoes back to parents their heartless abdication of their own humanity, the numbness of their feelings and the deadness of their own inwardness. (as-Sufi 1979a: 22–3).

Abd al-Qadir also criticises the current western society because it lets religious and moral values diminish. He describes the present society as 'an openly religious society whose worship is idolatry. The idol of today is the labour process, and the sacrament of the idolaters is the consumer product.' He writes:

Within fifty years all sexual taboos and moral limits have been destroyed. Adultery was declared not only a norm but a sign of upward social mobility. Pre-marital sex was declared a sign of political tolerance, opposition to it a sign of incipient fascism. Women were defined as being like Negroes or Jews and had to be liberated ... Everybody was free to be different ... the populace had been reduced to slavish obedience. Controlled by an anti-education of laissez-faire tactics in childhood, in dialogued and monitored sexual expression in adolescence, in forced isolation in the work nexus, lonely in youth, lonely as a nuclear family, lonely in old age – the free urban animal was the most abject and culturally barren human being in the history of the world. (as-Sufi, 1982: 57–8).

The dialectic of Abd al-Qadir with regard to politics is based on terms such as usury, power system and debt. Abd al-Qadir believes that usury is at the root of the injustices of our time, and that until it is confronted and eliminated, other issues cannot be adequately dealt with: 'They are branches, usury is the root. The corruption of business, the poverty; the starvation in Africa is the direct result of the usury system.'[19] In one of his latest books, For the Coming Man, he writes: 'Debt is the mechanism of the enslavement of men, and an inhibiting factor in the creation of the free man. Usury is the instrument of the perpetualisation of debt by a mathematical model which will assure its unpayability in the spiral of interest which makes liberation from the debt an impossibility.' (as-Sufi, 1988: 34). So the first act of a Sufi, he says, is the consciousness that usury must be abolished, 'this is the spiritual awareness'. That is why he views politics necessary: 'We have no escape from the political to be spiritually developed.' He asserts that power has passed from nations to international monetary and banking system since the Second World War.[20] He always urges his followers to put this message against usury across in their relationship with non-Muslims: 'Thousands of people are losing their houses. Tell them they are the victims of this system because they don't know the wisdom of Islam. We must call English people to Islam. We must infiltrate non-believers by marriage, by business ... to lift them up from slavery.'[21]

Conclusion

The *Murabitun* movement with its past and present has a wide reputation among Muslims throughout the world as well as that of Britain. The movement also seems to have been one of the most successful groups in attracting non-Muslims to Islam in Britain. Abd al-Qadir's movement in the seventies has emerged as the first big Sufic movement in the West which is led by a western convert to Islam and is predominantly made up of Westerners. It has then appealed to the people of the sixties who were depressed and disillusioned with their life-style for one reason or another, which led them to the rejection of western culture in its totality. Yet the authoritarian character and some ideas of Abd al-Qadir, such as moving into the countryside, eventually brought a split in the community and the majority of the people pulled out. So the number of members, which was described as hundreds before, came down to tens which eventually led Abd al-Qadir to emigrate to Spain and continue his mission there.

It is evident that in the first phase of his mission, Abd al-Qadir had rejectionist ideas which suggested isolation from the greater society and that induced the dissolution of the community. As it has become clear in the last two sections on the group of Shaykh Nazim and Abd al-Qadir, it is at this point that the two leaders' teachings diverge from each other, though they both started a Sufic/Islamic movement in Britain. The former has never suggested isolation while the latter did so. Nonetheless, in the second period of his mission Abd al-Qadir changed his policy so far as the greater society is concerned. It is now him who asks his followers to seek the ways of infiltration into the society to call people to Islam.

Sufism understood by Abd al-Qadir is distinctive from other Sufic movements as well as from that of Shaykh Nazim. Abd al-Qadir believes that the political dimension of Islam must be made available to Westerners and it must be explained to them 'why this society is getting corrupted' whereas Shaykh Nazim avoids this point in general. While Abd al-Qadir primarily targets man's intellect Shaykh Nazim is concerned with the 'heart', the 'soul', and the 'self'.

Finally, one of the significant features of the *Murabitun* is that their call to Sufism/Islam is an indirect one. They ask the people they target to question their culture and think about the problems facing them in this society. It is here again the two movements differ. While one, Shaykh Nazim's movement, makes available what it has in hand to offer people and focuses on it at the first stage of the mission, the other, Abd al-Qadir's mission, asks people to question and become fully aware of what is missing or wrong with what they currently have so that they can fully understand the problems of the whole world and fight to alter the existing system.

CONCLUSION

Conversion is necessarily a multifaceted experience, and it is obvious that not all conversions are of the same type. The conversions to Islam studied here are usually a complex and gradual process prepared over a long period. They are volitional, not as a result of a sudden resolution of spiritual conflicts. They are generally conversions of adults who are often oriented towards points of doctrine.

Researchers have conventionally approached conversion as something that happens to a person. This approach may be termed 'passivist'. According to this view the individual is destabilised by external forces first and then brought to commit himself to a conversionist group by social-interactive pressures applied by that group. There is an alternative approach to the phenomenon which may be termed 'activist' and sees conversion within a contextual world hypothesis as an accomplishment on the part of the convert, rather than as the effect of social, psychological or other forces. The activist approach regards the convert as a seeker who attempts to construct a personally satisfying life, whether at a philosophical level of 'meaningfulness', or at a practical level of freedom from stress (see Straus, 1979: 161). So far as this study's findings are concerned, the two approaches are not antagonistic, but rather complementary. However, this study proposes that the conversion experience itself is a conscious adoption of a new set of beliefs and principles to reshape one's life.

Many studies (Deutsch 1975: 166; Ullman, 1989: 11) of converts to new religious movements indicate that new religious movements have a special appeal to disorganised, disturbed youth alienated from their family of origin. They report that an unhappy childhood and adolescence is characteristic of these converts. The present study does not strongly support other studies which found a relationship between conversion and childhood/adolescent turmoil. In general the converts painted a normal or happy (but rarely very happy) picture of their childhood although there were extreme cases. Twenty one (30%) of the 70 described their childhood as unhappy while only 17 (24%) reported an unhappy adolescence. Adolescence, this study suggests, prepares the ground for conversional change, not because the converts had a particularly troubled adolescence, but because it was the period in which they partly/completely rejected the religion of their parents. However, the converts tend to come from families where there was no strong identification with any religion.

In the psychological literature there is a convention which looks on conversion experience as being an adolescent phenomenon. The sociological literature, mostly on new religious movements, finds that conversion occurs in early twenties. Conversion ages for the present sample show a great deviation from most of the studies of religious conversion. The average conversion age for the present sample is 29.7, with the majority (61%) falling into 23–45 years age-group (see table 2. 3). The present research proposes that conversion is a gradual psychic process occurring beyond adolescence.

The finding that the conversions of the subjects interviewed usually occurred in their late twenties after they had rejected their childhood religion at adolescence may well be explained by the Eriksonian concept of a 'moratorium' period during which other spiritual options are sometimes explored. Erikson (1962: 43) observed that many adolescents struggling with the integration process opt to 'retreat' for a period of time in order to work out a plan of self-reorganisation or integration. He posited that moratorium individuals go through a period 'before they come to their crossroads, which they often do in the late twenties'. During the moratorium period the majority of the converts studied here seem to have been neglectful of religion or were experimenting with religious beliefs other than Islam. For some this period provided a time for careful consideration of the pros and cons of a variety of alternatives. Twenty nine percent of the converts got involved in new religious movements after they broke up with religion of childhood (see table 3.3). Only 11 percent described themselves as practising their religion of upbringing prior to conversion. Others were either nominal or atheist (13%). However, it must be stated that their drift from their religion may be part of a general social movement. The 'psychological set' which accepts parental or environmental religious beliefs and which had previously been the norm did not seem to be the case for them.

Conversion at a later age may also be explained by Kohlberg's (1984: 172ff) cognitive-developmental theory of moral reasoning, which includes the 'preconventional', 'conventional', and 'post-conventional' levels. The postconventional level is reached by a minority of adults and is usually reached only after the age of 20. This level includes such mature concepts as self-chosen direction, a more universal ethical outlook, evaluation of options, and personal ethical principles that move one to ethical decisions. All these changes require cognitive conversion in areas of morality. This profile is of an individual who holds the standards on which a good society must be based (Kohlberg, 1984: 178ff). In short, Kohlberg implies that conversion of a moral variety demands a certain maturity of thought and cognition which occurs only later in life and may be more appropriate for this pattern of conversion.

The accounts given by those interviewed suggest that the over-secularisation of society led them to seek for an alternative way of life. They initially became interested in Islam because they felt that it had strong, clear values on things they felt concerned about. Their revolt was not directed against religious beliefs, but against certain practices (like moral permissiveness) legitimised by their former religion. Some of those (29%) who were involved or became interested in new religions were in search of an alternative to the secular and materialistic perspective of society. It is apparent that this shift is not about departure from (nominal) Christianity to Islam, but it is about a growing tendency towards the sacred or spiritual.

Most of the studies on religious conversion, especially those on new religious movements seem to disregard cognitive style and put emphasis on a turbulent background. The psychodynamic approach to conversion maintains that converts experience increased emotional upheaval in the period preceding conversion as well as in childhood. A significant number of the reports of converts in this study give accounts of troubled lives before entrance into Islam. Almost half of the sample's (49%) preconversion lives were judged to contain emotional distresses caused by events like a broken marriage. These distressful incidents seem to have sparked them to think about religion. For one fifth of the converts the emotional turmoil that characterised their descriptions of childhood and adolescence was also apparent in the immediate antecedents to the conversion experience. Their unhappiness in childhood and adolescence was, in most cases, caused by parental marriages which either ended up in divorce or nearly broke up, and they described this as the major trauma of their lives (see table 3.5). A single emotional 'trauma' or shock may condition an individual and may bring personality change or a conversion experience (Clark, 1958: 215). This is not to say that an emotional turmoil or trauma is enough for conversion or personality change, but that the effective crisis that causes turmoil after the incident could simply cause a process which leads to conversion. However, the final decision for conversion may depend on intellectual elements. Some cases of conversions in the present sample seem to follow the above description. However, the material from the sample studied suggests that conversions did not occur as a direct result of the emotional turmoil or personal distress. This may be associated with conversion, but it is not necessarily a predisposing condition. In the preconvert there may be an unconscious conflict, and a 'psychological set', but these factors alone may in many cases not be enough. There must be an immediate force at the same time. This force is likely to be cognitive and existential questions (47 percent reported specific concerns that could be designated as cognitive or existential during the two years period prior to conversion). The stories of many converts suggest that an active, continuous and relentless search for meaningful answers to questions about the nature of life and death precipitated their conversion. They had been asking questions about the meaning and purpose of human life and compelled to reexamine and reevaluate their previous beliefs and life-styles. These people believed that the cognitive problems that used to bother them had been met by conversion to Islam because it had offered them a complete philosophy in life; it had proclaimed the responsibility of man, a future life, and a day of judgement. It had answered to their questions like 'what is man's place in the universe?' The course that the preconversion period often takes is that the emotional turmoil or personal distress of the individual leads them to a stage where they develop cognitive concerns. Those who had a turbulent background, and an unstable world view stated that Islam had seemed to promise a release from anxiety if they transferred to it, and functioned so. They also pronounced that it had provided answers as to why they had been in emotional turmoil in the first place.

The converts interviewed entered into the fold of Islam by various means and for a variety of reasons. Some accepted it after studying it for a long time, and some entered it in order to be able to marry a Muslim or after marrying a Muslim. Many converts recounted that their conversion was the result of the positive examples of Muslims. Contact with a follower of Islam may have increased the likelihood of conversion and been instrumental in the process. In general, conversions in the present sample rarely occurred without human contact. However, it must be emphasised that the converts interviewed were already oriented towards a religious quest at the time of their contact. The pattern that emerges from this study is that people decide to play roles and get involved in new beliefs and practices with a more thoroughgoing acceptance of beliefs occurring later in the process. The present finding regarding the experimental motif (60%) which stresses the activistic view of conversion shows that one cannot avoid the part played by the converts. At the same time it is important to realise that conversion is a social phenomenon, with affective and emotional ties playing key roles in the affirmative decision.

Conversion from one religion to another means changes that involve large areas of personality, and these vary according to the religion itself. Conversion for the present sample required a major transformation in basic religious identity. Along both structural and subjective dimensions of the religious change, the interviewees reported an identity change. They all experienced a profound change not only in beliefs but also in practices and life-style, though the extent of the latter varied.

There are social, psychological and religious preconditions out of which new religious movements in the West developed. They were/are seen as filling the spiritual emptiness. Conversion to Islam through Sufism can be understood in these terms by taking into account that by joining Sufi groups in the first place, people were/are rejecting western culture rather than traditional religion. The Sufi groups observed here offered the Sufi subjects a new social identity and provided them with companionship and a sense of belonging that some of them had previously failed to attain within society. This process was further accelerated by the past events such as family disorders which many Sufis had experienced. The Sufi subjects seem to differ from non-Sufis in their conversion experiences and backgrounds. The pattern of conversion for the Sufis seems to be affectional whereas it looks likely to be intellectual for the non-Sufis. Sufis tended to come from a background in which they were involved in new religious movements. Reported traumatic events by Sufis also show a higher rate when compared to non-Sufis.

In his article, 'The Problem of Christianity in Muslim Perspective', Kerr (1981: 158) discusses whether the moral permissiveness of Christianity gives Muslims a chance to propagate Islam. He writes: 'Evidence of the failure of Christianity in the West is further adduced from what many Muslims see to be the rampant moral permissiveness, which, they argue, is the inevitable consequence of secularism. The multitude of criticism made on this issue can be grouped under three interrelated categories: the devaluation of the dignity of women through commercial exploitation of sex, resulting in the disintegration of the family of which the mother is the traditional pivot, resulting in juvenile delinquency (drugs, alcohol, etc.). These are all matters that gravely concern Muslims living in Britain.' Like Kerr, Muslims living in Britain believe that the modesty of Muslim women, the stability of Muslim family life, the absence of drinks, drugs, and sex-related crimes and the overall discipline of Muslims living in the West will itself send powerful signals to non-Muslims, since the moral values of Christianity are diminishing in the society. However, these attractions of Islam may be offset by lack of effective missionary strategy and by the perception of Islam in the West as a religion of half-civilised Middle-Eastern people.

GLOSSARY

Ahl al-Kitab: 'People of the Book'. Those whom the Koran cites as having received revealed scriptures. i.e., Jews and Christians.

Ahmadi: A member of the heterodox sect founded by Mirza Ghulam Ahmad (1835–1908).

Barakah: It is grace in the sense of a blessing or spiritual influence which God sends down. *Barakah* may be found in persons, places and things. Certain actions and circumstances may also be a vehicle for blessing, as other actions and circumstances can dispel grace.

Da'wah: Literally call, invitation, summoning. In the religious sense it is mission to exhort people to embrace Islam as the true religion.

Dhikr: Remembrance of God, making mention of God. It refers to invocation of the Divine Name. For the Sufis, *dhikr* is a spiritual method of concentration, the invocation of a Divine Name under the direction of a spiritual master belonging to an authentic chain of transmission.

Imam: Leader in public prayer, one whose leadership or example is to be followed. The legal title given to the leader of the Muslims.

Jamaat: Group (of people), band, party, community.

Naqshbandiyyah: A prominent Sufi order founded by Muhammad Bahaad-Din Naqshband (1317–1389).

Raj: Kingdom; commonly used for British rule in India.

Ramadan: The nineth month of Islamic calender which is month of fasting. Muslims refrain from eating, drinking and sexual relationship during the hours of daylight.

Shahadah: Islamic profession of faith which enjoins the believer to announce that there is no God but Allah, and Muhammad is His messenger.

Shari'ah: The path to be followed; the totality of Islam; the divine law.

Shaykh: A venerable old man or man of authority. A spiritual master, the head of a Sufi order.

Sufi: A Muslim mystic, so called after the early ascetics in Islam who wore garments of coarse wool (suf).

Sunnah: Literally habit, path or way, a manner of life. Technically the spoken and acted example of the Prophet.

195

Tabligh: The action of calling non-Muslims to the religion of Islam or those Muslims to practice it regularly.

Tariqah: Literally 'path'. A generic term referring to the doctrines and methods of mystic union, and rightly synonymous, therefore with the terms of esoterism and mysticism; it refers also to a 'school' or 'brotherhood' of mystics, of which there are very many, all ultimately linked to a single source.

Ummah: A people, a community; a nation, in particular the 'nation' of Islam which transcends ethnic or political definition.

NOTES

1 Muslims in Britain

1 The unemployment rate among Muslims is significantly high. The Department of Labour estimates that unemployment among young people (16 to 24 years of age) of Pakistani and Bengali extraction is currently running at 37 percent, the highest of any ethnic or age group in Britain (Evans, 1989: 12).

2 Matthew Paris, *Chronica Majora* (Rolls Society, 1872–1884; Corpus Christi, Cambridge MS16; Cotton Collection MS Nero D5; Harleian Collection MS 1620), Historia Majora Matthei Paris Monachi Albenensis (1571); cited by Daniel, 1975: 108–9.

3 Matthew Paris, Ibid; cited by Ronay, 1978: 29–30.

4 'Sheikh Abdullah Quilliam', *The Islamic World*, 1896, pp. 202–13.

5 *The Islamic World*, July 1896, pp. 68–70.

6 *The Islamic World*, July 1896, 72, 116.

7 *The Islamic World*, July 1896, 99.

8 *The Islamic World*, July 1896, 98.

9 *The Islamic World*, July 1896, 86–7.

10 *The Islamic World*, July 1896, 98; Clark, 1986: 39.

11 New York Times, 21 December 1913, cited in *The Islamic Review*, 1933, 4–5, 110.

12 Lord Headley's presidential address at British Museum Society, *Islamic Review and Muslim India*, 1915, 13, 9–16.

13 Ibid.

14 *Islamic Review and Muslim India*, 1915, 12, 607.

15 *Islamic Review and Muslim India*, 1915, 5, 217.

16 *Islamic Review and Muslim India*, 1915, 2, 60.

17 *The Islamic Review*, 1924, 3, 118–20; Clark, 1986: 41.

18 *The Islamic Review*, 1935, 3, 81.

19 This figure was estimated by *The Society for British Muslims* and *Islamic Cultural Centre* in London as well as converts who are involved in this study; see also Nielsen, 1992: 43.

20 Leaflet distributed by the Islamic Party of Britain, The Way Ahead: Islamic Party of Britain, nd.

21 Interview with A. Hankin, the spokesman of the *Islamic Party* on economics, by the author in January 1991.
22 'Islamic Party Loses its Deposit', *The Muslim News*, 23 November 1990.
23 *The Independent*/Election 1992 results, 10 April 1992, p. 10.
24 'Muslims Divided About the Party', *New Horizon*, November 1989, p. 21.
25 Interview with Daoud Rosser-Owen, the president of the *Association for British Muslims*, by the author in January 1991.
26 There are around 30,00–50,000 French converts to Islam in France. There are over 5,000 German converts in Germany. There are around 5,000 Dutch converts in the Netherlands. See Nielsen, 1992: 11, 26, 61.

2 *On the Way to Conversion*

1 Scholars who take this perspective on conversion include Sanctis, 1927; Fowler, 1981; Gillespie, 1991.
2 'Absent' covers deficient and absent fathers; 'withdrawn' includes psychologically absent, hostile/aggressive, unstable, withdrawn, weak/ineffective fathering; 'normal' covers overprotective, neutral, and positive. See Ullman, 1989: 204.
3 These questions were also asked by Ullman, 1989: 46.
4 For further discussion see Ullman, 1989: 46–7.
5 For a wider discussion of these points see Cox, 1979: 7–21; Ullman, 1989: 126.
6 P. Johnson, *The Psychology of Religion*, NY: Abingdon, 1959, 127; cited by Christensen, 1963: 210.
7 D. Offer and J. L. Offer, *From Teenage to Young Manhood*, NY: Basic Books, 1975; cited by Ullman, 1989: 123.
8 S. Jacobson, *The Achievement and Moratorium Identity Status*, Unpublished Doctoral Dissertation, N. York University, 1977; cited by Marcia, 1980: 169.
9 The term 'conventional' means conforming to and upholding the rules and expectations and conventions of society or authority just because they are society's rules, expectations, or conventions.

3 *Conversion Process*

1 P. Brierley (ed.), *UK Christian Handbook*; cited by K. Thompson, 1988: 224; see also Hunter, 1985: xi.
2 The data analysis suggests that previous involvement with NRMs is strongly associated with Sufism (chi-square with continuity correction = 11.15, df=1, p<.001).
3 The data analysis found the relation between Sufi and experiencing a traumatic event to be significant (Total chi-square = 4.09, df=1, p<.05).
4 To find out the presence/absence of conversion patterns two people (the author and a psychologist) independently assessed the motifs for each convert using Lofland and Skonovd's criteria, since where

decisions are being taken about presence/absence of a particular feature in behaviour/discourse, etc. one person's opinion may not be totally reliable. 85.2 percent overall agreement was reached, which was considered satisfactory. In order to emphasise the fact that conversions typically emerged by going through many motifs rather than one, the judges pointed out every motif operational in the process rather than just the primary one.

5 The data analysis found the relation between the presence/absence of intellectual motifs and cognitive concerns before conversion to be significant. Of the 33 who reported cognitive concerns before conversion, 28 were judged to have gone through an intellectual motif (chi-square with continuity correction = 4.336, df=1, p<.05). Other variables, education, gender, and age of conversion were not found statistically significant.

6 The data analysis found the relation between the affectional motif and being married to a Muslim at the time of the conversion to be significant (chi-square with continuity correction = 4.316, df=1, p<.05).

7 (chi-square with continuity correction = 5.898, df=1, p<.02).

8 The data analysis found the relation between Sufi and affectional motif to be significant (chi-square with continuity correction = 5.52, df=1, p<.02). It is also found that the relationship between Sufi and mystical motif is significant (chi-square with continuity correction = 9.392, df=1, p<.01).

9 Of the 23 Sufis 15 (65%) reported use of drugs such as marijuana and hallucinogens when they were younger, while only 3 (13%) reported that they were taking drugs prior to conversion. The data analysis suggests that there is an association between Sufi and previous drug-use (chi-square with continuity correction = 8.65, df=1, p<.01). Of the 47 non-Sufis only 12 (25%) reported previous drug use. Of the 12 only 3 (6%) were using drug prior to conversion. The use of drugs by converts not prior to conversion, but at a younger age may well be explained by two facts. *First,* many have come to Sufism/Islam after trying one of the NRMs in which they were helped to recover from it. And also being involved in new religious movements naturally led to conversion at an older age when one gets fed up with bad habits like drugs and attempts to give up. *Second,* many of them were youngsters in the early seventies when using drugs was normative in some young highly-educated groups.

10 See Snow and Phillips, 1980: 444; Stark and Bainbridge, 1980a and 1980b; Ebaugh and Vaughn, 1984: 148; Greil and Rudy, 1984: 318.

5 Conversion through Sufism

1 Irina Tweedie once argued her point on a TV programme called 'Sufism: The Heart of Islam' screened on Channel 4 on 18 December 1990. Irina Tweedie holds regular meetings in which she gives talks on Sufism which are attended by many British people.

2 *Subud* was founded by an Indonesian, Muhammad Subuh (1901–1987), in 1934. It is described as 'a way to make contact with Power of God, the Great Life Force.' It is neither a kind of religion nor a teaching, but a spiritual experience awakened by the Power of God leading to spiritual reality free from the influence of passions, heart and mind. In the *Subud* meeting, called *latihan*, the member waits for certain experiences, believed to be the working of God within him.

3 L. Rocher and F. Cherqaoui, *D'une foi l'autre: Les conversions à l'islam en Occident*, Paris: Seuil, 1986, 147–8; cited by Gerholm, 1988: 264.

4 See P. Clarke, 'Religion: Old and New in the 1990s', paper presented at the conference on 'The future of Theology and Religious Studies: The Agenda for 1990s' sponsored by Department of Theology and Religious Studies, King's College London on 25 October 1990; see also Clarke, 1984: 1.

5 Only three (13%) reported use of drugs prior to conversion.

6 For more information about the group of Shaykh Nazim see Atay, 1994.

7 Shaykh Nazim seems to be attracting German converts more than any other nationality and the growth of his mission seems to be faster in Germany than in Britain.

8 A Booklet by Sheikh Hisham titled 'About Our Master Sheikh Nazim', nd.

9 In Arabic *'hoo'* means 'he' which here refers to Allah.

10 The meeting in London School of Economics was held in March 1991.

11 Quoted from a talk by Shaykh Nazim given to local teachers at Spurley Hey School, Rotherham, Sheffield, on 26 May 1988; for written testimony see Sheikh Nazim, 1988–1991: 4.

12 *Islam: Journal of the Darqawi Institute*, 1977, pp. 26–31.

13 *Islam: Journal of the Darqawi Institute*, June 1976, 1.

14 P.A.I.D, People Against Interest Debt, A Murabitun Organisation, P.O. Box 436, Norwich NR3, Leaflet entitled 'The Interest Economy: A New Form of Slavery', nd.

15 Leaflet by P.A.I.D. titled 'What is the Common Factor', nd.

16 Tape-cassettes of A. as-Sufi which contain his talks over the years. See also as-Sufi, 1978: 46.

17 Leaflet by the Murabitun, nd.

18 A. as-Sufi made this point when he appeared on Channel 4, 18 December 1990, in a programme titled 'Sufism: the Heart of Islam.'

19 Tape-cassettes of A. as-Sufi.

20 Tape-cassettes of A. as-Sufi.

21 Talk given by A. as-Sufi in Regent's College, London, 10 March 1991.

BIBLIOGRAPHY

Abdullah, A. (1986), 'Khurram Murad: Worker and Thinker', *Arabia: The Islamic World Review*, December, 63

(el)-Affendi, A. (1988), 'A False Dawn', *Inquiry*, 1, 50–6.

Allen, S. (1971), *New Minorities, Old Conflicts: Asian and West Indian Migrants in Britain*, NY: Random House.

Allison, J. (1969), 'Religious Conversion: Regression and Progression in Adolescent Experience', *Journal for the Scientific Study of Religion*, 8, 23–38.

Allport, G. (1951), *The Individual and His Religion*, London: Constable.

Ally, M. M. (1982), *The History of Muslims in Britain*, MA thesis, University of Birmingham.

Anthony, D., T. Robbins, M. Doucas, and T. Curtis (1977), 'Patients and Pilgrims: Changing Attitudes toward Psychotherapy of Converts to Eastern Mysticism', *American Behavioral Scientists*, 20, 861–86.

Anthony, D. and T. Robbins (1982), 'Spiritual Innovation and the Crisis of American Civil Religion', *Daedalus*, 1, 215–34.

Anwar, M. (1979), *The Myth of Return: Pakistanis in Britain*, London: Heinemann.

Anwar, M. (1980), 'Religious Identity in Plural Societies: The Case of Britain', *Journal of Institute of Muslim Minority Affairs*, 2, 110–121.

Anwar, M. (1986), *Young Muslims in a Multi-Cultural Society: Their Educational Needs and Policy Implications: The British Case*, Leicester: The Islamic Foundation.

Argyle, M. and B. Beit-Hallahmi (1975), *The Social Psychology of Religion*, London: Routledge & Kegan Paul.

Atay, T. (1994), 'Naqshbandi Sufis in a Western Setting', Unpublished PhD Thesis, University of London.

Austin, R. L. (1977), 'Empirical Adequacy of Lofland's Conversion Model', *Review of Religious Research*, 3, 282–7.

Baer, H. A. (1978), 'A Field Perspective of Religious Conversion: The Levites of Utah', *Review of Religious Research*, 3, 279–94.

Balch, R. W. (1980), 'Looking Behind the Scenes in a Religious Cult: Implications for the Study of Conversion', *Sociological Analysis*, 2, 137–43.

Balch, R. W. and D. Taylor (1977), 'Seekers and Saucers: The Role of the Cultic Milieu in Joining a UFO Cult', *American Behavioral Scientists*, 20, 839–60.

Ball, H. (1987), *Why British Women Embrace Islam?*, Leicester: Muslim Youth Educational Council.

Barker, E. (1984), *The Making of a Moonie: Brainwashing or Choice?*, Oxford: Blackwell.

Barker, E. (1989), *New Religious Movements*, London: Her Majesty's Stationery Office.

Barker, I. and R. Currie (1985), 'Do Converts Always Make the Most Committed Christians?', *Journal for the Scientific Study of Religion*, 3, 305–13.

Batson, C. D. and W. Ventis (1982), *The Religious Experience*, Oxford: Oxford University Press.

Baumeister, R. F. (1986), *Identity: Cultural Change and the Struggle for Self*, Oxford: Oxford University Press.

Bawany, I. A. (ed.), (1961), *Islam Our Choice*, Cairo: Dar al-Kitab al-Misri.

Beckford, J. A. (1991), 'Politics and Religion in England and Wales', *Daedalus: Journal of the American Academy of Arts and Sciences*, 3, 179–201.

Beit-Hallahmi, B. (1989), *Prolegomena to the Psychological Study of Religion*, London: Associated University Press.

Bellah, R. (1974), 'Comment on the Limits of Symbolic Realism', *Journal for the Scientific Study of Religion*, 13, 487–89.

Bellah, R. (1976), 'The New Religious Consciousness and the Crisis of Modernity', in *The New Religious Consciousness*, (eds), C. Glock and R. Bellah, Berkeley: University of California, 333–52.

Berger, P. (1969), *The Social Reality of Religion*, London: Faber and Faber.

Berger, P. and T. Luckman (1971), *The Social Construction of Reality: A Treatise in the Sociology of Knowledge*, London: Penguin Books.

Bird, F. and W. Reimer (1983), 'Participation Rates in New Religious and Parareligious Movements', in *Of Gods and Men* (ed.), E. Barker, Macon: Mercer University Press, 215–38.

Bossy, J. (1970), 'The Counter-Reformation and the People of Catholic Europe', *Past and Present: A Journal of Historical Studies*, 47, 51–70.

Bossy, J. (1985), *Christianity in the West: 1400–1700*, Oxford: Oxford University Press.

Bouquet, D. (1932), *Religious Experience*, Cambridge: Heffer and Sons.

Bragan, K. (1977), 'The Psychological Gains and Losses of Religious Conversion', *British Journal of Medical Psychology*, 50, 177–80.

Brierley, P. (ed.), (1982), *UK Christian Handbook 1983*, London: Bible Society, MARC Europe.

Brown, L. B. (1987), *The Psychology of Religious Belief*, London: Academic Press.

Burfoot, J. (1983), 'The Fun-Seeking Movement in California', in *Of Gods and Men*, (ed.) E. Barker, Macon GA: Mercer University Press, 147–64.

Carmel, A. (1964), *So Strange My Path: A Spiritual Path*, NY: Bloch.

Cavenar, J. O. and J. G. Spaulding (1977), 'Brief Communication: Depressive Disorders and Religious Conversion', *The Journal of Nervous and Mental Disease*, 3, 209–12.

Chittick, W. C. (1989), *The Sufi Path of Knowledge*, NY: State University Press.

Christensen, C. W. (1963), 'Religious Conversion', *Archives of General Psychiatry*, 9, 207–16.

Clark, G. K. (1962), *The Making of Victorian England*, Mass: Harvard University Press.

Clark, P. (1986), *Marmaduke Pickthall: British Muslim*, London: Quartet Books.

Clark, W. H. (1958), *The Psychology of Religion*, NY: Macmillan.

Clarke, P. B. (1983), The Sufi Path in Britain – The Revivalist Tendency, *Update: A Quarterly Journal of New Religious Movement*, 3, 12–16.

Clarke, P. B. (1984), 'New Paths to Salvation', *Religion Today*, 1, 1–3.

Coe, G. A. (1917), *The Psychology of Religion*, Chicago: The University of Chicago Press.

Collins, S. (1957), *Coloured Minorities in Britain*, London: Lutterworth.

Conn, W. E. (1985), 'Merton's "True Self": Moral Autonomy and Religious Conversion', *Journal of Religion*, 4, 513–29.

Cox, H. (1979), *Turning East*, London: Allen Lane, Penguin Books.

Dahya, B. (1973), 'Pakistanis in Britain: Transients or Settlers?' *Race: The Journal of Institute of Race Relations*, 3, 241–277.

Daniel, N. (1975), *The Arabs and Medieval Europe*, London: Longman.

(ad)-Darqawi, Mawlay al-Arabi (1979), *The Darqawi Way*, Norwich: Diwan Press.

Deikman, A. J. (1979), 'Sufism and Psychiatry', in *The World of the Sufi*, (no editor mentioned), London: Octagon, 175–98.

Deutsch, A. (1975), 'Observations on a Sidewalk Ashram', *Archives of General Psychiatry*, 32, 166–75.

Dollah, M. A. (1979), 'The Social Psychology of Religious Conversion', Unpublished M. Litt. Thesis, Glasgow University.

Downton, J. V. (1973), *Rebel Leadership*, London: Collier-Macmillan.

Downton, J. V. (1980), 'An Evolutionary Theory of Spiritual Conversion and Commitment: The Case of Divine Light Mission', *Journal for the Scientific Study of Religion*, 19, 381–96.

Ebaugh, H. R. and S. L. Vaughn (1984), 'Ideology and Recruitment in Religious Groups', *Review of Religious Research*, 2, 148–57.

Eickelman, D. F. (1981), *The Middle East: An Anthropological Approach*, NY: Prentice Hall.

Enroth, R. (1977), Youth, *Brainwashing, and Extremist Cults*, Exeter: The Patemoster Press.

Erikson, E. H. (1962), *Young Man Luther*, London: W. Norton.

Erikson, E. H. (1964), *Insight and Responsibility*, London: Faber and Faber.

Erikson, E. H. (1968), *Identity: Youth and Crisis*, London: Faber and Faber.

Evans, R. (1989), 'Political Emergence of Britain's Muslims', *Geographical Magazine*, December, 11–2.

(al)-Faruqi, I. R. (1986), *The Path of Da'wah in the West*, London: The UK Islamic Mission.

(al)-Fasi, A. (1967), 'The Need of the Day in the World of Islam is the Organising of Missionary Work: A Few Practical Suggestions', *The Islamic Review*, December, 3–4.

Fowler, J. W. (1981), *Stages of Faith: The Psychology of Human Development and the Quest for Meaning*, London: Harper & Row.

Francis, L. J. (1984), *Teenagers and the Church*, London: Collins.

Frankl, V. E. (1988a/1946), *Man's Search For Meaning*, London: Hodder and Stoughton.

Frankl, V. E. (1988b/1969), *The Will to Meaning*, NY: Meridian.

Freud, S. (1937), 'Group Psychology and the Analysis of the Ego', in *A General Selection from the Works of Sigmund Freud*, (ed.) J. Rickman, London: Hogarth, 195ff.

Freud, S. (1961/1928), 'A Religious Experience', in *The Standard Edition of the Complete Psychological Work of S. Freud*, (ed.) James Stracey, vol. 21, 169–72.

Freud, S. (1978/1928), *The Future of an Illusion*, Translated by W. Scott, London: Hogarth.

Galanter, M. (1980), 'Psychological Induction into the Large-Group: Findings From a Modern Sect', *American Journal of Psychiatry*, 12, 1574–9.

Galanter, M. (1982), 'Charismatic Religious Sects and Psychiatry: An Overview', *American Journal of Psychiatry*, 139, 1539–48.

Galanter, M. and P. Buckley (1978), 'Evangelical Religion and Meditation: Psychotherapeutic Effects', *Journal of Nervous and Mental Disease*, 10, 685–91.

Gallagher, E. (1990), *Expectation and Experience: Explaining Religious Conversion*, Vol. II, Atlanta: Scholars Press.

Gartrell, C. D. and Z. Shannon (1985), 'Contacts, Cognitions, and Conversion: A Rational Choice Approach', *Review of Religious Research*, 1, 32–48.

Gay, J. D. (1971), *The Geography of Religion in England*, London: Duckworth.

Gellner, E. (1992), *Postmodernism, Reason and Religion*, London: Routledge.

Gerholm, T. (1988), 'Three European Intellectuals as Converts to Islam: Cultural Mediators or Social Critics?', in *New Islamic Presence in Western Europe*, (eds) T. Gerholm and Y. G. Lithman, London: Mansell, 263–77.

Gerlach, L. P. and V. Hine (1968), 'Five Factors Crucial to the Growth and Spread of a Modern Religious Movement', *Journal for the Scientific Study of Religion*, 1, 23–40.

Gilbert, A. D. (1980), *The Making of Post-Christian Britain: A History of the Secularization of Modern Society*, London: Longman.

Gillespie, V. B. (1991), *The Dynamics of Religious Conversion*, Alabama: Religious Education Press.

Greil, A. L. (1977), 'Previous Dispositions and Conversion to Perspectives of Social and Religious Movements', *Sociological Analysis*, 2, 115–25.

Greil, A. L. and D. Rudy (1984), 'What Have We Learned From Process

Models of Conversion? An Examination of Ten Case Studies', *Sociological Focus*, 4, 305–23.

Guénon, R. (1942), *The Crisis of the Modern World*, trans A. Osborne, London: Luzac.

Haddad, Y. and A. Lummis (1987), *Islamic Values in the United States*, NY: Oxford University Press.

Hall, G. S. (1920), *Adolescence: Its Psychology*, Vol. I-II, London: Appleton.

Haqq, K. A. (1930), 'The Mosque at Woking', *The Islamic Review*, July, 18, 242–4.

Harrison, M. I. (1974), 'Sources of Recruitment of Catholic Pentecostalism', *Journal for the Scientific Study of Religion*, 13, 49–64.

Hastings, A. (1986), *A History of English Christianity: 1920–1985*, London: Collins.

Headley, Lord (1927), 'The Strength of Islam', *The Islamic Review*, 7, 234–46.

Headley, Lord (1933), 'The Passing of a Great Muslim', *The Islamic Review*, 4–5, 109–14.

Heeren, F. (1966), 'Why I Embraced Islam', *Muslim News International*, January, 29–30.

Heirich, M. (1977), 'Change of Heart: A Test of Some Widely Held Theories about Religious Conversion', *American Journal of Sociology*, 83, 653–80.

Hewitt, I. (1990), 'British Converts Caught Between Two Cultures', *The Independent*, 6 January.

Hiro, D. (1971), *Black British White British*, London: Eyre & Spottiswoode.

Hogg, A. (1990), 'Islam Treks Over the Boer Frontier', *The Sunday Times*, 17 June.

Holm, J. (1977), *The Study of Religions*, London: Sheldon.

Hourani, A. (1991), *Islam in European Thought*, Cambridge: Cambridge University Press.

Howe, D. W. (1976), 'Victorian Culture in America', in *Victorian America*, (ed.) D. W. Howe, University of Pennsylvania Press, 3–28.

Hunter, A. G. (1985), *Christianity and Other Faiths in Britain*, London: SCM Press.

Hunter, K. (1962), *History of Pakistanis in Britain*, Publisher's name is missing.

Islahi, A. (1978), *Call to Islam and How the Holy Prophets Preached*, Kuwait: Islamic Book Publishers.

James, W. (1962/1902), *The Varieties of Religious Experience*, London: Collins.

James, W. (1945/1892), *Psychology: Briefer Course*, NY: H. Holt.

Jantzen, G. (1990), 'Mysticism and New Religious Movements', *Religion Today*, 5, 10–12.

Johnson, A. B. (1977), 'A Temple of Last Resorts: Youth and Shared Narcissisms', in *The Narcissistic Condition*, (ed.), M. Nelson, NY: Human Sciences Press, 27–65.

Johnson, G. (1976), 'The Hare Krishna in San Francisco', in *The New Religious Consciousness*, (eds) C. Glock and R. Bellah, Berkeley: University of California, 31–51.

Johnstone, P. (1981), 'Christians and Muslims in Britain', *Islamochristiana*, 7, 167–99.

Josselson, R. (1980), 'Ego Development in Adolescence', in *Handbook of Adolescent Psychology*, (ed.) J. Adelson, NY: Wiley, 188–210.

Jung, C. G. (1973/1933), *Modern Man in Search of a Soul*, London: Routledge & Kegan Paul.

Kabbani, R. (1986), *Europe's Myths of Orient: Devise and Rule*, London: Macmillan.

Kerr, D. (1981), 'The Problem of Christianity in Muslim Perspective: Implications for Christian Mission', *International Bulletin of Missionary Research*, 4, 152–62.

Kettani, M. A. (1986), *Muslim Minorities in the World Today*, London: Mansell.

Kildahl, J. P. (1977), 'The Personalities of Sudden Religious Converts', in *Current Perspectives in Psychology of Religion*, (ed.) H. Malony, Michigan: W. Eerdmans, 238–48, originally published in *Pastoral Psychology*, 1965, 16, 37–44.

Knowles, D. (1958), 'Religious Life and Organisation', in *Medieval England*, (ed.) Austin Lane Poole, Oxford: Clarendon, Vol. II, 382–438.

Kohlberg, L. (1984), *The Psychology of Moral Development*, London: Harper & Row.

Krailsheimer, A. J. (1980), *Conversion*, London: SCM Press.

Levin, T. M. and L. Zegans (1974), 'Adolescent Identity Crisis and Religious Conversion', *British Journal of Medical Psychology*, 47, 73–82.

Levtzion, N. (1979), 'Towards a Comparative Study of Islamisation', in *Conversion to Islam*, (ed.) N. Levtzion, London: Holmes and Meier, 1–23.

Lewis, P. (1994), *Islamic Britain: Religion, Politics and Identity among British Muslims*, London: I. B. Tauris.

Lings, M. (1981), *What is Sufism?* London: Unwin Hyman.

Lofland, J. (1977a), *Doomsday Cult: A Study of Conversion, Proselytisation, and Maintenance of Faith*, Enlarged Edition, London: Irvington.

Lofland, J. (1977b), 'Becoming a World-Saver Revisited', *American Behavioral Scientists*, 6, 805–18.

Lofland, J. and N. Skonovd (1981), 'Conversion Motifs', *Journal for the Scientific Study of Religion*, 4, 373–85.

Lofland, J. and R. Stark (1965), 'Becoming a World-Saver: A Theory of Conversion to a Deviant Perspective', *American Sociological Review*, 30, 862–75.

Lonergan, B. (1972), *Method in Theology*, London: Darton, Longman & Todd.

Long, T. E. and J. K. Hadden (1983), 'Religious Conversion and the Concept of Socialization: Integrating the Brainwashing and Drift Models', *Journal for the Scientific Study of Religion*, 1, 1–14.

Lynch, F. R. (1977), 'Toward a Theory of Conversion and Commitment to the Occult', *American Behavioral Scientists*, 20, 887–907.

McHugh, F. (1990), 'Allah's English Daughters', *Telegraph Weekend Magazine*, 31 March, 34–8.

Marcia, J. E. (1966), 'Development and Validation of Ego-Identity Status', *Journal of Personality and Social Psychology*, 5, 551–8.

Marcia, J. E. (1980), 'Identity in Adolescence', in *Handbook of Adolescent Psychology*, (ed.) L. Adelson, NY: J. Wiley, 159–87.

Martin, D. (1967), *A Sociology of English Religion*, London: SCM Press.

Mawdudi, A. A. (1967), 'Problems of Islam and Muslims in Britain', *Muslim News International*, 1, pp. 29–33.

Mayer, E. (1987), *Love and Tradition: Marriage Between Jews and Christians*, NY: Schocken Books.

Meadow, M. J. and R. Kahoe (1984), *Psychology of Religion*, London: Harper & Row.

Melton, J. G. (1985), 'The Revival of Astrology in the United States', in *Religious Movements: Genesis, Exodus, and Numbers*, (ed.) R. Stark, NY: Pragon House, 279–300.

Mohammad, S. R. (1991), *Islam in Britain: Past, Present and the Future*, Leicester: Volcano Press.

Murad, K. (1983), *Islamic Movement in the West*, Leicester: Islamic Foundation.

Murad, K. (1986), *Da'wah Among Non-Muslims in the West: Some Conceptual and Methodological Approach*, Leicester: The Islamic Foundation.

Murghani, S. S. (1987), 'When in Rome . . .', *Arabia: The Islamic World Review*, May, 46–7.

Nasr, S. H. (1968), *The Encounter of Man and Nature: The Spiritual Crisis of Modern Man*, London: Allen and Unwin.

Nicholson, R. A. (1963), *The Mystics of Islam*, London: Routledge & Kegan Paul.

Nielsen, J. (1984), 'Muslims' Immigration and Settlement in Britain', *Research Papers*, Muslims in Europe, 21, 1–20.

Nielsen, J. (1992), *Muslims in Western Europe*, Edinburgh: Edinburgh University Press.

Nordquist, T. (1978), *Ananda Cooperative Village: A Study in the Beliefs, Values and Attitudes of a New Age Religious Community*, Uppsala: Borgströms Tryckeri AB.

Owen, D. (1991), 'What's It Like to be a UK Muslim', *The Independent*, 26 August, 14.

Paloutzian, R. F. (1983), *Invitation to the Psychology of Religion*, London: Scott, Foresman.

Parrucci, D. J. (1968), 'Religious Conversion', *Sociological Analysis*, 29, 144–54.

Poston, L. (1992), *Islamic Da'wah in the West: Muslim Missionary Activity and the Dynamics of Conversion to Islam*, Oxford: Oxford University Press.

Pratt, J. B. (1948/1920), *The Religious Consciousness: A Psychological Study*, NY: Macmillan.

Rambo, L. R. (1982), 'Current Research on Religious Conversion', *Religious Studies Review*, 2, 146–59.

Rambo, L. R. (1993), *Understanding Religious Conversion*, New Haven: Yale University Press.

Renard, J. (1987), 'Jesus and Other Gospel Figures in the Writings of Jalal Al-Din Rumi', *Hamdard Islamicus*, 2, 47–64.

Rex, J. and R. Moore (1967), *Race, Community and Conflict*, London: Oxford University Press.

Richardson, J. T. (1985), 'The Active vs. Passive Convert: Paradigm Conflict in Conversion/Recruitment Research', *Journal for the Scientific Study of Religion*, 2, 163–79.

Richardson, J. T. and M. Stewart (1977), 'Conversion Process Models and the Jesus Movement', *American Behavioral Scientists*, 6, 819–38.

Rizzuto, A. (1979), *The Birth of the Living God*, London: The University of Chicago Press.

Robbins, T., D. Anthony and J. Richardson (1978), 'Theory and Research on Today's New Religions', *Sociological Analysis*, 2, 95–122.

Robbins, T. (1988), *Cults, Converts and Charisma*, London: Sage.

Rochford, E., S. Purvis, and N. Eastman (1989), 'New Religions, Mental Health, and Social Control', in *The Social Scientific Study of Religion*, (eds) M. Lynn and D. Moberg, London: JAI Press, vol. I, 57–82.

Rodinson, M. (1974), *Islam and Capitalism*, trans. B. Pearce, London: Allen Lane.

Rodinson, M. (1988), *Europe and the Mystique of Islam*, trans. R. Veinus, London: I. B. Tauris.

Ronay, G. (1978), *The Tartar Khan's Englishman*, London: Cassel.

Rose, E. B., et al. (1969), *Colour and Citizenship: A Report on British Race Relations*, London: Oxford University Press for the Institute of Race Relation.

Salisbury, W. S. (1969), 'Religious Identification, Mixed Marriage and Conversion', *Journal for the Scientific Study of Religion*, 8, 125–9.

Salzman, L. (1953), 'The Psychology of Religious and Ideological Conversion', *Psychiatry*, 16, 177–87.

Sanctis, Sante de (1927), *Religious Conversion*, trans. H. Augur, London: Kegan Paul.

Sardar, Z. (1991), 'In Three Ways Cursed to Remain in a Ghetto', *The Independent*, 23 August, 19.

Scroggs, J. and W. Douglas (1977), 'Issues in the Psychology of Religious Conversion', in *Current Perspectives in Psychology of Religion*, (ed.) H. Malony, Michigan: W. Eerdmans, 254–65.

Shafranske, E. P. (1992), 'Religion and Mental Health in Early Life', in *Religion and Mental Health*, (ed.) J. F. Schumaker, Oxford: Oxford University Press, 163–76.

Shah, I. (1980/1968), *The Way of the Sufi*, London: Octagon.

Sharma, A. (1985), 'The Rajneesh Movement', in *Religious Movements: Genesis, Exodus, and Numbers*, (ed.) R. Stark, NY: Pragon House, 115–28.

Shaw, A. (1988), *A Pakistani Community in Britain*, Oxford: Basic Blacwell.

Sheikh Nazim (1981), *Mercy Oceans' Endless Horizons*, London Talks Delivered in Summer 1981.

Sheikh Nazim (1982–3), *Mercy Oceans' Pink Pearls: Selected Lectures of Sheikh Nazim*, Summer 1982 England and Germany, Winter 1983 Cyprus.

Sheikh Nazim (1983–4), *Mercy Oceans' Divine Sources: The Discourses*

208

of Sheikh Nazim, Summer 1983 England and Germany, Winter 1984 Cyprus.

Sheikh Nazim (1984–5), *Mercy Oceans of the Heart: The Discourses of Sheikh Nazim*, Summer 1984 Germany and Switzerland, Winter 1985 Cyprus.

Sheikh Nazim (1985–6), *Mercy Oceans' Rising Sun: The Discourses of Sheikh Nazim*, Summer 1985 and Winter 1986 Cyprus.

Sheikh Nazim (1986), *Mercy Oceans' Lovestream: The Discourses of Sheikh Nazim*, Summer 1986 London, Germany, Switzerland.

Sheikh Nazim (1987), *The Secrets Behind the Secrets: Talks by Sheikh Nazim in Switzerland*, 1987.

Sheikh Nazim (1990), *From Here to Hereafter*, Cyprus Talks, 1990.

Sheikh Nazim (1988–91), *Messages for Mankind*, Sheffield Talks 1988–91.

Sheikh Nazim (nd), *The Naqshbandi Way*.

Sheldrake, K. (1915), 'The British Muslim Society: Public Meeting in the Mosque, Woking', *Islamic Review and Muslim India*, 1, 4–7.

Shibutani, T. (1955), 'Reference Groups as Perspectives', *The American Journal of Sociology*, 6, 562–9.

Sicard, S. V. (1976), 'Contemporary Islam and its World Mission', *Missiology: An International Review*, July, 343–61.

Siddiq, S. M. (1934), 'Islam in England', *The Islamic Review*, 1–2, 14–25.

Singer, M. (1980), 'The Use of Folklore in Religious Conversion: The Chassidic Case', *Review of Religious Research*, 22, 170–85.

Snow, D. and R. Machalek (1983), 'The Convert as a Social Type', in *Sociological Theory*, (ed.) R. Collins, London: Jossey-Bass, 259–89.

Snow, D. and C. Phillips (1980), 'The Lofland-Stark Conversion Model: A Critical Reassessment', *Social Problems*, 4, 430–47.

Spilka, B., R. Hood and R. Gorsuch (1985), *The Psychology of Religion*, New Jersey: Prentice Hall.

Starbuck, E. (1911/1899), *The Psychology of Religion*, London: The Walter Scott.

Stark, R. (1985), 'Europe's Receptivity to Religious Movements', in *Religious Movements: Genesis, Exodus, and Numbers*, (ed.) R. Stark, NY: Pragon House, 301–43.

Stark, R. and W. S. Bainbridge (1980a), 'Networks of Faith: Interpersonal Bonds and Recruitment to Cults and Sects', *American Journal of Sociology*, 6, 1376–95.

Stark, R. and W. S. Bainbridge (1980b), 'Toward a Theory of Religion: Religious Commitment', *Journal for the Scientific Study of Religion*, 19, 114–28.

Straus, R. A. (1979), 'Religious Conversion as a Personal and Collective Accomplishment', *Sociological Analysis*, 2, 158–65.

as-Sufi, Abd al-Qadir (1976), 'The end of a Civilisation and After', *Islam: Journal of the Darqawi Institute*, June 1, 3–10.

as-Sufi, Abd al-Qadir (1978), *Jihad: A Ground Plan*, Norwich: Diwan Press.

as-Sufi, Abd al-Qadir (1979a), *Indications from Signs*, Atlanta: Iqra.

as-Sufi, Abd al-Qadir (1979b), *Resurgent Islam*, Arizona: Iqra.

as-Sufi (ad-Darqawi), Abd al-Qadir (1981), *Letter to an African Muslim*, Norwich: Diwan Press.

209

as-Sufi (ad-Darqawi), Abd al-Qadir (1982), *Kufr: An Islamic Critique*, Norwich: Diwan Press.

as-Sufi (al-Murabit), Abd al-Qadir (1988), *For the Coming Man*, Norwich: Murabitun Press.

Taylor, B. (1975), 'Sociological Factors in Patterns of Religious Conversion and in their Investigation', Unpublished PhD Thesis, University of Aberdeen.

Thompson, E. P. (1967), 'Time, Work-Discipline, and Industrial Capitalism', *Past and Present: A Journal of Historical Studies*, 38, 56–97.

Thompson, K. (1988), 'How Religious are the British?', in *The British: Their Religious Beliefs and Practices, 1800–1986*, (ed.) T. Thomas, London: Routledge, 211–39.

Thomson, A. (1989), *Blood on the Cross: Islam in Spain*, London: Ta Ha Publishers.

Thouless, R. H. (1979/1923), *An Introduction to the Psychology of Religion*, Cambridge: Cambridge University Press.

Tipton, S. (1982), *Getting Saved from the Seventies*, Berkeley: University of California Press.

Travisano, R. V. (1970), 'Alternation and Conversion as Qualitatively Different Transformations', in *Social Psychology Through Symbolic Interaction*, (eds) G. P. Stone and H. A. Farberman, Massach.: Xerox College Publishing, 594–606.

Ullman C. (1982), 'Cognitive and emotional Antecedents of Religious Conversion', *Journal of Personality and Social Psychology*, 43, 183–92.

Ullman, C. (1988), 'Psychological Well-being Among Converts in Traditional and Nontraditional Religious Groups' *Psychiatry* 51, 312–22.

Ullman, C. (1989), *The Transformed Self: The Psychology of Religious Conversion*, London: Plenum.

Vahanian, G. (1967), *The Death of God: The Culture of Our Post-Christian Era*, NY: George Braziller, Fourth Printing.

Wallis, R. (1984), *The Elementary Forms of New Religious Life*, London: Routledge & Kegan Paul.

Wallis, R. and S. Bruce (1986), *Sociological Theory, Religion and Collective Action*, Belfast: The Queen's University Press.

Watt, W. M. (1972), *The Influence of Islam on Medieval Europe*, Edinburgh: Edinburgh University Press.

Weber, M. (1968), *Economy and Society: An Outline of Interpretive Sociology*, (eds) G. Roth and C. Wittich, NY: Bedminster Press.

Wilson, B. (1976), *Contemporary Transformation of Religion*, Oxford: Clarendon.

Wilson, B. (1982), *Religion in Sociological Perspective*, Oxford: Oxford University Press.

Wilson, B. (1991), ' "Secularisation": Religion in the Modern World', in *The Study of Religion, Traditional and New Religion*, (eds) S. Sutherland and P. Clarke, London: Routledge, 195–208.

Wright, J. E. (1982), *Erikson: Identity and Religion*, NY: The Seabury Press.

X, Malcolm (1964), *The Autobiography of Malcolm X*, with the assistance of Alex Haley, NY: Grove Press.

Yakan, F. (1984), *Islamic Movement*, Indianapolis: American Trust Publications.

Yusuf, I. (1989), 'Islam in America: A Historical Social Perspective', *Hamdard Islamicus*, 4, 79–86.

INDEX

Abd al-Qadir as-Sufi 2, 20, 21, 50, 142, 146, 175–86, 188
Abdullah Yusuf Ali 18
adolescence 2, 31, 32, 35–7, 43, 44, 46–66, 82, 93, 118, 120, 153, 190, 192
agnostic 37, 39
Ahl al-Kitab 20
Ahmad, K. 29
Alawiyyah 177, 178
Allison, J. 33, 36, 37, 54
Allport, G. 81
Ananda Marga 150, 157
Anglicanism 72
Argyle, M. 55
Association for British Muslims 24, 25
Augustine, St 48, 62, 82

Babaji Centre 158
Bainbridge, W. S. 110
Ball, H. 21
Bangladesh 6
Batson, C. D. 93
Baumeister, R. F. 48, 75
Beit-Hallahmi, B. 55, 132
Berger, P. 75, 133
Bible 70, 74, 107, 139
Bleher, S. M. 21, 23
Bouquet, D. 48
Bruce, S. 163
Buddhism 47, 69, 79, 84, 89, 90, 127, 169
Burckhardt, T. 143

Burfoot, J. 154

Catholic 38, 39, 52, 54, 57, 63, 67, 70, 84, 88, 118, 137
childhood 1, 2, 3, 31–8, 62, 69, 81–3, 117, 118, 123, 186, 190–2
Christensen, C. W. 31, 46, 47
Christianity 11, 16, 18, 40, 46, 47, 52, 53, 69, 70–3, 93, 116, 129, 134, 143, 156, 161, 173, 174, 191, 194
Church of England 19, 38, 39, 52, 67
circumcision 131
Coe, G. A. 45, 46
cognitive approach 95
cognitive issues 48, 51, 66, 81, 86, 87, 91–4, 121, 122, 191–3
conversion
    age 37, 46, 47, 93, 149, 190
    antecedents 4, 36, 81, 82, 86, 192
    causes of 1
    cognitive approach 81, 92
    definition 1, 69, 125
    gradual 43, 48, 66, 69, 112, 124, 189, 190
    maintenance of 132
    moral 65, 66
    motifs 4, 95, 96, 98, 103, 106, 108, 109, 123, 193
    new beliefs 61, 123, 140, 193
    postconversion 125
        dress 131
        new name 128

213

relations with the society 137
preconversion 53, 54, 66, 82, 86,
    94, 95, 128, 141, 192
  religious affiliation 67, 117
process 67, 81, 84, 92, 97, 103,
    109, 110, 113, 114, 119, 127
process model 119, 120, 122
psychoanalytic view 40
psychodynamic approach 81,
    191
rebellion 54–8
sudden 42, 43, 46, 69, 165
converts
  educational level 80
  gender 80
  marital status 80
Cox, H. 144, 145, 147

da'wah 9, 13, 22, 25–30, 180
  strategy 3, 29
  strategy in Britain 25
Darqawi Institute 178
Darqawiyyah 176–8
death 32, 35, 58, 69, 82, 87, 88–90,
    192
deprivation theory 110
Deutsch, A. 32, 34, 47, 51, 109, 168
dhikr 146, 149, 151, 158–60, 162,
    163, 170, 180, 182
Divine Light Mission 47, 50, 69,
    133, 149, 150, 152
Diwan Press 178
Downton, J. V. 164
drug-use 37, 86, 109, 131, 150, 183

Eaton, G. 21
emotional issues 32, 41, 48, 49, 51,
    81–6, 94, 109, 122, 124, 171,
    191–3
Erikson, E. H. 51, 54, 59–62, 66,
    190
existential questions 51, 65, 86, 87,
    90, 91, 93

Faruqi, I. R. 25
father figure 33–8
Fowler, J. W. 61
Frankl, V. E. 81, 91, 92
Freud, S. 40–3, 81, 164, 185

Galanter, M. 47
Gellner, E. 77
Gillespie, V. B. 64, 126
Green, A. 23
Greil, A. L. 92, 133
Guénon, R. 52, 143

Hadden, J. K. 133
Hall, G. S. 46
Hankin, A. S. 23
haqiqah 184
Hare Krishna 32, 47, 69, 97, 118,
    133, 149, 150, 152
Headley, Lord 15, 16, 18
Heirich, M. 54, 55, 92
Hewitt, I. 136
Hinduism 69, 84, 89, 109, 168
Hyde Park 15, 178

identity 37, 43, 48, 59–66, 75, 79,
    82, 97, 113, 125–7, 130, 133, 134,
    139, 155, 168, 171, 193
image of Islam 11, 90
India 5–7, 14, 15, 19, 79, 145, 157
individualism 74, 151
individuation 37, 38, 57
industrialisation 72, 73
Islam, Yusuf 20, 115
Islamic Cultural Centre 9, 19, 21
Islamic Foundation 9, 29
Islamic Party of Britain 21–3
Islamic Propagation Centre 9

Jamaat-i Islami 6, 26, 29
James, W. 69, 140
Jesus 28, 53, 56, 94, 98, 107, 118,
    129, 135, 143, 144, 167
Jew 38, 39, 58, 67, 80, 116, 131, 143,
    147, 162
Josselson, R. 57
Judaism 58, 59, 69, 129, 143, 161
Jung, C. G. 48, 81

Kahoe, R. 133
Kerr, D. 194
Khwaja Kamal-ud-Din 14, 15, 18
King John 11
Kohlberg, L. 65, 66, 191

Koran 11, 18, 26, 28, 56, 88, 90, 107, 111, 112, 182

Lévi-Strauss, C. 185
Levin, T. M. 37, 46
Lings, M. 21, 143
Lofland, J. 2, 4, 65, 85, 92, 96, 98, 109, 110, 119, 120–2, 126
Lonergan, B. 65
Long, T. E. 133
Luckman, T. 133

Malcolm, X. 101, 102
Marcia, J. A. 60, 61
marriage 20, 32, 82, 84, 104, 108, 109, 111, 114–21, 130, 138, 139, 187, 192
Martin, D. 76
Marx, K. 185
Mawdudi, M. 26, 27, 29
Meadow, M. J. 133
Methodist 38, 39, 67
modernisation 72, 73, 77
moratorium 59–66, 120, 153, 190
Muhammad an-Naseer 11
Murabitun 20, 181, 182, 187, 188
Murad, K. 29, 30
Muslim Parliament 9
Muslims in Britain
  education 6
  geography 7
  history of 5
  mosques 9
  organisations 7, 9, 10
  population 7
  religious observance 8
  settlement 5, 7, 8

Naqshbandiyya 157, 159
Nasr, S. H. 91
Native British Muslims
  contemporary 19
  history of 10
  population 19
new religious movements 2, 32, 53, 68, 79, 95, 97, 110, 119, 120, 133, 144–57, 189–91, 193, 194
Nicholson, R. A. 143
Nordquist, T. 111

Oedipus complex 40–3
Owen, D. 24

Pakistan 5–8, 19, 29, 183
parents
  reaction 137, 138
  religious affiliation 38, 38
Parrucci, D. J. 126
Paul, St 48
Phillips, C. 85, 86, 121
Pickthall, M. 18, 19
Pidcock, D. 23
Poston, L. A. 47, 108
Pratt, J. B. 46
Protestantism 79
psychodynamic approach 81, 191

Quilliam, W. H. 12–16, 24

Rajneesh 69, 79, 169
rebellion conversion 54–8
religion in Britain 52, 72
religious experience 2, 32, 40, 41, 48, 52, 93, 108, 109, 171
Rizzuto, A. 42
Rudy, D. 133
Rushdie, Salman 21
Russell, B. 12

Salisbury, W. S. 116
Salzman, L. 42, 57, 58
Schuon, F. 143
secularisation 73–8, 145, 147, 191
seekership 87, 93, 110, 120, 121, 133, 173, 189
Shadhiliyyah 176
shahadah 56, 90, 117, 128, 129, 159, 171
shari'ah 181, 184, 185
Sharma, A. 156
Shaykh Daghistani 158
Shaykh Nazim 155–7, 175
Shaykh Nazim's group
  basic teachings 161
  initiation to the group 158
  leader-member relations 163
  mission in Britain 157
  psychotherapeutic treatment 168

Singer, M. 126
Skonovd, N. 96, 98
Snow, D. 85, 86, 121
social influence 110, 113
social network theory 110
socialisation 1, 36, 55, 92, 132, 133, 140
socialism 63, 70, 89, 106, 153
Spain 11, 157, 180, 181, 183, 185, 187
spirituality 79, 111, 147, 150, 165, 173, 184
Stanley, Lord 12
Starbuck, E. 46, 165
Stark, R. 2, 4, 65, 85, 92, 95, 109, 110, 119–22, 126, 145
Subud 69, 143, 147
Sufism 4, 20, 131, 142–161, 173, 175, 176, 180, 184, 188, 193

Tablighi Jamaat 6, 9
Taoism 69

Thouless, R. H. 65
Tolstoy 48
traumatic events 3, 32, 82, 83, 136, 194
Trinity 53, 94, 129
Turkish Cypriots 6–8
Tweedie, I. 143

UK Islamic Mission 9, 25
Ullman, C. 35, 36, 38, 43, 47, 49
Unification Church 46, 48, 97, 121, 133, 145, 152
usury 186, 187

Ventis, W. 93

Wallis, R. 145, 147, 163
Weber, M. 163
Wilson, B. 74–6, 148
Woking Mission 14, 15, 18
Wood Daling Hall 178, 179

Zegans, L. 37, 46

21146416R00127

Printed in Great Britain
by Amazon